OUTLINES OF
MORAL THEOLOGY

OUTLINES OF
MORAL THEOLOGY

VERY REV. FRANCIS J. CONNELL, C.Ss.R., S.T.D., LL.D.

PROFESSOR OF MORAL THEOLOGY
DEAN OF THE SCHOOL OF SACRED THEOLOGY
CATHOLIC UNIVERSITY OF AMERICA

THE   BRUCE   PUBLISHING   COMPANY
Milwaukee

Imprimi potest: JOHN SEPHTON, C.Ss.R., *Superior Provincialis*
Nihil obstat: JOHN A. SCHULIEN, S.T.D., *Censor librorum*
Imprimatur: ✝ MOYSES E. KILEY, *Archiepiscopus Milwauchiensis*
    March 9, 1953

To the
MOST REV. PATRICK A. O'BOYLE, D.D., LL.D.
Archbishop of Washington
Chancellor of The Catholic University of America

FOREWORD

The movement of theology for the layman is gathering increasing force with the years, as any casual observer can see. It manifests itself in college circles where educators are more and more taking up the cry: "Let us restore theology to its proper place in the curriculum of the Catholic college." It is to be seen also in religious communities of Sisters and Brothers, where Superiors have become seriously concerned about a systematic program in theology for their subjects and the prospective members of their groups. The growing number of special summer sessions in theology for religious is part of this same trend. In this connection also mention should be made of the numerous and well-attended adult education courses in theology offered both by institutions of higher education, by religious communities, in particular the Dominican Fathers, and also by some members of the Hierarchy. In short, the movement of theology for the layman in the United States has become a worthy counterpart of similar activities in foreign lands, notably in Italy and France.

The great obstacle to the even wider spread of this movement in the United States is the lack of suitable books, both textbooks for classroom (nonseminary) purposes and reference books to supplement the textbooks, to say nothing of popular works on theological subjects to be read by persons of a general cultivated taste. This serious lack can easily be explained. Theology has for altogether too long a time remained the almost exclusive possession of the specialist in the theological seminary. Textbooks have been designed for the theological seminary, where the author of these textbooks could presuppose both a thorough grounding in philosophy and a fairly broad knowledge of the technical terms of the science of theology. In fact this presupposition had taken such a hold on the minds of Catholic educators that for many years (and often even today) it was assumed that no one could understand theology or was justified in studying it unless he had already become somewhat versed in philosophy.

Fortunately this block is rapidly being broken down. Educators, including some theologians, are now beginning to believe that it is possible to teach theology with a minimum use, if not a total absence, of highly technical terms, and without any previous knowledge of philosophy. From this conviction flows the belief that theology can be taught in college for the entire period of four years, simultaneously with and even before philosophy. The whole vista, also, of theology for the average man who is interested in a thorough scientific knowledge of his religion as an added bulwark for his faith now looms large. Several series of textbooks on theology for the college student, we know from personal experience, are in preparation. Some have already begun to appear on the market. The dearth of works for supplementary reading in formal courses, as well as for general study, is also beginning to be met. Special works to solve this difficulty are being freshly composed, and works in foreign languages written for this same purpose are being translated into English.

Father Connell's work, OUTLINES OF MORAL THEOLOGY, about which he himself is entirely too modest, is an important contribution to the movement of theology for the layman. First of all it assumes no great amount, if any, of previous training in theology or philosophy. Technical terms are avoided, or if used clearly explained when used. The work is well organized from the pedagogical point of view and clearly written as well. Yet, with all this, it may be called a scientific work, since sources are appropriately and systematically cited throughout.

To our mind, OUTLINES OF MORAL THEOLOGY will have a threefold usefulness: (1) as a textbook in college and adult education classes for the particular field which it professes to cover, (2) as a very valuable work for supplementary reading in these same classes, if not used as a textbook, and (3) as general reading to be enjoyed by many laymen who are eager for a more scientific knowledge of their faith. We predict great success for the book, and with all our heart wish it Godspeed.

ROY J. DEFERRARI
Secretary General
The Catholic University of America

AUTHOR'S PREFACE

This work is based on a series of lectures delivered during three successive sessions of the Summer School of The Catholic University of America in the course entitled "Theology for the Laity." Those who attended this course, not only lay persons but also a considerable number of religious Brothers and Sisters, manifested a most enthusiastic and encouraging interest in the exposition of the truths of morality as contained in God's message to mankind and proposed by the Catholic Church, which has urged me to publish these lectures. It is my fervent hope that, after the example of these diligent and zealous men and women, many others, both lay persons and religious, will make use of this work to acquire a deeper knowledge of that most sublime science, Sacred Theology.

I have entitled this book OUTLINES OF MORAL THEOLOGY to indicate that it is not intended to present in full detail a course in moral theology such as is given to candidates for the priesthood. A project of such proportions would require several volumes. However, I have endeavored to incorporate into this single volume in concise form all the fundamental doctrines of Catholic theology in the field of morality together with the chief applications of these teachings to the ordinary problems of human life.

Above all, I have tried to make this work a truly scientific study of the many topics with which it deals, rather than a merely popular presentation of Catholic ethical doctrine. Hence, it is a work that requires study — if possible, under the direction of a trained theologian. It is intended especially for the students of a Catholic college or the members of a parish study club, who can have the guidance of a priest in reading and discussing its contents. However, I believe that any intelligent Catholic, even though he has not the opportunity of obtaining such professional guidance, can derive much benefit from this book. It is encouraging to note that the number of zealous lay Catholics, anxious to acquire a thorough understanding of the Church's teachings, is rapidly increasing in the United States. They realize that to appreciate their faith fully and to refute its adversaries effectively they must possess a truly scientific knowledge of the Church's teachings, and are desirous of the opportunity of receiving this type of knowledge.

It is my hope, also, that priests and seminarians will find in OUT-LINES OF MORAL THEOLOGY a helpful summary of their more complete course, and a handy reference work for a brief solution of moral problems that may be presented to them. For this reason the Index is very complete and detailed.

To keep the book within due limits, I have followed the plan of proposing the commonly accepted theological teachings, without discussing to any extent views that may have been proposed by a few theologians but have not found favor with the great majority. And since most of the doctrines here presented are found in all the standard works on moral theology, I have reduced the number of footnotes to the minimum.

I wish to express my gratitude to all who have helped me in preparing this work, particularly my sister, Miss Margaret T. Connell, who gave me great assistance in compiling my notes for publication.

Since the sacred science of theology is the very keystone in the majestic arch of Catholic education, it is my earnest prayer that all who make use of this book in the quest of a deeper knowledge of our holy faith will receive from Him who is the Light of the World, through the intercession of Mary, the Seat of Wisdom, a profound understanding of the harmonious and inspiring doctrines of the Catholic Church on the way in which men must live to merit life eternal.

FRANCIS I. CONNELL, C.Ss.R.

August 2, 1952
Feast of St. Alphonsus Liguori
Patron of Moralists and Confessors

CONTENTS

PART I
GENERAL MORAL THEOLOGY

PART II
THE VIRTUES IN PARTICULAR

PART III
THE SACRAMENTS

OUTLINES OF
MORAL THEOLOGY

INTRODUCTION

The Nature of Moral Theology

Theology in general is the science that treats of God and of created things in as far as they are related to God. That species of theology which limits itself to those truths that can be perceived by the light of natural reason, such as the existence of God, the unity of the divine nature, God's omnipotence and eternity, is called *natural* theology. That species of theology which is based on the truths revealed by God, such as the Holy Trinity, the Real Presence of our Lord in the Holy Eucharist, is called *supernatural* theology.

Speculative theology is concerned with the mere knowledge of truth; *practical* theology is concerned with human acts in as far as a man ordains them to God or exercises them in a manner contrary to God's will. Speculative natural theology is called *theodicy*. Speculative supernatural theology is called *dogmatic theology*. Practical natural theology is called *ethics;* practical supernatural theology is called *moral theology*.

Supernatural theology finds its principles in the truths of divine revelation; but it employs natural reason to deduce conclusions from these principles and to augment them by arguments from natural reason. This is especially true in the sphere of moral theology, which accepts and amplifies many of the arguments adduced in the natural science of ethics.

$$
\text{Theology} \begin{cases} \text{Natural} \begin{cases} \text{Speculative } (\textit{Theodicy}) \\ \text{Practical } (\textit{Ethics}) \end{cases} \\ \text{Supernatural} \begin{cases} \text{Speculative } (\textit{Dogmatic Theology}) \\ \text{Practical } (\textit{Moral Theology}) \end{cases} \end{cases}
$$

Moral theology, as understood nowadays, deals mainly with human acts inasmuch as they are *obligatory*. However, in its broader and more traditional meaning, moral theology treats also of works of *counsel* and acts of *virtue*. Hence, moral theologians follow two distinct methods of dividing their treatises — according to the commandments or according to the virtues. In our course we shall follow the second method.

We can distinguish general moral theology and special moral theology. General moral theology comprises the treatises on the final end of man, human acts, law, conscience, sins, and the virtues in general. Special moral theology embraces the treatises on the particular virtues (theological and moral), together with the sins opposed to them, and the sacraments.

The earlier theologians usually treated both dogmatic and moral theology as two aspects of the one science of theology. Since the seventeenth century there has been a tendency to discuss them separately, so that the impression is given that they are two distinct sciences. This is incorrect; for theology, whether speculative or practical, is one science in as far as its formal object or motive is the same, divine revelation, as analyzed and applied by human reason. However, because their material objects are very different (what we should believe, what we should do) we treat them in different courses in our seminaries and universities. This work is devoted to the scientific treatment of moral theology, though pertinent doctrines of dogmatic theology will also be incorporated.

Division

This book is divided into three parts:

I. General Moral Theology
II. The Virtues in Particular
III. The Sacraments

PART I:

GENERAL MORAL THEOLOGY

CHAPTER 1 . . . *THE FINAL END OF MAN*

1. *Nature and Division of End*

End, as we treat it in moral theology, means *purpose*, or *that for the sake of which something is done.* We distinguish various types of ends:

1. The end of the *act* and the end of the *agent:* the former is that purpose to which an action by its nature is destined (*finis operis*); the latter is that purpose which the person performing the action intends (*finis operantis*). The two may coincide, or they may differ. Thus, the end of the act of almsgiving is the relief of the poor; but the end of the agent may be vanity. An evil *finis operantis* vitiates an act even when it has a good *finis operis.*

2. *Ultimate* end and *intermediate* end: an ultimate end is one which completely satisfies and terminates the desires of the agent; an intermediate end is one which is desirable in itself, and is also referred to a further purpose. An intermediate end differs from a *means,* in as far as this latter is desired only because of its service to a purpose. (A means may even be undesirable in itself, like bitter medicine used to cure a disease.) An ultimate end may be *relatively ultimate* (that is, the final purpose of a certain series of actions, such as admission to college after years of work to earn the money) or *absolutely ultimate* (the final purpose of one's entire life).

3. *Objective* end, *subjective* end, and *formal* end: the objective end is the thing which is sought; the subjective end is the person for whom it is sought; the formal end is the attaining of the objective end. Thus, the workingman's objective end is his salary; the subjective end is himself and his family; the formal end is the receiving of his salary.

In every human action a person acts for an end, and (at least implicitly) for an absolutely ultimate end. (A human action is an action performed by a human being deliberately and freely, such as praying, speaking rationally, stealing, blaspheming. We are not concerned with indeliberate actions, such as the beating of the heart, or

7

actions performed without the use of intelligence and free will, such
as evil language by a person bereft of reason.)

a) Whenever a human being performs a human action, he intends
some good for himself (though it may be for others also). But the
very act of intending good for oneself is acting for an end. (The
major premise is evident from experience. We all realize that when
we act freely, it is because we seek something regarded as a good for
ourselves. Even when a person deliberately commits a sin, he seeks
the forbidden object under the aspect of good, although he knows it
is morally evil. We speak of this as an *apparent* good. The minor
premise of this argument is evident from the very notion of acting for
an end — it is the same as acting for the attainment of some good.)

b) If a person had an unending series of actions in view, he could
never begin to act, since that which is ultimate in the order of
activity is first in the order of intention. Accordingly, unless there
were an absolutely ultimate end intended, there would be no first final
cause in the order of intention to motivate the act and to set the will
in motion. The ultimate end is not necessarily a determined, concrete
good. It may be happiness conceived in an abstract, indefinite way
(*beatitudo in communi*). Moreover, a person may tend to this end
only implicitly, or virtually — that is, without explicitly proposing to
act for his own happiness, though actually this is his fundamental
motive.

The absolutely ultimate end, therefore, is that which one conceives
as bringing him all the happiness he desires. Its influence enters into
every act a person performs. A person may change his ultimate end
in the course of his lifetime. For example, he may at one time place
it in created goods; at another time in God. This brings us to the
question of the true objective ultimate end of man.

2. Man's True Objective Ultimate End

On the part of God the purpose of all creatures is the manifestation
of His divine goodness. As the Vatican Council expresses it, God
formed creatures out of nothing "not to increase His happiness or to
acquire it, but to manifest His perfection by the goods which He
imparts to creatures."[1]

However, we are here concerned with the objective ultimate end
of human acts and of life itself on the part of man; and from this
standpoint we have the important truth that God alone is the true
ultimate end or complete objective beatitude of man.

St. Thomas proves this thesis in two ways. First, he argues from experience, by exclusion, proving that none of the various created goods that men desire, such as riches, honors, power, friendship, etc., actually satisfy man's craving for happiness. This is especially true since man can retain his created goods only for a brief time. Second, he argues, the will of man is capable of desiring universal good; hence, only universal good can perfectly satisfy him. In other words, no matter how many or how great created goods a person may possess, his intellect can always present more goods as possible and desirable, and the will of man will then naturally desire these possible goods. Hence, man can never be fully satisfied unless in some way he possesses unlimited good, and that is found only in God. In other words, God is the only true objective ultimate end of man.[2]

This is the idea proposed by St. Augustine when he said: "Thou hast made us for Thee, O God, and our heart is restless until it rests in Thee."[3]

Sometimes the statement is made that from the fact that there is in man a natural desire for happiness that can be satisfied only by an Infinite Being, we can draw an argument that an Infinite Being exists. But this deduction does not seem logical. For, before such an argument could be drawn, we should have to be certain that there is an orderly arrangement in nature, according to which every creature will attain to the end for which it is adapted; and the existence of such an orderly arrangement supposes the existence of an all-wise, all-good God.

3. Man's True Formal Ultimate End

Since God is the only true objective ultimate end of man, his formal ultimate end — or perfect happiness — must consist in some manner of possession or attainment of God. This must take place through acts of man's spiritual faculties, rather than through the faculties of his body, since a spiritual object (God) can be attained only by spiritual acts. In other words, to be perfectly happy, man must possess God through acts of the intellect and the will, the faculties of knowledge and love respectively.

If man had been created in a purely natural state — as God could have created him — his soul in the future life would have possessed natural knowledge and love of God that would have given him natural happiness fully satisfying his natural desire for happiness. In that event the knowledge of God would have been provided by created intellectual species, which would have represented the divine nature only analogously, as in the present life. The knowledge in that case would have been far more perfect than any knowledge man could have acquired on earth, but it would not have represented the inner life of God, whereby He exists in His Trinity of Persons.

However, from revelation we now know that man has been elevated to the supernatural order, from the beginning of the human race, and that all human beings, beginning with the first man and woman, Adam and Eve, have been destined to a manner of possessing God in the next life similar to the manner in which God knows and loves Himself. This means particularly that man is destined in the future life to what is called an intuitive perception of the divine nature — a perception which takes place without the medium of any created species, since the divine essence itself, as possessed by the Three Divine Persons, is the immediate object of the intellect, elevated to the power of direct perception by the *light of glory.*

This is the doctrine enunciated by St. Paul when he says that we shall see God "face to face,"[4] and by St. John when he says: "We shall see him just as he is."[5] This is known as the beatific vision, to which we find a reference in the words of our Lord: "Blessed are the pure of heart, for they shall see God."[6]

Since man's destiny to the beatific vision is something supernatural, it is not due to his nature, and is not naturally desired, and can be known as actually designated for man only from revelation. On this point some Catholic scholars in recent years fell into error by teaching that God necessarily destines intellectual beings to the beatific vision. Pope Pius XII, in the encyclical *Humani Generis,* condemns this error, when he rejects the doctrine of those who "destroy the gratuity of the supernatural order, since God, they say, cannot create intellectual beings without ordering and calling them to the beatific vision."[7] We cannot, therefore, say that the soul of man naturally desires the *beatific vision,* though we can say that it naturally desires to possess *God.* At most, one could say that there can be in the human will an inefficacious conditional natural desire of the beatific vision. It is in this sense that St. Thomas is to be understood when he says[8] that man has a desire of the beatific vision.

When the human intellect intuitively perceives the infinite goodness of the divine nature, the will is necessarily drawn to love God. For an object that fully satisfies the will's desire for goodness draws the will to itself without any freedom of choice. This beatific love is followed by a measure of joy corresponding to the degree of the knowledge and love, and this in turn is commensurate with the degree of sanctifying grace with which the soul entered eternity. This necessary love of God by its very nature excludes from the will of those who behold the beatific vision the freedom to sin.

All theologians hold that the blessedness of heaven embraces the acts of intellect and will just enumerated. However, it is a matter of dispute between the Thomists and the Scotists which of the two acts — vision in the intellect, love in the will — is to be regarded as the more fundamental. The Thomists say it is the act of the intellect, the Scotists say it is the act of the will.

The soul which has left this earth in sanctifying grace, on being admitted to the beatific vision (after purification in purgatory, if necessary), no longer retains faith, since faith has for its object divine truth that is not directly perceived, and in the beatific vision the soul directly perceives divine truth. In place of faith the intellect receives *the light of glory,* enabling it to see God face to face — as He is in Himself. Similarly, the virtue of hope departs from the soul, since hope has for its object something not yet possessed, and the soul then possesses God, the supreme object of its hope on earth.

From revelation we know that on the last day the bodies of all who have ever lived will be reunited to their souls, and that the bodies of the blessed will share for all eternity the glory of their souls, while the bodies of the wicked will share in their punishment. It is a matter of dispute among theologians whether the resurrection of the body can be proved from reason — in other words, whether a resurrection would have taken place (at least in the case of the just) even if men had been created for a purely natural end. Father Merkelbach, O.P., argues that a resurrection is called for (at least in the case of those who have merited eternal happiness) from the very fact that man naturally desires happiness for his entire being, and the body is a portion of man's being; hence the body must be reunited to the soul for the attainment of perfect happiness.[9] This seems to have been the view of St. Thomas also.[10]

The happiness of the blessed in the possession of God is by its nature eternal. For, unless one in possession of the Sovereign Good is assured that this happiness will last forever, he could not be perfectly happy.

The particular type of glory given to the bodies of the just in the present order — glory like to that of the risen Christ — can be known only from revelation.

FOOTNOTES

1. *DB*, 1783; cf. 1805. (By *DB* is meant Denzinger-Bannwart's *Enchiridion Symbolorum, Definitionum et Declarationum*, a collection of the authoritative teachings of the Church.)
2. *Summa*, I–II, q. 2.
3. *Conf.*, I, n. 1 (Migne, *Patrologiae Latinae Cursus Completus*, 32:661).
4. 1 Cor., 13:12.
5. 1 Jn. 3:2.
6. Mt. 5:8.
7. N. 26.
8. *Summa*, I–II, q. 3, a. 8.
9. *Summa theologiae moralis*, I, 41.
10. *Contra Gentiles*, IV, 79.

CHAPTER II . . . HUMAN ACTS

1. *Nature and Division of Human Acts*

The human act is one that is proper to a human being, an act that proceeds from the free will of man. It presupposes in the intellect some knowledge of the particular purpose of the act, and in the will freedom of choice to perform it or not to perform it. A human act (*actus humanus*) is different from an act of man (*actus hominis*). This latter is performed by a human being, but does not proceed from his free will. Thus, the beating of the heart, talking in one's sleep, the grasping of a toy by a baby, are acts of man, but not human acts. It can even happen that a person is so overcome by sudden passion that he does something that is objectively gravely sinful, yet it is not a human act. For example, a man enters his home and finds his wife murdered, the murderer being still in the room. The husband might be so overcome by grief and anger that he would kill the murderer, yet not be guilty in conscience of any sin, because his emotions deprived him temporarily of the use of intellect and free will. Theologians call such acts *first-primary acts* (*actus primo-primi*). When the use of intellect and free will is partially impeded, an act is called *second-primary* (*actus secundo-primus*). Such an act, even though objectively it were a mortal sin, would be subjectively only a venial sin.

Human acts are distinguished as follows:

1. *Elicited* and *commanded:* An elicited human act is one that proceeds immediately from the will, and is consummated in the will, such as an act of love for God. A commanded act is one that proceeds immediately from another faculty, but at the command of the will, such as the act of walking down the street. Physically the act of the will is distinct from the act of the commanded faculty; but morally the two are regarded as a single act.

2. *Internal* and *external:* An internal act proceeds from an internal faculty, such as the intellect, the will, or the memory; while an external human act proceeds from an external faculty at the direction of the will, such as the hand or the tongue. An external human act is always a commanded act; but an internal act can be either elicited

(if it proceeds immediately from the will) or commanded (such as an act of faith elicited by the intellect at the command of the will).

A human act is sometimes called a voluntary act (*voluntarium*). However, in theological terminology, a voluntary act is wider in scope. It includes even the necessary act of the will loving God as perceived through the beatific vision.

The omission of an act, to be voluntary and imputable, must proceed from a positive act of the will, deliberately choosing not to perform the act, or at least deliberately choosing not to will to perform the act, as takes place when a person chooses to perform an action incompatible with the act of obligation. For example, if a person decides to play golf all Sunday morning, knowing that thus he will be unable to hear Mass, he is guilty of the sin of missing Mass, even though he does not expressly will: "I will not go to Mass."

An act may be *voluntary in cause*. This takes place when a person performs an action foreseeing that a certain effect will follow, even though he may not will this effect in itself. Thus, a man may realize that if he becomes intoxicated, he will blaspheme. He may not wish to blaspheme; nevertheless, if foreseeing this consequence, he gets drunk, he is guilty in cause of the blasphemy. However, it must not be inferred from this that a person is never allowed to perform an action when he foresees that some evil effect will flow from it. According to the principle of the double effect (to be explained later) a person may perform an action with the prevision that there will be a bad effect, as long as he does not will this effect (but merely permits it) and there will be a good effect also, following immediately from the action, sufficiently desirable to justify the permitting of the bad effect. Thus, a man would be allowed to take ether to undergo an operation, even though he foresees that under the influence of the anesthetic he will blaspheme, for that would be only a material sin.

When a person does something to which his will is positively opposed (e.g., not realizing what he is actually doing) the act is *involuntary,* as in the case of the hunter who shoots his friend, thinking he is aiming at an animal. When he does something to which his will is not opposed, though in this instance he did not will it, the act is *nonvoluntary,* as in the case of the hunter who inadvertently kills an enemy whom he would gladly kill anyway.

2. Impediments to Freedom of Human Acts

Four factors may prevent or diminish the freedom of a human act.

Two of these — violence and fear — come from extrinsic causes; two come from the person himself — ignorance and passion.

Violence is physical force brought to bear on a person to compel him to do something which he does not will. For example, a man might be compelled by violence to drink an excessive amount of intoxicating liquor, a girl might be physically forced to submit to a sexual attack. When violence is complete — that is, when the victim resists physically as much as he can — any action performed by force of the violence is *involuntary*. At times, however, there is no obligation to use as much physical resistance as one can — that is, when there is question of merely submitting to another's evil act, not of performing a bad act oneself. Thus, if an attacker threatens a girl that he will kill her if she attempts resistance, she may submit passively, as long as her will is opposed to the deed, and there is no proximate danger that she will give consent to the resultant sensual pleasure. In such a case her part in the attack is *nonvoluntary*. If the victim resists less than he should, because he really wishes the evil deed to take place, there is strictly no question of violence, and the bad act is really voluntary on his part, though it can be said to be partially involuntary (*voluntarium simpliciter, involuntarium secundum quid*). This would be the case if the man being forced to drink too much liquor resists half-heartedly, because he really wishes to get drunk.

The "confessions" which are extorted from the victims of Communist aggression behind the Iron Curtain today are examples of violence. The tortures and drugs employed on these poor persons evidently retain their power for some time after they have been inflicted, so that the statements made by these accused persons are often involuntary. Consequently, they are not responsible utterances.

Fear, or mental anxiety because of an impending or future evil, may at times be so overwhelming that it deprives a person temporarily of the use of reason; and in that event an action by the instigation of that fear is not a human act, and consequently not imputable. However, ordinarily fear, however great, does not take away the use of reason and hence does not justify a person in performing an action which is *intrinsically* wrong, such as denying the faith or committing murder (e.g., abortion), though it might diminish the culpability to some extent. Fear could at times excuse one from the observance of a *positive* law, such as the observance of the Sunday obligation. Thus, if a person had good reason to fear that his enemy would shoot him if he set out for Mass on Sunday, he would be excused from the positive (ecclesiastical) observance of hearing Mass. Moreover, by special legislation of the Church, certain acts performed under the influence of fear are null and void. For example, grave fear inducing a novice to make profession renders the vows invalid.[1] Similarly, a marriage is invalid if it is entered into through grave, unjust fear exerted by another person, in such wise that a person is forced to choose marriage in order to rid himself of the fear.[2]

Ignorance is lack of knowledge in a person who should possess such knowledge. Thus, in a physician lack of medical knowledge is ignorance, but not lack of knowledge of astronomy. From the moral standpoint inadvertence, failure to apply one's habitual knowledge to present circumstances, is equivalent to ignorance.

Ignorance is *invincible* or *inculpable* when it is not due to one's own fault. Thus, if a person is sick on Sunday and cannot attend Mass and in consequence does not learn that Wednesday is a day of abstinence, he is guilty of no sin if he eats meat on Wednesday, for his ignorance is inculpable, and consequently acts proceeding from it are involuntary or nonvoluntary as far as their morality is concerned. But if on Tuesday a person gets the idea that perhaps tomorrow is a day of abstinence and can easily settle the matter by calling up a neighbor or the priest, but neglects to do so, and then eats meat on Wednesday with the thought: "I'm not sure about this, so I'll consider myself free," he commits sin, for his ignorance is *vincible* or *culpable*. It should be noted that the neglect to acquire knowledge necessary to observe the law is sinful (even though one does not wish the ignorance in itself), since in that event the ignorance is voluntary in cause, as in the case of a doctor who neglects to study sufficiently about a rare disease afflicting one of his patients, because the study is too irksome. A person is still more guilty if he directly wills to remain in ignorance, so that he may have greater freedom of action, as in the case of a doctor who will not attend lectures on medical ethics, lest he learn that certain of his practices are condemned by the Catholic Church as opposed to the law of God.

Passion (sometimes called concupiscence) is a tendency of the sensitive appetite toward some pleasurable good — e.g., intoxication, impurity. Like fear, it can sometimes deprive a person temporarily of the use of reason and free will, and in that event an action performed under the influence of passion is not voluntary or culpable. When it does not go this far, it diminishes the imputability of the act and the gravity of sin, sometimes to the extent of rendering what is objectively a mortal sin only a venial sin (a *second-primary* act).

This applies to *antecedent passion,* which precedes the use of free will. Passion can be *consequent* — that is, it can be deliberately brought on, and in that event it rather increases the guilt. Thus, a man may arouse his anger by dwelling on the insults he has received from his neighbor. Again, a person may deliberately frequent some occasion of impurity, knowing that his passions will thus be aroused; and in that case the subsequent sins are in nowise diminished by the fact that he committed them under the influence of strong passion.

If a person has contracted a bad habit, so that he frequently commits an evil act with very little or no advertence, but is now seriously trying to eradicate the habit, any acts which proceed from this habit without advertence are involuntary. But, on the other hand, if he adverts to the habit and decides to do nothing about it, he sins, and acts which subsequently follow from the habit are voluntary in cause. Usually, however, even in this event there is sufficient actual advertence to render these actions voluntary in themselves, especially if they are gravely sinful, such as impure desires or blasphemy.

3. *Morality of Human Acts*

Morality in the strict sense can be predicated only of human acts or of the persons who perform them. Thus, we say it is good to pray, it is bad to steal; and the man who does the former is a good man, the one who does the latter is a bad man. It is only by an extension of the term that we speak of bad books or bad pictures. What we mean is books or pictures calculated to arouse morally evil thoughts and desires in the minds of the spectators.

Nowadays, outside the Catholic Church the ultimate basis of morality is placed by many in custom or human legislation. This is the theory of positivism, according to which all actions are good or bad merely because human beings have decided to consider them such, or because civil laws have determined that it should be so. From this it logically follows that actions which are morally good at one time will become morally bad at another period, or vice versa. Two Americans who have done much to propagate this theory are Judge Oliver Wendell Holmes and John Dewey. In *Newsweek* for December 25, 1950, Raymond Moley says: "Despite the wide veneration accorded these two men, it is well to note the havoc they have created in the thinking of contemporary America and the perversions of their teaching."

Some actions are commanded or forbidden by positive legislation — divine, ecclesiastical, or civil. Consequently, as Catholic theologians express it, some actions are good because they are commanded or bad because they are forbidden. Thus, by divine positive law we are commanded to receive Holy Communion, and forbidden to receive Confirmation a second time. By ecclesiastical law we are commanded to go to Mass on Sunday and forbidden to eat meat on Friday. By civil law we are commanded to pay our taxes and forbidden to drive through a red light.

But there are other actions which are good or bad by their very nature; and these are commanded because they are good, forbidden because they are bad. It is the morality of these actions which we are now considering.

By morality we mean a transcendental relation of a human act, either of agreement or of disagreement, to a norm or rule of goodness and evil, based on man's nature considered in its entirety. A transcendental relation is one that is inherent in the act itself.

To understand this principle, we must bear in mind that a thing is called good or bad in as far as it acts in accordance with its nature or does not act in this way. An ax is a good ax if it cuts well, an automobile is a good automobile if it runs properly. On the contrary, an ax that is dull and cannot cut well is not a good ax, an automobile that is constantly stalling is not a good automobile.

So, too, a man is a good man and his actions are good when those actions are in accordance with human nature and the purposes for which that nature was made. On the other side, actions which are contrary to man's nature are bad. It should be noted that we must determine this rule or norm from the consideration of man's nature *in its entirety,* and not merely from the consideration of an individual faculty. Thus, sexual gratification is adapted to the sexual faculty considered in itself; but it is not always conformable to man's nature taken in its entirety.

When we analyze human nature, we find that it has three essential characteristics, in as far as man is a *social* being, a *rational* being, a *created* being. When man performs actions in accordance with his nature under these aspects, the actions are good, and he thus fulfills his obligations toward his neighbor, toward himself, and toward God.

Man by his nature is meant to live in the society of his fellow men;

consequently, those actions whereby social life is promoted are morally good, those actions whereby society is injured are morally bad. Thus, it is good to be kind and just toward others, to obey the laws passed by legitimate human authority, to propagate the human race in the married state (in which alone the welfare of the offspring is assured). On the contrary, it is detrimental to society (and consequently morally evil) to be unkind, to lie, to steal, to disobey lawful authority, to use the sexual faculties outside of marriage.

Man is also a rational being, which means that a spiritual soul animates his material body, and is intended by nature to be the dominating element, and to exercise reasonable guidance over the body so that it may remain healthy and strong as long as nature permits. Consequently, man performs good actions when he eats and drinks in moderation, when he uses reasonable means to preserve his health and life, when he keeps his emotions in proper check. On the contrary, he performs bad actions when he risks his life immoderately, when he mutilates himself or commits suicide, when he eats immoderately, and especially when he drinks excessively and thus subjects the soul to the cravings of the body.

Man is also a created being, and as such he has obligations toward his Creator. Hence, he performs good actions when he worships and loves and thanks God; he performs bad actions when he blasphemes or neglects to worship God.

Thus, an analysis of man's very nature furnishes the basic norm of what is right and wrong. This is what we mean when we say that human nature is the *constitutive* norm of morality. This norm is within the capacity of human reason, which is the *manifestative* norm of morality. This does not mean that every individual by his own intellectual efforts can discover all the rules of morality. There are certain questions on which men would disagree if left to their own reasoning powers — for example, whether divorce, by public authority, is ever lawful. But every human being endowed with the use of intelligence is able to realize that certain actions are in accordance with human nature while other actions are at variance with human nature. In other words, every human being can know at least the basic norms of the moral law.

Father Slater, S.J., expresses this doctrine of the constitutive norm of morality in these words: "The teaching of St. Thomas and many others seems to be that the fundamental norm of morality is rational human nature as such. Good, in general, is that which is conformable to the rational nature of man considered in itself and in all its relations. . . . The fundamental norm of right conduct is man's moral nature; morally right conduct is conduct in conformity with man's nature in itself and in all its relations."[3]

While human nature is the *proximate* constitutive norm of morality, the *remote* norm is the divine nature, which is the efficient cause and the prototype of human nature, so that whatever is in accord with human nature is necessarily in accord with the divine nature, whatever is opposed to human nature is also opposed to the divine nature.

Supernatural good is never opposed to the natural good, but is superior to it. Accordingly, what is naturally good — e.g., marriage — may meritoriously be renounced for a higher supernatural good, such as a greater opportunity to love God and to practice works of divine charity.

Besides the *constitutive* and the *manifestative* norm of morality, there is also a *preceptive* norm. The remote preceptive norm is the eternal law of God, the proximate objective norm is the natural law; the proximate subjective norm is conscience.

4. *The Factors of Morality*

To determine whether an individual act is conformable to the norm of morality or opposed to it — in other words, whether it is good or bad — three factors (known technically as the *fonts* of morality) must be considered. These are called respectively the *object*, the *circumstances,* and the *end*.

By the object of an act we mean its primary moral aspect; by its circumstances we mean those moral aspects which are present as accessories or additions to the primary aspect; by the end we mean the purpose of the person performing the act (*finis operantis*). Actually, the end is one of the circumstances; but it is given a separate classification because it has a very important bearing on human actions.

For example: A man steals money belonging to the Church, his purpose being to buy liquor in order to get drunk. The object of the act is a sin of injustice; an essential circumstance is the fact that the money belongs to the Church; the end is a sin of intemperance. Again, a man is extraordinarily generous in taking care of his sick father, because in this way he hopes to atone for the sins of his past life. The object of his actions is charity; a circumstance is filial piety; the end is penance. Just as an evil act is made worse by additional bad circumstances or ends if they are foreseen, so a good act is rendered better by additional good circumstances or ends, if they are foreseen and intended.

To be truly good, an action must be good in object, circumstances, and end. The theological axiom expressing this is *Bonum ex integra causa, malum ex quocumque defectu* ("Good is from the entire cause, evil is from any defect"). The reason is that moral goodness consists in conformity to a certain measure or norm, and conformity demands that a thing meet the standards of the norm in all respects. E.g., a beam to be used in constructing a house is no good for the purpose if even one measurement is defective, even though the other measurements are correct. So, too, all the factors of a human act must be good if the act is to be accounted as morally good. This is the reason why a good end does not justify a bad means. Thus, a person would not be permitted to tell a lie, even though by means of it he could bring about many conversions to the faith. A man would not be allowed to deny his Catholic faith even though he could thereby gain a very desirable job in which he could effect much good for religion.

Under circumstances are included chiefly *place* (e.g., the commission of a sin *in church*); *time* (e.g., working three hours unnecessarily *on Sunday*); *person's state* (e.g., a sin against chastity *by a religious*); and *manner* (e.g., theft *by violence*).

There are two classes of circumstances — those which change the species of the act, and those which merely increase or diminish the moral goodness or evil of the act within the same species. When a circumstance of the first type is present, the act is endowed with two species of virtue or of sin. Thus, the religious who overcomes a temptation against chastity practices both chastity and (because of the vow) religion. When a sinful act is accompanied by a gravely evil circumstance changing the species of the sin, this circumstance must be told in confession.[4] Thus, a boy who has seriously injured his father by giving him a beating must confess not only that he gravely injured another (fifth commandment) but also that this other was his father (fourth commandment).

The other type of circumstances does not change the specific nature of the sin, but makes it more or less grave within the same species. Thus, if a person steals money from a blind beggar it is a more despicable act than if he stole from one in good health; but it would not add a new species of sin. Similarly, a person who assists at Mass with great fervor performs a better act than one who assists with very little devotion, but there is no new *species* of goodness added.

The fact that a circumstance of this latter type was present in a sin does not have to be made a matter of confession. Thus, the thief described above would satisfy his obligation by confessing, "I committed a mortal sin of theft," without mentioning the fact that the victim was poor or blind. However, if a circumstance is such that it renders a sin mortal which otherwise would or could be venial, it must be confessed. Thus, a person who steals $100 commits specifically the same sin as one who steals 5 cents, but the circumstance that a large sum was taken must be told. In such a case we say that the circumstance, though it is merely aggravating as far as the *moral* species of the sin is concerned, changes the *theological* species of the sin.

In discussing the end of an action, theologians consider the case of one who performs an action in order to obtain pleasure from it. The Church teaches that it is sinful to eat and drink and to exercise conjugal relations (even when these actions are objectively lawful) *merely* for the sake of pleasure. However, there would be no *mortal* sin, as long as the acts themselves are lawful. Moreover, a person does not act merely for pleasure in performing an action within the bounds of temperance as long as he has at least implicitly the intention of procuring reasonable *recreation,* a morally good end. Such an act can be raised to the state of a supernaturally meritorious act by a good intention, even though the desire of pleasure is also present. These ideas are emphasized in order to offset any false ascetical notions, which might propose the seeking of natural pleasure in a moderate degree as something sinful.

It is the more common teaching of theologians that no human act can be morally indifferent in the concrete. In other words, every deliberate human act is either good or bad. The reason is that, even though an act may be morally indifferent as regards its object (in the abstract), such as the act of walking, there will always be an end on the part of the agent, which will be either good or bad, and this will render the act in the concrete either good or bad.

5. *The Principle of the Double Effect*

A principle that is often employed in moral theology is known as the principle of the double effect. It means that under certain conditions a person may perform an action even though he foresees that one of the effects will be evil, either physical or moral. Four conditions must be fulfilled in order to justify one in acting thus:

1. The action which is to be performed by the agent must be morally good, or at least morally indifferent by its nature.

2. The bad effect may be only permitted; it may not be willed in itself.

3. The good effect must be caused at least as directly as the bad effect. In other words, the bad effect may not be a means to produce the good effect. Sometimes this condition is expressed by the phrase that the good effect must be at least equally immediate with the bad effect. But this immediacy refers to the order of *causality,* not the order of *time.* In the order of time the bad effect may precede the good effect.

4. The good effect must be sufficiently beneficial to compensate for the permitting of the bad effect. Many factors must be considered in determining this condition. Thus, a greater good is *per se* required to compensate for the permitting of a *morally* bad effect (the sin of another) than for the permitting of a *physically* bad effect; a greater good is required when the bad effect is *sure* to follow than when it will only *probably* follow; a greater reason is required only when the bad effect is injurious to the *common* good than when it is harmful only to an *individual.*

SOME PRACTICAL CASES: The bomber can attack an enemy ammunition base, even though he foresees that some innocent civilians will very likely be killed, as long as the military benefit to his country from the destruction of the base will be very great. On the other hand, if the number of civilians who will be killed is so great that the benefit anticipated from the attack will not compensate for the loss of many lives (and, of course, it is not easy to establish a proportion between these two terms), the attack is unlawful. (For this reason, the use of the A-bomb on the Japanese cities in 1945 was immoral. Too many civilians were killed in comparison with the military objectives gained. Some tried to argue that by killing so many civilians our armies terrorized the people and induced them to surrender, so that eventually more lives were spared than were destroyed by the bomb. But such an argument fails to take into consideration the third condition. It results in a bad means to a good end.)

Four men are on a raft, and after a while it is discovered that the raft will hold only three. With four it will sink. One may jump off the raft, even though he knows that he will soon perish. But if the crisis is insufficient food, one may not jump off, though he may voluntarily abstain from food, even though it will result in death from starvation. These cases revolve around the third condition, the difference being that in some instances the good effect flows directly from the act (or omission), in other instances only through the causality of the bad effect.

SOME PROBLEMS TO BE DISCUSSED: The hunger strike as a protest against governmental injustice. . . . The shooting of a gangster by a policeman when the gangster is trying to shoot the policeman and is holding a child in front of himself. . . . The man who shoots himself when trapped in a burning building. . . . The man who leaps from the twentieth story of a burning building to escape the flames. . . . The aviator who dashes his plane into an enemy warship, knowing that he will be killed, but hoping at the same time to inflict great damage on the vessel. . . . The priest who goes into a burning building to baptize a child, knowing that he will be unable to escape.

The principle of the double effect can be applied to the case of one who goes into the proximate occasion of sin, so that at times he will be justified in doing this, as long as there is a sufficiently grave reason for doing so. For example, a man may go into a saloon which is a proximate occasion of sin to him, in order to persuade his son to come home. But a person is not justified in doing this unless he also uses means for rendering remote the proximate occasion, especially prayer. Moreover, a person may never use this principle if he is sure to sin. But one may sometimes lawfully perform an action foreseeing that it will be an occasion of sin to another, as will be treated under the subject of scandal.

6. The Merit of Human Acts

Merit in the concrete sense is an act deserving of reward. In the abstract, merit is that quality of a good work whereby it is rendered worthy of a reward, or it is the right of the person to receive a reward.

Since every human act is either good or bad, every human act is either meritorious or demeritorious in the sight of God. A work can be *naturally* meritorious or *supernaturally* meritorious, depending on whether its motive is natural or supernatural. We are concerned here only with supernatural merit.

Supernatural merit is either condign or congruous. It is condign when a reward is due in justice; it is congruous when a reward is due only out of fitness. Congruous merit is again subdivided into infallible and fallible, the former being present when God has promised a reward, the latter when no such promise has been made. For example, when a sinner makes an act of perfect contrition, he merits congruously but infallibly[5] the restoration of the state of grace. However, if a person offers even heroic acts to obtain the grace of a religious vocation, he can merit it only congruously and fallibly.

A person can merit condignly (supposing the fulfillment of the conditions enumerated below) an increase of sanctifying grace, heavenly glory, and an increase of glory corresponding to the measure of his sanctifying grace.[6] No one (except Christ, divinely established as the head of the human race) can merit condignly for others. Of the three values that can be in a good work — merit (condign), satisfaction, and impetration — the second and the third can be transferred to others, but the first remains one's own.

CONDITIONS FOR CONDIGN MERIT: 1. On the part of the person meriting. He must be (a) in the present life. No one can merit after death. Not even our Lord merited after His death on the cross.[7] (b) In the state of sanctifying grace, for merit always implies an increase of grace, and no one can increase in grace unless he already possesses it.

2. On the part of the work. (a) Morally good, at least by reason of the end of the agent. It stands to reason that no one can merit by an evil deed. (b) Free — that is, the agent must have the power of will to perform the work or not to perform it; for merit comes to us from our giving something to God, and the only acts we can give to God are those over which we have power by free will. It is not necessary that an act be morally free in order to be meritorious. In other words, we can merit by deeds of obligation. (c) Supernatural — that is, it must be directed toward God and aided by actual grace.

3. On the part of God. He must have promised a reward. That God has made such a promise in regard to our good deeds is abundantly evident from revelation.[8]

Theologians are not in agreement as to the nature of the direction to God (Condition 2, c) required for a meritorious work. Some think that this is fulfilled as long as the person is in the state of grace. The better and the safer view, however, is that an *act* of love of God must be made, directing the work to Him because He is all-good in Himself. However, even in this view it suffices that the influence of charity persevere *virtually* from the previous act. Thus, if a person directs all his acts to God several times in the course of the day by an act of divine charity, all his good acts — even those that in themselves are only naturally good — are raised to the rank of supernaturally meritorious actions.

FOOTNOTES

1. Can. 572. (This refers to a particular canon, or law, in the *Codex Juris Canonici*, the official code of ecclesiastical law, which began to bind in 1918.)
2. Can. 1087.
3. *Manual of Moral Theology*, p. 156.
4. *DB*, 917.
5. Jn. 14:23.
6. *DB*, 842.
7. Jn. 9:4.
8. Mt. 20:1–16; 25:34 ff.

1. *Nature of Law*

Law is defined as an ordinance of reason, promulgated for the common good by one who has authority over a society.[1] It is called an ordinance of *reason* because it is the product of the practical reason of the legislator. Hence, a law that would be unreasonable would be no law. A law is directed to the common good of the society in which it prevails, not to the good of only a few individuals.

A law differs from a precept inasmuch as the latter is intended for the benefit of an individual or a few persons. Thus, a bishop might impose on one of his diocesans the precept of abstaining from reading certain books, even though these might not be forbidden by general law. Moreover, a law by its nature is permanent, whereas a precept ordinarily ceases to bind with the death or passing from office of the one who imposed it.[2] Furthermore, a law binds the subjects of the lawgiver only within the territory of the lawgiver, unless the opposite is stated. In other words, a law is territorial, not personal, unless the lawgiver positively asserts it is personal.[3] But a precept is personal, binding the person wherever he is. A law can be passed only by a person or body possessing jurisdictional power, but a precept can be imposed by virtue of dominative power, such as a parent possesses over his children.

A law must be promulgated before it possesses the power to bind. This means that a notice of its existence must be communicated to those whom it is intended to bind. A law is sufficiently promulgated when measures have been taken which of themselves are sufficient to notify all the subjects, even though accidentally some of them do not become aware of the law. There is no precise method established for promulgating a law; it is left to the legislator to determine the means to be used. The usual way in which laws of the Holy See are promulgated is by publication in the *Acta Apostolicae Sedis,* and (unless the nature of the law demands it or the opposite is stated) they begin to bind three months after the date of the issue in which they appear.[4]

A law is affirmative if it commands that something be done (e.g., the law that we must assist at Mass on Sunday); it is negative if it

27

forbids something (e.g., the law of Friday abstinence). Some laws are both affirmative and negative, although they may be expressed in only one of these forms. For example, the seventh commandment: "Thou shalt not steal," forbids theft, and commands the payment of debts.

Theologians refer to some laws as *purely penal*. This means that the legislator does not intend to bind the subjects *in conscience* to the thing commanded (as in the case of a preceptive law) but merely requires that they submit to a certain penalty if they transgress the law and are convicted of the transgression. A good example of such a ruling is the keeping of a book from a library over the stipulated time. It is no sin, as long as the person who does so is willing to pay the fine. Some theologians are quite lenient in applying the idea of penal law to civil legislation. Father Davis, S.J., says: "It is indeed disputed whether state law is anything more than penal in England."[5] But others incline to the view that all civil laws are preceptive, binding in conscience, as long as the opposite is not evident.[6] This latter view alone seems tenable. We must always remember that all legitimate civil authority comes from God,[7] and that civil rulers, however mistaken their views may be on matters of religion, have a right to command obedience to their laws in conscience and that usually their primary intention seems to be to require obedience to their laws in as far as they have the right to demand it. Consequently, civil laws should be regarded as binding in conscience unless the opposite is evident.

2. *Divisions of Law*

Law is either eternal or temporal. The temporal law is either natural or positive. Positive law is either divine, ecclesiastical, or civil.

$$\text{Law} \begin{cases} \text{Eternal} \\ \text{Temporal} \begin{cases} \text{Natural} \\ \text{Positive} \begin{cases} \text{Divine} \\ \text{Ecclesiastical} \\ \text{Civil} \end{cases} \end{cases} \end{cases}$$

There are certain other subdivisions. Thus divine positive law is divided, by reason of different stages in human history, into Primitive, Mosaic, and Christian. Civil law is either national or international. In our country we can divide civil national law into state law and federal law. It is to be noted that only those who possess public power of jurisdiction can make laws — e.g., the Pope, a bishop, the state legislature, Congress. A pastor or a local superior of a religious community cannot make laws.

3. *The Eternal Law*

The eternal law is defined by St. Thomas as "the plan of divine wisdom inasfar as it directs all acts and motions toward the end of the universe."[8] From the very fact that God is all-wise it follows that He must have a plan for the activities and the objectives of all His creatures. However, there is a great difference in the way that different creatures follow out this plan. Irrational creatures obey it necessarily, being guided by the forces of nature, without any free choice on their part. But intellectual creatures, angels and men, are endowed with the faculties of intelligence and free will, whereby they can obey the eternal law voluntarily. However, even in regard to those who disobey God's law we can say that the eternal law is fulfilled, inasmuch as they are compelled to submit to punishment according to His just decrees. Hence, it is true to say that no one can evade the eternal law.

4. *The Natural Law*

The natural law is the participation of the eternal law in the rational creature. In other words, it is that portion or aspect of the eternal law which governs human beings. As was stated in the preceding chapter, the proximate foundation of the natural law, or the proximate constitutive norm of morality, is human nature considered in its entirety. Actions which are in accordance with human nature considered in all its aspects and relations are morally good; actions which are in disagreement with human nature are morally bad. The remote foundation of the natural law, or remote constitutive norm of morality, is the divine nature, which created human nature with its inherent characteristics and propensities.

St. Paul speaks of the natural law as perceptible by the Gentiles, who did not have the Mosaic law, saying: "They show the work of the law written in their hearts."[9] The natural law is promulgated by God through man's own reason (the manifestative norm of morality) which tells him that certain human actions are good, others evil, because they are respectively in accordance with or opposed to human nature in its entirety. From this it follows that a person can be aware of certain moral laws (and hence be able to commit sin) even though he is not aware (temporarily) of God's existence.

We do not hold that all men can perceive clearly and with certainty *all* the prescriptions of the natural law by their own unaided power of reason. We distinguish three classes of commandments of natural law: (1) *Most universal principles,* such as "Good must be done, evil avoided." (2) *Immediate deductions from the former,* such as "It is wrong to steal, to murder, to commit adultery." (3) *More remote conclusions,* such as "Things that are found must be restored to their owner, fornication is always wrong, direct suicide is always forbidden."

Catholic theologians commonly hold: (1) Everyone with the use of reason perceives the most universal principles. (2) Normally every mature human being perceives the immediate deductions, but by exception (particularly in the case of one brought up without any religious or moral training) a person might be in invincible ignorance of some of these precepts for a time. (3) It is quite possible for a person to be in invincible ignorance of some of the more remote conclusions, even all his life, when he has no guidance from revelation and the Catholic Church. Thus, there are certainly non-Catholics who in all sincerity believe that birth control and divorce are permissible under certain conditions.[10]

Is a dispensation from the natural law ever permissible? The majority of Catholic theologians say that a dispensation in the strict sense from the natural law can never be given even by God Himself. However, at times what appears to be a dispensation has been granted by God. In these events, however, what actually took place is that in God's plan the purpose of a particular law yielded to a higher good, so that actually the final objective of law, the glory of God, was procured in another way. As some theologians express it, in these instances the *matter* of the law was changed.

We have examples of these quasi dispensations in the command God gave to Abraham to slay his son Isaac,[11] and in the dispensation God granted for polygamy and divorce in the Old Law, as well as in the Pauline privilege in the New Law. But it should be noted that such quasi dispensations can be given only in regard to laws that are directed immediately to the good of creatures. There can be no modifications or exceptions in regard to laws imposing on man obligations directly toward his Creator. Thus, under no circumstances could there be a permission for a person to blaspheme or to offer God a false form of worship.

Since the natural law is essentially joined to human nature, all rational creatures are bound to observe it. Hence, even a person who is deprived of the use of reason commits a material sin if he does something opposed to the natural law. Accordingly, one who would induce an infant (one below the age of reason) or an imbecile to perform an act against the natural law, such as an act of impurity, would be guilty of grave sin, even though the sin on the part of the agent himself would be merely material.

Frequently the mode of expressing the natural law — even by the Almighty in the promulgation of the ten commandments — is abbreviated, so that the precise meaning can be found only through a certain measure of interpretation and expansion. Thus, the commandment: "Thou shalt not kill," does not forbid the killing of any creatures save man, and even then the prohibition must be qualified, so that the commandment in its fullness would be expressed thus: "Thou shalt not kill directly an innocent person, apart from a special divine authorization." Similarly, the commandment: "Thou shalt not steal," does not absolutely forbid us to take the goods of another. It merely forbids us to take his goods *against his reasonable will*. Hence, a person in extreme need of food may take enough to satisfy his needs from another in possession of more than he strictly needs, even against the latter's will, since in such a case the owner would be unreasonable in his unwillingness to share his possessions.

5. *The Divine Positive Law*

In addition to the natural law, the human race has always been subject to the divine positive law, because men have been destined to the beatific vision, a supernatural end, since the creation of the human race. However, in the early centuries there were few precepts other than the obligation to strive to serve God as He had revealed Himself and to have faith in the Redeemer to come. Hence, this was known as the law of nature, although actually it was a supernatural, divine positive law.

For His chosen people, the race of Abraham, the Almighty promulgated many commandments through the prophet Moses. It should be noted, however, that the ten commandments (except the third) were not positive-divine legislation in the strict sense, since they were only expressions of the natural law.

The Mosaic legislation passed away with the promulgation of the Christian law, as far as ceremonial and judicial precepts were concerned. For, the Mosaic law contained commandments of three types

— ceremonial, judicial, and moral.[12] The first two passed away absolutely; the moral commandments passed away in as far as they were prescribed in the Old Law, but they remained in as far as they are expressions of natural law and in as far as they have been renewed by Christ.

The New Law, the law of Christ, will endure until the end of time. The chief positive prescription of the New Law is the obligation to accept the teachings of Christ and to enter His Church.[13] It also contains the obligation on those who have entered the Church to receive the sacraments of Penance (if needed) and the Holy Eucharist. Prümmer teaches that the divine positive law of Christ obliges the members of the Church to assist at Mass occasionally.[14] And, since Christ has given His Church the right to make impediments and to legislate for Christian marriage, civil governments are bound by the law of Christ the King to yield in this matter the right they would have by virtue of the natural law.

6. Civil Law

Civil authorities have the right to pass laws binding in conscience, because they are the representatives of God Himself.[15] However, a civil law that is in opposition to a higher law — natural, divine, or ecclesiastical — does not bind in conscience, for it is actually not a law at all. Civil laws which require good order within the jurisdiction for which they are passed, such as laws forbidding the carrying of weapons, bind externs as well as citizens; but the general principle is that civil laws bind only the citizens of the territory for which they are passed.

7. Ecclesiastical Law

The power to legislate was given by Christ Himself to the rulers of His Church,[16] and is exercised by those who possess public jurisdiction such as the Pope for the entire Church, and bishops for their respective dioceses. Pastors do not possess legislative power. The Code of Canon Law contains the laws of the Holy See, which, however, for the most part bind only Catholics of the Latin rite.[17] The Church has the right to impose laws on all baptized persons, whether they are Catholics or non-Catholics. Some laws certainly bind all baptized persons, such as the impediment of consanguinity or blood relationship in relation to marriage. Other laws certainly do not extend to all baptized persons, such as the obligation to appear before a priest for a valid marriage, which does not bind a couple, both of whom were baptized and brought up as non-Catholics and never converted to the Catholic Church. In regard to certain laws, such as the Friday abstinence, there is a dispute among theologians whether or not they extend to those who have been baptized and brought up as non-Catholics. The rights of the Church in regard to unbaptized persons are limited to the right to preach and to interpret to them the truths of faith and morals and to receive them into the Church by baptism, irrespective of civil laws.

Some ecclesiastical laws are founded on the presumption of a common danger, and these bind even those persons who are actually not endangered. Thus, the prohibition of books by the Index extends even to those persons who could safely read these books, unless they have received permission to read them.

Laws that are merely ecclesiastical bind only those who have reached the age of reason and are at least seven years old (and, of course, are baptized), unless the law itself states differently.[18] The law of annual confession and Holy Communion, since it is basically a divine law, binds even those who are under seven, once they have reached the use of reason.

Ecclesiastical law imposes an obligation that is grave or light in accordance with the importance of the matter involved and the intention of the legislator. When grave matter is involved the legislator is presumed to bind under mortal sin, although even in this case he *can* impose the obligation as binding under venial sin only. When the matter is light and its violation would involve no grave consequences, the legislator cannot impose it under pain of mortal sin. It should be noted, however, that the gravity of the consequences is sometimes measured, not from the standpoint of an individual violation, but from the great harm that might ensue on a more general scale if individual violations were not forbidden under pain of mortal sin — e.g., the law of the eucharistic fast.

The Church has the right to punish those who violate her laws; and *per se* this power extends to the imposition of fines and imprisonment. Nowadays, however, the Church generally confines her punishments to spiritual penalties, such as excommunication and suspension. Some penalties are incurred by the very fact that a person commits a crime when he is aware of the existence of the penalty (e.g., the excommunication inflicted on one who lays violent hands on a cleric or religious); others are prescribed by the Code to be inflicted by ecclesiastical authorities, such as the deposition from office, after the second offense, of a religious superioress who manifests displeasure when a nun goes to confession to a priest who is not the regular confessor.[19]

The question sometimes arises as to whether those who are in a diocese or country only transiently are bound by the ecclesiastical laws prevailing in that place. We must distinguish between those who are *wanderers* (*vagi*), people who have no fixed abode anywhere, and those who are *travelers* (*peregrini*), people who have a home someplace else. The former are bound by the ecclesiastical laws, both general and particular, of the place where they happen to be. In other words, for the time being, they become the subjects of the bishop in whose territory they happen to be.

In regard to travelers, the general principles are these: They are bound by any law of the Universal Church that binds in the particular locality they are visiting, even if this law does not bind in their own home territory. On the other hand, travelers are not bound by a law of the universal Church which has been dispensed from (or for some other reason does not bind) in the particular territory which they are visiting. Furthermore, they are not *per se* bound by a particular law of the territory which they are visiting, though *per accidens* they may be obliged to observe it, especially if otherwise they would give scandal.

For example, a Catholic from the U.S.A. visiting Canada would be obliged to attend Mass on January 6 (because the Epiphany is a holyday by universal law, from which a dispensation is not granted in Canada), but he would not have to go to Mass on August 15 (which is a holyday by universal law, but there is a dispensation granted from its observance in Canada). But a Catholic from the U.S.A. visiting Ireland would not have to attend Mass on March 17 (a holyday in Ireland by particular law), unless he was a person without any fixed abode, or unless by not attending Mass he would give scandal.

To obey a law it is not necessary to have the explicit intention of *fulfilling the law;* it suffices to have the intention of *doing what the law prescribes.* For example, if a person accustomed to hear Mass every day goes to Mass on Sunday morning, thinking it is Saturday and convinced that he is performing a supererogatory work of devotion, he would not be bound to hear another Mass later when he realizes that it is Sunday. Similarly, a person who has received Holy

Communion in the course of the Easter season does not have to receive the Holy Eucharist again, even if at the time of the former Communion he expressly planned to make a subsequent Communion his Easter duty.

In the matter of the private celebration of Mass, the private recitation of Office, the reception of Holy Communion, and the observance of fast and abstinence, one may follow any recognized system of time — e.g., sun time, standard time, daylight-saving time, etc.[20] Furthermore, one may be inconsistent in formally different actions.[21] For example, in a place where daylight-saving time is in use, a person could eat meat between midnight and 1 a.m. on Saturday morning (daylight-saving time) and yet receive Holy Communion or celebrate Mass later on that day. But one must observe twenty-four hours as a day of fast or abstinence.

8. *Causes Excusing From Ecclesiastical Law*

A person is excused from observing an ecclesiastical law when he is physically or morally unable to observe it. Thus, a person sick in bed is physically incapable of going to Mass. A person is said to be morally unable to fulfill an ecclesiastical precept when the observance would involve grave inconvenience to himself or someone else. Thus, a mother is morally unable to go to Mass when her sick child needs her care; a laboring man is morally unable to observe the strict law of fast because of his hard work. To excuse a person from abstinence a graver reason is required than to excuse him from fast.

A *dispensation* from an ecclesiastical law means the relaxation of the law for a good reason in a special case. The reason need not be so great as to excuse him; for in that case he would need no dispensation. The Pope can dispense from any ecclesiastical law. By the prescription of the Code a bishop and a pastor can dispense their respective subjects as well as visitors in their respective territories from the common law of the observance of Sundays and holydays (Mass and servile work) and from the observance of fast and abstinence. This power, however, can be extended only to individuals and to individual families; but a bishop can also dispense the whole diocese for reasons of public health, or because of a great gathering of people.[22] This same power, in regard to individual subjects and other persons who live in the religious house, at least over a day and a night, is possessed by superiors of exempt clerical religious orders. Finally, a bishop can dispense in a particular case from the general law of the Church when it is difficult to have recourse to the Holy See and there is danger of some grave evil in delay, and the dispensation is one that the Holy See is accustomed to grant.[23] By virtue of special faculties from the Holy See (known as the quinquennial faculties, since they are granted for a period of five years at a time) the bishops of the United States enjoy the right to grant a considerable number of dispensations, such as from certain marriage impediments, from the required age for the reception of the priesthood, from the lack of dowry in the case of sisters or nuns, etc.

If a superior dispenses from his own law the dispensation is valid, even though there is no sufficient reason for it; but it is illicit, since it involves a sin of *acceptance of persons* on the part of the superior, a sin against distributive justice. But if a lower superior dispenses from the law of a higher superior without sufficient reason (e.g., a bishop dispensing from a general law of the Church), the dispensation is invalid. However, when there is a doubt as to the sufficiency of the reason the subject may lawfully seek and the superior may lawfully grant the dispensation.[24]

At times a person may reasonably judge that the observance of an ecclesiastical law is so onerous and difficult that it can be reasonably presumed that the legislator did not intend to bring this particular case within the scope of the law. In that event he need not observe the law. Of course, great prudence is required in making such a judgment, lest one grow lax as regards the Church's laws. This manner of excusing oneself from the observance of a law is known as *epicheia*. For example, if a young man on the day of his ordination or first Mass broke his fast, he could receive Holy Orders or celebrate the Holy Sacrifice through a reasonable use of *epicheia*. Similarly, a person who cannot fast could receive the Holy Eucharist once at Paschal time. (It is to be noted that one who finds it difficult or impossible to observe the eucharistic fast can sometimes obtain a dispensation from the Holy See, at least when the approval of his own diocesan authorities has been received. Moreover, the new regulations on the eucharistic fast which went into effect on January 16, 1953, render the observance of this law much easier than it was previously.)

FOOTNOTES

1. St. Thomas, *Summa*, I–II, q. 90, a. 4.
2. Cf. Can. 24.

3. Can. 8.
4. Can. 9.
5. *Moral and Pastoral Theology*, I, p. 164.
6. Cf. Crowe, *The Moral Obligation of Paying Just Taxes* (Washington, D. C.: Catholic University Press, 1944), p. 94 ff.; Herron, *The Binding Force of Civil Laws* (Miami, Fla.: Brower Press, 1952).
7. Rom. 13:1.
8. *Summa*, I–II, q. 93, a. 1.
9. Rom. 2:15.
10. Cf. Bertke, *The Possibility of Invincible Ignorance of the Natural Law* (Washington, D. C.: Catholic University Press, 1941).
11. Gen. 22:2.
12. *Summa*, I–II, q. 99.
13. Mk. 16:16.
14. *Manuale theologiae moralis*, II, 487.
15. Rom. 13:1.
16. Mt. 18:18; Lk. 10:16.
17. Can. 1.
18. Can. 12.
19. Can. 2414.
20. Can. 33.
21. Cf. Bouscaren, *Canon Law Digest Supplement* (1948), p. 4.
22. Can. 1245.
23. Can. 81.
24. Can. 84.

CHAPTER IV . . . CONSCIENCE

1. *Nature of Conscience*

Conscience, as we are considering it here, is *moral* conscience, different from *psychological* conscience, the perception of one's own existence and actions, which is better called in English *consciousness*. Moral conscience is either consequent or antecedent. Consequent conscience concerns past actions, and is a judgment as to their moral goodness or wickedness. It is in this sense that we speak of examining our conscience. Antecedent conscience is concerned with an action the performance of which one is considering for the future. It has reference only to acts as to be performed by *oneself*. It is an act of the intellect, judging that an action must be performed as obligatory, or must be omitted as sinful, or may be performed as lawful, or is advisable as the better course of action. Thus, we have four types of conscience — commanding, forbidding, permitting, counseling.

Conscience is not, therefore, in the strict sense, *habitual* knowledge of right and wrong. This is *moral science*. Neither is conscience in the strict sense an habitual attitude toward moral problems, although we use the term sometimes in this sense, as when we speak of a scrupulous conscience or a lax conscience. But in the true sense, conscience is an *act* of the practical intellect, concerned with a particular action which one is contemplating doing or omitting in the future. (Many people, particularly non-Catholics, regard conscience as an emotional faculty. They "feel" that something is right or wrong, and are guided in their conduct by this feeling. Of course, this norm is entirely unreliable. The more intelligence and the less feeling enter into conscience, the more likely it is to be correct.)

2. *Division of Conscience*

Conscience is *true* or *correct* when it presents the morality of an action as it truly is; it is *erroneous* when it presents the moral aspect of an action incorrectly. Thus, a Catholic whose conscience tells him that it is a mortal sin to eat meat on Friday without a justifying reason has a correct conscience. A Catholic has an erroneous conscience if he thinks it is only a venial sin to transgress the law of Friday abstinence, whatever amount of meat he eats, or if he thinks that it is a mortal sin to eat even a small quantity of meat on Friday.

The proper norm of conduct *per se* is a true conscience, and a person is obliged to follow such a conscience when it commands or prohibits something. Thus, *per se* the Catholic is obliged to abstain from meat on Friday, and to observe the laws of the Church in regard to matrimony. However, *per accidens,* because the individual is bound to seek what is true in the sphere of morality according to his own intellectual ability, a conscience that is invincibly or inculpably errone- ous may be the proper rule of morality, so that a person with such a conscience may be subjectively obliged to abstain from a certain act or to perform a certain act under pain of formal sin. Thus, the Baptist who believes that he is obliged by the law of God to uphold his religion would commit a sin if he became a Catholic. However, it should be noted that such a person cannot be said to have a *real right* to follow his (erroneous) conscience, even though he thinks he has a right to do so. For a *real right* is something objective, and no one can be said to have a real right to commit sin. We can say that a person with an inculpably erroneous conscience has a *purely subjective* right to do what his conscience commands, and that God will reward him for sincerely following his conscience; but we cannot say that God wills the (materially) sinful act the person performs. Further- more, those who have authority over a person may prevent him at times from following the dictates of an erroneous conscience, how- ever sincere he may be. Thus, the authorities of a country that is Catholic in population and tradition may prevent heretical propa- ganda as injurious to the Catholic citizens, even though those who strive to spread heresy are sincere in their desire to do God's will. From this it can be seen that it is incorrect to say: "Everyone has a right to practice any religion he deems to be true." No one has a *real right,* as far as God's law is concerned, to practice any religion save the religion which God has imposed on all mankind.

A person who has a vincibly or culpably erroneous conscience is obliged to seek to correct it before he acts; and in the meantime he may not act unless he follows the safer side, the course that is surely free from sin. Thus, if a man is vincibly ignorant as to whether or not today is a day of abstinence, he must make reasonable efforts to find the truth before he may eat meat, and in the meantime he is obliged to abstain from meat. Of course, if he prefers to abstain, he is not bound to make inquiries, since he is willing to follow the safer side.

A conscience is *certain* when a person, without fear of the opposite being true, judges an act to be good, bad, permissible, or advisable. A conscience is *doubtful* when a person's judgment is suspended, either because he has good reasons for both sides, or no good reasons for either side. In practice, whenever we speak of a doubtful conscience we mean that a person is in doubt between law and liberty — in other words, he is uncertain whether or not he is bound by some obligation.

3. *Use of Conscience in Action*

A person may not act in favor of liberty unless he is *certain* that he may do so without danger of committing sin. For, one who acts while conscious that he may be committing sin, and willing that it should be so, shows that he is willing to offend God, and by that very fact commits sin. However, as will be seen presently, this has reference to a practical doubt that one is sinning, since it is possible to have *practical certainty* that one is not sinning, even though there is a *speculative doubt* as to the lawfulness of the action.

There are different kinds of certainty even in the moral sphere. (We are not considering here the types of certainty known as metaphysical and physical.) There can be absolute moral certainty, which excludes the possibility of the opposite. Thus, a person can be absolutely certain that today is Thursday, so that he is certain, without the possibility of the opposite, that he is not forbidden to eat meat. Similarly, a person may have this high type of certainty that he paid a debtor his bill yesterday, and hence that he has satisfied his obligation of justice toward this man. Again, a person is absolutely certain that if he kills this child he will be guilty of grave sin.

However, it is frequently impossible to have this type of certainty in regard to the lawfulness of a certain act, because there are so many contingencies in human affairs, so many circumstances to be considered when we are faced with a moral problem. Hence, we reasonably presume that God will not demand this measure of certainty that we are not committing sin whenever we act in favor of liberty, otherwise life would become unbearable to one who really desires to serve God. In other words, we hold that moral certainty in a broader sense suffices in order to act licitly in favor of liberty. This type of certainty does not exclude the *possibility* or even some probability that we are acting unlawfully when we act for liberty, but is based on sufficiently strong arguments to permit us to act in favor of liberty.

This type of moral certainty is divided into two classes. The first is that which is present when the arguments in favor of liberty are so strong that of themselves (directly) they exclude all reasonable probability from the opposite side. For example, a young man preparing for the priesthood procures his baptismal certificate from the parish church and that gives sufficient certainty that he may lawfully receive the sacrament of Holy Orders without any reasonable fear that he was not baptized validly. One could imagine the *possibility* that he was never baptized — e.g., that the priest inadvertently said the wrong words, that the water did not flow sufficiently, etc. — but such doubts are imprudent, devoid of all reasonable probability, and it is God's will that they be rejected. Again, a person makes a slightly uncharitable remark about a neighbor. It is *possible,* through some peculiar combination of circumstances, that the remark may be doing great harm; but it is not *probable;* and so, the person who has made the remark should not be worried about any *grave* obligation to correct the impression he has given.

The second class of moral certainty of this broad type is that which is obtained when there are probabilities on both sides, some in favor of law, others in favor of liberty. As the case stands thus, one could not lawfully act in favor of liberty, because he must have certainty that he is free from the obligations of the law. But by the use of certain general principles (reflex principles, as they are called), a person can in these circumstances form a conscience that is *practically certain.* Theologians disagree as to the measure of probability one must have in favor of liberty before he can form his conscience in his favor by the use of these reflex principles, but all agree on the general principle that an opinion that is speculatively only probable can become practically certain by the use of these reflex principles.

For example: I have taken something to eat late at night, and immediately the thought occurs to me that perhaps I have broken the eucharistic fast, and I may not receive the Holy Eucharist. Two clocks are available, both good, as far as I know. According to one, it was a minute before midnight when I took the food; according to the other, it was a minute after midnight. I can say that it is equally probable that I may receive Holy Communion, and that I may not. In such a case I may apply the reflex principle that "the condition of the one in possession takes precedence" (*Melior est conditio possidentis*). In other words, I may consider myself as possessing the right to receive the Holy Eucharist until the law proves that there is a reason why I may not. But, as long as the law can offer no better argument against my receiving Holy Communion than my argument for the right to receive, my liberty remains in possession, and I may receive Holy Communion. Again, if a man who is a practical Catholic, accustomed to avoid mortal sin, doubts whether or not he consented to an internal temptation, he need not confess the doubtful sin. He can use the general or reflex principle: "From what usually happens one may form a prudent judgment" (*Ex communiter contingentibus prudens fit praesumptio*). In other words, from the fact that he ordinarily resists temptation to grave sin he can prudently judge that he did not yield in the present instance, and hence he has sufficient *practical* certainty that he is free from the obligation to confess a mortal sin. In such cases one has indirect certainty in favor of liberty.

4. *Exceptions to the Use of Reflex Principles*

There are certain cases in which it is not permitted to act in favor of liberty by forming a practically certain conscience through the application of reflex principles. Such cases occur when there is danger that from the use of the opinion in favor of liberty some evil may occur which the reflex principles will not avert — in other words, some evil in addition to material sin. For, it must be noted that when one uses probabilism in the manner above described an evil is likely to follow, even when the opinion in favor of liberty is much more probable, the evil of material sin. But since it is only a *material,* not a *formal,* sin, we reasonably conclude that God will allow us to run the risk of such a sin, since otherwise our life would be burdened with all manner of restrictions and anxieties. But the case is different when another evil may follow, either to ourselves or to another. In such a case we must follow the view in favor of the law if we can do so — in other words, we must follow the safer side (*pars tutior*), if this is possible. Theologians generally classify such cases under these three headings:

1. When there is danger that by following the opinion in favor of liberty a sacrament will be given invalidly, the safer side must be followed. For example, if the liquid which I am going to use for baptism is only very probably water, or the liquid I am going to use

for Mass is only very probably wine, I am not free to go ahead and to baptize or to say Mass. I must procure what is *certainly* water or wine. For the use of a reflex principle will not eliminate the danger of giving or confecting these sacraments invalidly.

2. When there is danger that some grave evil, either spiritual or temporal, may come to myself, I may not use probabilities; I must follow the safer side, even though the opinion for liberty is much more probable. For example, if it is really probable that I will sin *formally* by going to a certain movie, I must stay away, even though it is much more probable that I will not sin.

3. When there is danger that some grave evil, either spiritual or temporal, may come to a neighbor through my use of a reflex principle I may not use a probable opinion in favor of liberty. I must follow the safer side. For example, a druggist has twenty bottles bearing the label of a helpful remedy; but he knows that in some way poison has got into one of the bottles. He may not sell even one of the bottles to a customer desiring the remedy, even though it is much more probable that the bottle contains good medicine; but he must destroy the entire lot. He must fulfill the law that he may not inflict even probable danger on his neighbor; he must follow the safer side. Again, a jury may not render a verdict of guilty against a man on trial for murder, even though it is much more probable that the man is guilty. There must be direct (though not necessarily absolute) moral certainty of his guilt before he may be convicted.

(In these cases we are supposing that a *certain* means is available for warding off the danger in question. For, there are times when one may use probabilism even in some of the cases described — namely, when the non-use of probabilism may also have evil results. For example, if an unbaptized child is dying, and the only liquid available is something that is only probably valid matter, I may use it to administer the sacrament of Baptism conditionally. Of course, if I later obtain what is certainly water, I must repeat the baptism conditionally. Again, if a person is dying for lack of the medicine mentioned in No. 3, I may give him one of the bottles, even though there is a probability that it contains poison, because if I do not act thus, he will *certainly* die.)

5. *The Various Moral Systems*

Among Catholic theologians there have been various schools of thought in regard to the question: "How probable must an opinion in favor of liberty be in comparison to the opinion in favor of law in order that one may be justified in accepting it, with the use of reflex principles, as a safe norm for acting in favor of liberty?" (The exceptions just enumerated are supposed in all the systems.)

The two most extreme views have been condemned by the Church. The extreme of rigorism held that one must have direct certainty that he is not bound by a law in order to act in favor of liberty, so that one may not follow even the most probable opinion.[1] The most lax view held that any view expressed in print, even though the author is young and modern, must be regarded as probable (and safe to follow) as long as it has not been condemned as improbable by the Holy See.[2]

However, between these two extremes various systems for forming the conscience have been proposed by reliable Catholic theologians, and have not been condemned by the Church. For example, Probabiliorism (held by very few today) taught that one may act in favor of liberty only when the opinion for liberty is certainly more probable than the opinion for the law. Among the outstanding exponents of this system was Billuart, a celebrated Dominican theologian of the eighteenth century.

Nowadays, however, most theologians are either probabilists or equiprobabilists. This latter system was upheld by St. Alphonsus Liguori, who has now been declared by the Church to be the patron of moralists and confessors.

According to Probabilism, one may follow a truly probable opinion in favor of liberty, even when the opinion for the law is certainly more probable. The probabilists use this principle both when the doubt is concerned with the existence of the law (Is there a law obliging me to do this?) and when it concerns the cessation of the law (I know I was held by a law, but am I dispensed from the law, have I fulfilled the law, or has the law been abrogated?). Their chief reflex principle is: "A doubtful law does not bind."

According to the equiprobabilists, when an opinion in favor of the law is certainly more probable than the opinion for liberty a person is obliged to obey the law. For, they say, if a person sincerely desires to know the truth, he will accept a more probable opinion and act on it in preference to a less probable opinion, since in this way he has the assurance of being correct in a greater number of cases in the long run.[3] Similarly, the equiprobabilists hold that when the opinion in favor of liberty is certainly more probable than the opinion for law, a person is not bound by the law.

However, when the opinions on both sides are about equal, the equiprobabilists make a distinction. They say that in this event, if the doubt concerns the *existence* of the law a person is not bound to obey the law, but may follow liberty. For, they say, in such a case liberty is in possession. The law has not proved that it has a claim on the individual, and so we apply the reflex principle: "In a doubt the condition of the one in possession takes precedence" (in English we have a parallel axiom: Possession is nine tenths of the law). But when the doubt concerns the *cessation* of the law, it would follow that the law must be obeyed, for in such a case the law certainly has been imposed on the person, and consequently is in possession. Hence, the individual must prove that the law is no longer in possession. This he cannot do unless he can present arguments that are certainly stronger than the arguments for the law.

CASES:

1. John Smith, living far out in the country, thinks that today may be a day of abstinence. The only persons he can consult are two neighbors, both good and intelligent men. One tells him that it is a day of abstinence, the other says it is not. What is John's obligation in regard to the observance of abstinence?

2. On another occasion, a Friday, John is told by one of these two neighbors that the bishop has given a dispensation from abstinence, while the other says that no such dispensation has been given. What may or must John do in the matter of abstinence?

3. William Brown, a Catholic, is cast on a desert island. He is sick for some time and loses track of the days. When he recovers, he finds that there is plenty of food available, both meat and fish. But he does not know which day is Friday. Is he bound to abstain on one day or every day or is he entirely free from the obligation of abstinence?

4. Mary Jones promised in prayer that if she managed to get Henry Williams as her husband she would abstain from candy three days every week. She won him; but now she doubts whether or not this was a vow, binding under grave sin, or only a resolution, binding in constancy, with a light obligation. Does she commit a mortal sin if she eats candy every day?

5. Alfred Stern inherited a valuable watch from his father. Sometime afterward one of his aunts informed him that the father had

stolen the watch from a jeweler; another equally reliable aunt told
him that the father had bought the watch. What may or must
Alfred do about the matter?

6. Father Pius goes to bed at 10 o'clock and falls into a deep
sleep. At 7 o'clock the next morning, he rises, quite refreshed, and
starts to prepare for Mass. Suddenly he remembers that in the
course of the night he had risen drowsily, taken a piece of candy,
and immediately returned to his slumbers. He has no idea as to
the precise time when this happened — it may have been 11 p.m.,
it may have been 2 a.m. May he say Mass?

7. Dr. Green left orders that the nurse should give the patient
some sleeping tablets, and wrote the prescription for her before
leaving the sickroom. On reaching his home he realizes that he
was somewhat distracted when he wrote the prescription, and has
a slight reason to fear that instead of prescribing two tablets he
prescribed twelve — sufficient to kill the patient. He feels, however, that it is much more probable that he wrote the prescription
properly. There is no telephone in the patient's house, and it is
a very stormy night; however, he could get back to the house
before midnight, the time for the giving of the tablets. What
should Dr. Green do?

8. Mary Taylor returned to the practice of her faith five years
ago, after leading a very wicked life, and made a fervent confession. Now she recalls a grave sin committed in the days of
her wickedness, and is in doubt whether or not she confessed it.
What should she do?

9. Harry Goodfellow is fond of conviviality, though in general
he is a good Catholic. On Saturday evening as he is preparing for
confession he remembers that in the course of the week he exceeded
the bounds of temperance on one occasion in the matter of cocktails.
He recalls that he felt very gay and made some foolish remarks;
but he is uncertain as to whether or not he was intoxicated in
the strict sense. Is he obliged to confess his intemperance as a
doubtful mortal sin?

10. Sister Josephine, in solemn vows and bound to recite the
Divine Office, is doubtful whether or not she recited Prime today.
However, she is accustomed to shift the string in her breviary as
she recites the Hours, and she finds the string now at the beginning
of Tierce. What is her obligation?[4]

NOTES:

1. The first obligation of one who is in doubt whether or not
he is bound by a law is to seek to acquire certainty, one way or

the other. He must use all reasonable methods to attain direct certainty before he is allowed to use reflex principles in order to attain indirect certainty.

2. A confessor has no right to impose his own opinions as to what is sinful or not on a penitent who is sufficiently instructed to form a reasonable judgment himself. For example, if a prudent man judges that his work is sufficiently burdensome to excuse him from the obligation of fasting in Lent, a confessor who takes a stricter view may not oblige the penitent to fast. But the confessor has the right and the duty to judge of the penitent's dispositions — that is, whether or not he is worthy of absolution. Furthermore, if the penitent is not sufficiently learned or prudent to form his own conscience on matters regarding what is right and wrong, or what must be confessed, he must follow the decision of the confessor in this matter, even if the confessor is somewhat stricter in these matters than are some other priests.

3. Although the Church allows a person to follow any of the moral systems described above (apart from the two condemned by ecclesiastical authority), it is evident that one who is always accustomed to follow the easiest opinion he can find worthy to be called probable is inclined to become lax in moral matters. The system which leads to the greatest proportion of correct judgments in matters of conscience is Equiprobabilism.

6. *Various Kinds of Conscience*

Although the word *conscience* strictly refers to an *act,* it is sometimes used to designate an habitual attitude toward moral problems. In this sense we can say that a person has a *lax* conscience or that he has a *scrupulous* conscience. The former is the attitude of a person who is too ready to judge that he is free from obligations — that is, when objectively he has not sufficient reason for such judgments. Such is the condition of a person who justifies the missing of Mass on Sunday because "he is tired." Nowadays, some Catholics have a lax conscience regarding the vice of contraception. The best remedy for a lax conscience is prayer and meditation on the eternal truths. A person is said to have a scrupulous conscience when without sufficient reason he judges his actions to be sinful, or sees grave sin when objectively there is only venial sin. The best remedy for a scrupulous conscience is meditation on the goodness of God and complete and literal obedience to one's confessor.

Finally, theologians sometimes speak of a *perplexed* conscience. This is the state of a person who hesitates as to which of two opposing

precepts should be observed, and fears that he will commit sin whichever side he chooses. Such, for example, is the mental state of a mother
taking care of a sick child on Sunday and fearing that she will sin
against the Church's law if she stays home to take care of the child,
and that she will fail against her maternal duty if she goes to Mass.
Generally speaking, when there is such a conflict of obligations one
should prefer to obey a divine law rather than a human law. Thus, a
priest who has inadvertently broken his fast on Sunday might give
scandal if he sent the people away without Mass, and in that event
it would be better for him to say the Mass. A person who acts with a
completely perplexed conscience commits no sin whichever side he
chooses, even though he may think he is sinning.

FOOTNOTES

1. *DB*, 1293.
2. *DB*, 1127.
3. Cf. J. O'Brien, "An Aspect of Equiprobabilism," *American Ecclesiastical Review*, Feb. 1941, pp. 97–106.
4. The answers to these cases are as follows:
   1. John is not bound to abstain, since his doubt is about the existence of the law, and the argument for liberty is as strong as the argument for the law (pp. 44–45).
   2. If John follows probabilism, he is free to eat meat. If he follows equiprobabilism, he must abstain, since the doubt concerns the cessation of the law.
   3. William may eat meat every day, since each day is more probably not Friday.
   4. If Mary's reasons for and against the existence of a vow are about equally weighty, she is not bound by vow to abstain from candy.
   5. Since Alfred acquired the watch in good faith, he may keep it, even though his right to own it is now doubtful, until it is proved that the watch was stolen. In the meantime he should make further inquiries. The matter of prescription might be involved (see p. 113).
   6. Fr. Pius may say Mass, since he is in a strict doubt, and liberty is in possession.
   7. Dr. Green must return to the patient's house and make sure that he did not prescribe a fatal dose, since this is a case in which probabilism may not be used (p. 43).
   8. If Mary accepts the system of probabilism, she is not bound to confess the sin. If she follows equiprobabilism and the reasons for believing that she did not confess it are as strong as those for believing that she did confess it, she must confess it when she next receives the sacrament of Penance. However, ordinarily the fact that she made a very good confession on her conversion would make it much more probable that the sin was properly confessed and relieve her of any further obligation.
   9. Harry is not bound to confess the doubtful mortal sin; but he should be sure that his contrition extends to it in the event that it was a grave sin, when he next goes to confession.
   10. Sister Josephine is not bound to recite Prime, since she can use the reflect principle: "From what usually happens, etc." (p. 42).

1. *The Nature of Sin*

Sin, in general, is a moral deordination. We distinguish original sin and personal (or actual) sin. Original sin is the deprivation of sanctifying grace inherited by every descendant of Adam (all mankind) because of his transgression. (Of course, we are excluding Christ Himself, who was incapable of sin because of His divine holiness, and also was free from original sin because of the miraculous mode of His conception. Moreover, it is a dogma of faith that the Blessed Virgin was preserved free from original sin from the first instant of her conception, by a special privilege, through the anticipated merits of her divine Son.)

Actual or personal sin is a positive act contrary to the law of God. We say it is a positive act because, even in the case of a sin of omission, the will acts to choose something at variance with God's will — even though this may consist merely in willing not to will to do the thing prescribed. We say that sin is contrary to the law of *God,* for, although sin may consist in the transgression of a human law, as far as its immediate object is concerned, it is always, at least remotely, against the law of God, which is the basis of all human legislation.

It is important to note, however, that a person need not have an intention of offending God in order to be guilty of sin. For, since the proximate constitutive norm of morality is human nature (in its entirety), a person can realize that a certain act is against one of the aspects of human nature (for example, theft, drunkenness), so that if he deliberately performs this act he commits a sin, even though he does not think of it as an offense against God. The Church has condemned the view of those who assert that a "philosophical sin" — that is, an act at variance with human nature and right reason committed by one who is ignorant of God or does not actually think of God — is not a mortal sin and does not dissolve the divine friendship or merit eternal punishment.[1]

In every sin there are two elements — a positive act of the will choosing as good what is really only an apparent good, and a defect of what should be present to make the act actually good. In a mortal sin the positive act is an inordinate turning to a creature; the negative element, or defect, is the turning away from the true final end, God. In a venial sin there is no turning away from God, but there is a deordination on the choice of the proper means to God.

A sin is not the same as an imperfection. An imperfection can be either negative or positive. A negative imperfection is simply the absence of greater perfection in an action, and this is present in every human act, however excellent it may be. A positive imperfection is the deliberate choosing of the less perfect of two possible courses of action, neither of which is commanded, though the more perfect is counseled, either by some outside authority (e.g., a sermon, an admonition from a superior, a spiritual book) or from within, by one's own intellect aided by grace. Thus, on a Sunday, a religious who has already heard Mass may have the opportunity of hearing another Mass, or he may spend the time in recreational reading. If he chooses to follow the latter course, it is a positive imperfection. Some theologians pass a strict judgment on imperfections of this type, classifying them as venial sins, inasmuch as it is unreasonable for a person to renounce the opportunity of gaining the additional merit that would come from these good works, unless there is some good reason for doing so. But, according to a more lenient view, which seems quite probable, these imperfections are not even venial sins. For, if they be ranked as such, there does not seem to be any real difference between what is of obligation and what is of counsel. But *per accidens,* there can be venial sin in such acts of imperfection, in the sense that they proceed from some immoderate inclination or sinful attitude, such as excessive love of ease or of pleasure. This same principle applies to the violation of those religious rules which do not bind under pain of sin.

That an act may be a sin, three conditions must be fulfilled: (1) There must be moral deordination or defect in the act, at least as the agent conceives it. (2) There must be some advertence of the intellect. (3) There must be some consent of the will (we are speaking of advertence and consent with reference to the *sinfulness* of the act, not merely to its *physical* entity). In the case of a sin that is voluntary in cause (e.g., blasphemy uttered in drunkenness), it suffices that the advertence and consent be present at the time the cause is placed, even though they are not present when the sinful act is performed. It is not necessary that the consent be given to the act in itself. It may even happen that the agent is opposed to this. But it suffices that he foresees the act and places the cause unjustifiably.

A sin is *material* when a person does something objectively wrong without adverting to its sinfulness (e.g., a Catholic eating meat on Friday, entirely forgetful of the day). A sin is *formal* when advertence and consent are present. It is possible to commit a formal sin which is not objectively a sin — e.g., a Catholic eating meat on Thursday, thinking it is Friday, and willing to commit sin.

2. *The Distinction of Sins*

Sins can be distinguished *specifically* and *numerically*. These distinctions have a practical bearing on the sacrament of Penance, since it is a divine law that sins be confessed according to *species* and *number.*[2]

Some theologians hold that sins are specifically distinguished according to their objects — that is, the matter about which they center, considered from the moral standpoint. Thus, a sin of detraction is specifically distinct from a sin of theft, because the former has for its object the unjust taking away of a person's reputation; the latter has for its object the unjust taking away of his temporal goods. Other theologians say that sins are distinguished specifically according to the virtues to which they are opposed. Thus, a sin of sacrilege is distinguished from a sin of heresy because the former is opposed to religion, the latter to faith. In practice, both norms are used, and it seems that they are not opposed to each other, but rather that the former is the more fundamental, the latter the more proximate.

At any rate, all admit that even within the sphere of the same virtue there can be specifically distinct sins, inasmuch as the goods protected by the virtue are different, or the virtue is violated by excess or defect or by a different manner of offense. Thus, the breaking of a vow is different from perjury, because one is the violation of a promise made to God, the other is the violation of the reverence involved in calling God to witness to the truth of a statement. Similarly, despair and presumption, though both opposed to the virtue of hope, differ from each other specifically, in that one fails by defect, the other by excess.

Sometimes it is not easy to judge whether different sins differ specifically or only in degree within the same species. Thus, some theologians say that detraction and calumny are specifically the same, even though the former is the narrating of true (though hidden) faults, and the latter is the narrating of something false. At any rate, contumely is specifically different from detraction, in as far as the former is the *dishonoring,* the latter the *defaming* of a neighbor; and honor is different from fame. Again, it is a disputed point among theologians whether a theft committed *in* church when the object stolen is not a sacred thing (possessed by the Church) is a sacrilege.

When a person is bound to the same act by different laws he commits only one sin by refusing to perform the act if the motives of both laws are the same; but if the motives are different there are two specifically distinct malices in the act of disobedience. Thus, a person commits one sin of irreligion by missing Mass on a Sunday that happens to be Christmas; but one who has a vow never to eat meat commits a sin that is specifically twofold if he eats meat on a Friday — a sin against temperance because of the law of the Church, and a sin against religion because of his vow.

As to the *numerical* distinction of sins, the general principle is that there are as many different sins numerically (in the same species) as there are (1) distinct acts of the will and (2) total objects of the acts. As regards the former it should be noted that in the case of sinful intentions leading to a completed act there is a *moral oneness,* so that a number of acts of the will, though physically distinct, are morally only one sin, identical with the completed act. Thus, if a man plans to rob a bank and for a period of several weeks renews this intention from time to time, making preparations, etc., he commits only one sin. Similarly, if a man misses his Easter duty, and as the months pass by, when the thought that he should receive the Holy Eucharist enters his mind, he simply renews his bad intention, he is said to have committed only one sin during the entire year. But, if a person retracts his bad intention, and then later returns to it, there is numerically a distinct sin committed. For example, if early Sunday morning a man makes the intention of missing Mass (having no justifying reason to do so) he commits a mortal sin. But, supposing that two hours later he decides that he will go to Mass, then later decides not to go, he commits numerically another sin. It should be noted that in the case of purely internal sins (bad thoughts, as they are generally called) every time they are physically interrupted and then resumed (unless the interval is very brief) a new sin (numerically) is committed, since there is no reference to an external act to link them together into one act.

The other foundation of the numerical distinction of sins — distinction of total objects of the act — means that when one act causes several distinct evils, involving different moral objects, so many distinct sins are committed. Thus, if a man accuses a whole family, made up of four members, of some serious crime unjustly, he is guilty of four (numerically) distinct sins. On the other hand, if the group is injured *as a body* there is only one sin — for example, when a person steals money from a firm all the members suffer, but there is only one sin, because they possess the money as a group, or moral person. However, there are certain rights that cannot be possessed in common, particularly bodily life and spiritual life. Thus, when a man kills a group of persons he commits as many sins as there are persons (in as far as he knows that so many are present) even though he accomplishes the deed by one (physical) act. Similarly, one who scandalizes a large number of persons — e.g., by obscene or blasphemous talk in the presence of a group — commits as many sins as there are persons scandalized (in as far as he could and should foresee it). These rules represent the more common view of Catholic theologians, though there are some who hold that only one sin is committed when a person by one act kills or scandalizes several persons.[3]

3. *Types of Sin*

Internal sins can be either *morose delectations, desires,* or *rejoicings.* The first concerns the *present,* the second the *future,* the third the *past.* It should be noted that only an act of the will can be a sin — not an act of the intellect. Hence, it is not strictly correct to speak of a sin of bad *thoughts.* Sin is present only when one *delights in something evil as presented by the intellect.* Merely to think of something evil is not in itself a sin, and may at times be useful or necessary — e.g., when one examines his conscience for confession. However, to think of something evil without a sufficient reason could be an occasion of sin, when it would be a grave incentive of sin, as in the case of sensual thoughts.

Sins of desire and of rejoicing are specified by the object as it actually exists. Thus, if a man desires to kill his enemy who happens to be a priest, he is guilty of both murder and sacrilege in desire. One who rejoices over a past sin of impurity with a married woman is guilty of the malice of both impurity and injustice. However, ordinarily a sin of morose delectation does not include the specific circumstances of the person involved. For example, a man who takes delight (without desire) in the thought of a sin with a particular woman ordinarily does not take into consideration the idea that she is married, and hence would not be guilty of any additional malice of adultery.

Any unlawful activity of the bodily faculties of a sexual nature is sinful if the person consents to it. When it arises without any fault on a person's part, there is no sin, so long as there is no consent of the will. The best mode of resistance is indirect. That is, a person can be indifferent to the imagination and the sensual activities, and keep his thoughts set on something good, especially if he accompanies this by a brief prayer. Even to place a cause from which it is foreseen that sensuality will be aroused is not a grave sin, if the act that is placed is something in itself lawful, such as attending a movie portraying a moderate amount of love-making, provided there is no grave danger of consent to the unlawful pleasure. And if there is a sufficient reason for placing such a cause, such as legitimate recreation, there is no sin at all in permitting the motions of sensuality. However, when a person performs actions which by their very nature tend to produce gravely sinful emotions, apart from some very serious reason (as might occur, for example, in the case of a surgeon required to perform an operation on a woman patient), he sins gravely even though he does not give consent to the resultant sexual pleasure. For this reason ardent love-making between an unmarried couple — "petting" as it sometimes is called — is a mortal sin.

Theoretically, a person may rejoice in a good effect that follows something evil. For example, if John Smith comes home intoxicated and causes so much trouble that his mother-in-law who is making an unlimited visit to his home decides to depart the next day, John may rejoice in her departure, even though he may not rejoice in the fact that he was drunk. A wife whose husband practices contraception (presuming that her co-operation with the act is lawful) may rejoice in her freedom from the burdens of childbearing, even though she may not rejoice in his sin. In practice, as is evident, the distinction is a fine one; so that at times it is dangerous to rejoice in the effect, lest one rejoice also in the cause. But, at any rate, a person may rejoice in a *physical* evil because of a greater natural good or because of a supernatural good. Thus, a mother may rejoice in the fact that her son has poor eyesight because it releases him from the dangers of military service. Or she could rejoice, when he has begun to go about with bad companions, if he is laid up with a severe injury that keeps him away from them until the friendship is ended.

The seven capital sins are so called, not because they are the worst type of sin, but because they represent the vices which offer the strongest incentives for committing sin. In a certain sense we can say that pride is the ultimate cause of all sins, in as far as whoever sins seeks inordinately his own excellence, and that is the fundamental note of pride. The seven capital sins are pride, covetousness, lust, anger, gluttony, envy, and sloth.

4. *Mortal and Venial Sin*

The essential objective difference between mortal and venial sin consists in the fact that the former is a transgression that involves an aversion from God, and the latter includes only an inordinate conversion to a created good, but no aversion from God. Venial sins, however numerous, can never coalesce into a mortal sin; but the matter of several sins, each of which taken by itself would be a venial sin, can coalesce into grave matter and thus constitute a grave sin — e.g., thirty acts of theft, each of two dollars, in the course of a day.

For a mortal sin three conditions must be verified: (1) There must be grave matter (or at least matter considered grave by the agent). (2) There must be full advertence of the intellect, which means that the agent must know or suspect that the matter is gravely sinful. (3) There must be full consent of the will to the act visualized as gravely sinful. If the first condition is lacking, but the other two present, the sin is deliberately venial. If the second and third conditions are not fulfilled, in the sense that the advertence and the consent are only partially present, the sin is a semideliberate venial sin. Such can be the case of one who does something wrong when he is only partially awake, or when he is taken off his guard by a sudden burst of passion. According to the Council of Trent[4] no one can long avoid venial sins without a special privilege; and it is commonly held that this refers to slight semideliberate venial sins. It is also a common teaching of theologians that the Blessed Virgin alone received this privilege.

We distinguish mortal sins into those that are mortal *by their whole nature* (*ex toto genere suo*) and those that are mortal *by their nature* (*ex genere suo*). The former admit no lightness of matter (parvity of matter), so that every sin of this kind that is fully deliberate is a mortal sin — e.g., blasphemy, impurity. The latter admit lightness of matter, so that even when it is deliberate a violation of the virtue to a small degree is only a venial sin, such as theft, sacrilege. A sin is *venial by its nature* when it is never of itself mortal, not only because of circumstances, such as a sin of lying, ingratitude, curiosity.

Venial sins, however numerous, do not diminish a person's degree of sanctifying grace or the merit previously gained. The chief evil of venial sins, when they are fully deliberate, is that they dispose to mortal sin. Venial sins are remitted by acts of perfect contrition (as long as the act extends to them), and also probably by acts of attrition (even without the sacrament of Penance) and perhaps even by acts of the opposite virtue, in as far as these contain implicitly a detestation of the venial sins.

FOOTNOTES

1. *DB*, 1290.
2. *DB*, 899.
3. Cf. Noldin, *Summa theologiae moralis*, I, n. 315.
4. *DB*, 833.

1. *The Nature of a Virtue*

A virtue is a species of habit. A habit is a mode or quality inhering in a being, with a certain measure of permanence or stability. If it inheres in the very substance of the being, it is called an *entitative* habit — for example, health in the body, sanctifying grace in the soul. If it inheres in a faculty it is called an *operative* habit. Some operative habits are morally indifferent, such as facility in writing, speaking a language, or playing the piano, or the habits of understanding and science (these are sometimes called intellectual virtues). Other habits are morally bad or good. Morally bad habits are called vices, e.g., the habit of intemperance. A morally good habit is called a virtue — for example, the habit of acting justly, charitably, etc.

The most notable characteristic of a virtue in the natural order is that it imparts facility of action, and sometimes even makes the repetition of a certain type of action pleasant. Thus, a person who has acquired the habit of temperance, finds it easy to refrain from excess of food and drink and even derives pleasure from this moderation.

A virtue resides in the will or in some faculty directly subordinate to the dominion of the will: the intellect and the sensitive appetites. A facility of operation residing in a faculty not subject directly to the will in its operations, such as the eye, would not be accounted a virtue.

2. *The Natural Virtues*

A natural virtue is a morally good operative habit directed toward good acts of the natural order. A virtue of this kind is acquired and strengthened by repeated acts. A natural virtue is in harmony with the natural law, and is directed toward God as the Author of nature, even though the person who possesses and practices it does not explicitly advert to this — e.g., the man who practices honesty because he realizes that it is demanded by rational nature.

The natural moral virtues are classified under the four general headings of prudence, justice, fortitude, and temperance. Prudence is in the intellect, justice in the will, fortitude in the irascible appetite (that

57

is, the appetite which inclines one to do things involving difficulty), and temperance in the concupiscible appetite (that is, the appetite inclining one to what is pleasurable to the senses).

These four are known as *cardinal* virtues (literally "hinge" virtues) because the moral life of man depends on their exercise as a door depends on the activity of its hinges. All the other moral virtues are subordinated to these in one way or other. Thus, the *integral* parts are certain dispositions or conditions that are required for the practice of a cardinal virtue, such as docility and circumspection in relation to prudence. The *subjective* parts of a virtue are those which are related to the cardinal virtue as species to genus. Thus, legal justice and commutative justice are subjective parts of the cardinal virtue of justice. The *potential* parts of a cardinal virtue are those which possess some of the characteristics of the cardinal virtue, but not all. Thus, humility and meekness are potential parts of temperance, and religion and gratitude are potential parts of justice.

A person can have one moral virtue *in a limited degree* without having the others. Thus, a person may be quite honest without being humble. But it is commonly taught by theologians that the moral virtues are so intimately related, and one so frequently demands the help of the others, that to have any virtue *in a perfect degree* a person must have all in a perfect degree.[1]

There is an axiom *Virtus in medio stat* — "Virtue consists in the golden mean." This does not mean that the proper thing is to practice only a limited measure of virtue. A person should strive for the highest perfection of every virtue. But it means that in determining the proper norm for each virtue we must avoid both excess and defect; otherwise, we do not practice the true virtue. Thus, true fortitude is between audacity and cowardice; humility is between pride and pusillanimity. The "golden mean" of justice is determined extrinsically. In other words, if a person owes another ten dollars, virtue demands that he pay ten dollars, no more and no less. But the "golden mean" of fortitude and temperance depends on the individual concerned. Thus an attempt to rescue a drowning person would be a deed of virtue for one who can swim, a deed of rashness for one who cannot swim.

3. *The Supernatural Virtues*

Since man is destined to a supernatural end, it is fitting that God should equip him with certain habitual inclinations and powers toward the attainment of that end, just as in the natural order God endows man with natural faculties, such as intellect and will. Accordingly, we expect in the supernatural sphere certain supernatural habits or virtues; and revelation informs us that such supernatural habits actually exist.

We can find a very close parallel between the natural and the supernatural order. Thus, in the natural order man possesses a principle of life (the soul), natural powers of operation (the faculties), and with the aid of God's natural concurrence he performs natural acts. Analogously, in the supernatural order man has a principle of supernatural life (sanctifying grace), habitual powers of supernatural operation (the supernatural virtues), and God gives supernatural help for the performance of supernatural acts (actual grace). Of course the analogy is not perfect in all respects. For example, the soul of man is a substance, whereas sanctifying grace is an accident, a created quality.

The supernatural virtues can be obtained only by infusion, the act of God conferring them directly on the soul. Since the habits of sanctifying grace and the supernatural virtues are a participation of the divine nature and of the divine powers respectively, only God through the operation of the divine nature can be the principal cause of their infusion. However, creatures can be the instrumental causes of the infusion of these supernatural habits — for example, the humanity of Christ and the sacraments.

It is characteristic of a natural virtue to give facility of action, making it possible to perform a certain type of action with ease and even at times with a certain degree of pleasure. However, this is not one of the characteristics of the supernatural virtues. The particular function of a supernatural virtue is to *supernaturalize* man's natural operative faculty, not to render supernatural acts easy or pleasant. Hence, a person who recovers the state of grace (accompanied by the infused virtues) after a long period of sinful conduct finds it just as difficult to perform good actions opposed to his vices as he did when he was in the state of sin. However, when a person habitually performs acts of a certain supernatural virtue a facility is certainly developed. The best explanation is that a supernatural act of virtue *contains* a natural act, and the repetition of these (contained) acts develops a natural virtue (which imparts facility) concomitantly with the development of the supernatural virtue.

In every virtue we can distinguish a *material object* and a *formal object*. The material object is the thing or things with which the virtue is concerned. Thus, the material object of faith is the truths revealed by God. The formal object is the motive which prompts the faculty to act as it does in regard to the material object. Thus, the formal object of faith is the authority of God revealing which prompts the intellect to accept the truths of revelation.

4. Different Species of Supernatural Virtues

We know from revelation that there are three virtues having God in the supernatural order as their immediate object. St. Paul tells us: "Now, there abide faith, hope and charity, these three; but the greatest of these is charity."[2] Faith has for its immediate object God as the supreme truth; hope has God as man's supreme good; charity has God as the supreme good in Himself. These three are called theological virtues, or divine virtues, because God is their immediate object, and we are made aware of them only because of divine revelation.

It is a common teaching of theologians that there are also supernatural moral virtues — virtues infused by God in connection with sanctifying grace, perfecting man's faculties to act properly in regard to the created means to the attainment of God in the supernatural order. These virtues are designated by the same names as the natural or acquired virtues, and are classified in the same manner under the cardinal virtues, prudence, justice, fortitude, and temperance. However, they are habits entirely distinct from the natural virtues; for even though they have the same *material* objects as these latter, they differ in their *formal* object, in that the formal object or motive of a natural virtue is made known by reason, and that of the supernatural virtues is made known by faith. One can have the supernatural moral virtues without having the corresponding natural virtues. Thus, a baptized infant has the infused moral virtues, infused together with sanctifying grace when he received Baptism, but he does not possess any natural virtues since these can be acquired only by the habitual exercise of good acts. On the other hand, a person may be in mortal sin (and hence devoid of the supernatural moral virtues) and yet have a considerable measure of some of the natural virtues.

Besides the theological virtues and the supernatural (infused) moral virtues, a person receives in conjunction with sanctifying grace the gifts of the Holy Ghost — created habits aiding one to be promptly obedient to the inspirations of the Holy Spirit. Seven such gifts are commonly enumerated — wisdom, understanding, counsel, fortitude, knowledge, piety, and fear of the Lord.[3] Some theologians have held that these gifts are actually nothing more than the theological and infused cardinal virtues as exercised under the special assistance of the Holy Ghost; but the more common teaching is that they are habits really distinct from the virtues. At any rate, they are not exercised only on those occasions when man is called on to perform extraordinary or heroic deeds, but they can be exercised even in the performance of ordinary deeds, when a person needs special help from God because his virtues are not adequate to meet the situation with which he is faced.

5. The Connection of the Virtues

The theological virtues, the supernatural moral virtues, and the gifts of the Holy Ghost are always conferred together with sanctifying grace, and in a measure corresponding to the measure of sanctifying grace. With the increase of sanctifying grace, whether through the reception of the sacraments (*ex opere operato*) or through the performance of supernaturally good (meritorious) deeds (*ex opere operantis*), these habits increase in their intensity. They are not diminished or destroyed by venial sin; however, by the commission of deliberate mortal sin sanctifying grace is expelled from the soul, and with it are expelled all the supernatural virtues, with the exception of faith and hope. Faith is expelled only by a mortal sin directly opposed to this virtue; hope is lost only by a mortal sin directly opposed to hope or by a sin that banished faith.

The order of dignity of the virtues and the gifts of the Holy Ghost is as follows:

1. Theological virtues (charity, faith, hope).

2. Gifts of the Holy Ghost (wisdom, understanding, knowledge, counsel, piety, fortitude, fear of the Lord).

3. The supernatural moral virtues (prudence, justice, fortitude, temperance).

4. The natural moral virtues (prudence, justice, fortitude, temperance).

In heaven, the blessed retain the virtues and gifts, except faith (because this is concerned with things not seen, and the blessed will see God) and hope (because this is concerned with things not possessed, and the blessed will possess God). However, not all the virtues will be exercised. For example, temperance will not be required to regulate the use of food and drink; fortitude will not be required to strengthen man against the fear of death.

FOOTNOTES

1. St. Thomas, *Summa,* I–II, q. 65, a. 1.
2. 1 Cor. 13:13.
3. Isa. 11:2.

PART II:

THE VIRTUES IN PARTICULAR

CHAPTER I . . . *FAITH*

1. *The Nature of Faith*

The word *faith* in connection with religion is often understood nowadays as a feeling of trust and confidence in God, a kind of blind acceptance of the divine presence and of divine help. This is somewhat similar to the Protestant concept of faith, proposed by Martin Luther, according to whom faith is a firm confidence that one has been justified through the merits of Christ. According to the original Protestant doctrine, this confidence is the essential factor of justification, which consists in the covering over of our sinfulness, as with a cloak, by the merits of Christ.

According to the teaching of the Catholic Church, faith is in the intellect, not in the will or in the feelings. Faith, in its widest concept (abstracting from religious connotation), is the acceptance of another's statement, based on his authority — his knowledge and his truthfulness. In other words, when we accept as true another person's statement regarding something which we do not perceive by our own faculties, the two qualities which we must first establish are his *knowledge* of the matter involved and his *veracity*. We must be sure that he understands the subject on which he is speaking and that he is speaking truthfully. Accordingly, faith is different from knowledge, which is the acceptance of something as true because it is evident to oneself. (This evidence can be immediate, as when I know that there is a tree outside the window or that one plus one makes two; or it can be mediate — through the use of my reasoning powers — as when I know that the sum of the angles of a triangle equals two right angles or that God exists.)

Divine faith is the virtue, infused by God together with sanctifying grace, inclining the intellect to assent firmly to all the truths revealed by God on account of the authority of God revealing, who can neither be deceived nor deceive.

2. *The Formal Object of Faith*

The formal object, or *motive*, of divine faith is the authority of

65

God revealing, who can neither be deceived nor deceive. In the words of the Vatican Council: "This faith, which is the beginning of human salvation, the Catholic Church professes to be a supernatural virtue by which, through the inspiring and helping grace of God, we believe as true the things revealed by Him, not on account of the intrinsic truth of the things perceived by the natural light of reason, but on account of the authority of God Himself revealing, who can neither be deceived nor deceive."[1] The "authority of God" is resolved into His divine wisdom and truthfulness, explained by the final clause "who can neither be deceived nor deceive."

It is evident from this that the authority of the Catholic Church is not even a partial motive of divine faith. In other words, if a person believed the mystery of the Holy Trinity, the divinity of Christ, etc., *because of the authority of the Catholic Church,* he would not be making an act of divine faith. For the motive of a *theological* virtue must be a divine attribute, some perfection of the *divine* nature.

However, besides divine faith, two other types of assent are demanded of Catholics — ecclesiastical faith and religious assent. By ecclesiastical faith we hold those truths that are not contained in divine revelation but are connected with it and have been defined by the Church with the exercise of its infallible power (for example, that Frances Cabrini is in heaven, that Anglican Orders are invalid). For, unless the Church could define such truths infallibly, it could not properly define and protect the deposit of divine faith. These truths constitute the *secondary* object of the Church's infallible teaching power; the truths contained in revelation constitute the *primary* object. In defining the primary object the Church is the infallible proponent, but her teaching authority does not constitute the motive; in defining the secondary object, the Church makes her own infallible authority the motive or formal object. Hence, we call the assent to such definitions *ecclesiastical* faith.

With *religious assent* we hold those truths which are *authoritatively* but not infallibly proposed by the Church. The Catholic must give to these an internal assent, based on the fact that the authoritative teaching power of the Church is assisted by the Holy Ghost and that the proponents of such doctrines take every precaution to insure the truth of their statements. Hence, a Catholic would ordinarily commit a grave sin of disobedience if he refused to accept such teachings, internally as well as externally. We say "ordinarily" because, in the case of one who is an expert in a particular subject, it is possible that in a very rare instance he may have good grounds for doubting or deny-ing one of these teachings. In that event, it is his duty to communi-cate his objections privately to the teaching authority, and to be silent publicly rather than contradict what has been taught. (For a Catholic to deny or to doubt a matter of ecclesiastical faith would always be a grave sin, though it would not be directed against the virtue of divine faith, and hence would not expel this theological virtue from his soul.)

Examples of doctrines which must be accepted with religious assent are the decisions of the Biblical Commission and the decrees of the Holy Office. Sometimes, especially in encyclicals, the pope makes state-ments which are to be accepted only with religious assent. On the other hand, the pope can enunciate in encyclicals truths to be accepted with divine faith or ecclesiastical faith. Hence, it would be incorrect to state as a general principle that the doctrines of the encyclicals bind Catholics only to religious assent. In the encyclical *Humani generis* Pope Pius XII asserts that frequently in encyclicals teachings are expounded which pertain to Catholic doctrine, and he reproves those who are inclined to underestimate such teachings on the ground that they are not infallible.

3. *The Material Object of Faith*

The material object of divine faith is all the truths revealed by God. All men are obliged to believe the public deposit of divine revelation — all truths contained in Scripture or in divine Tradition — no matter how unimportant they may seem to be in themselves. Thus a person would be guilty of a grave sin against divine faith if he denied that the dog of Tobias wagged his tail when his master returned.[2] For all truths contained in revelation have the same motive or formal object, the authority of God revealing.

A private revelation must be believed by those individuals for whom it is intended. However, no one is obliged to believe the statement of another that a private revelation has been made for him unless good assurance has been given that it is really from God. Usually such assurance is given through evident miracles. Persons for whom the revelation is not intended are not bound to accept it as a divine mes-sage, although they would do wrong if they positively denied it or derided it when there is good evidence that it came from God.

Not only what is explicitly contained in public revelation but also what is implicitly contained in explicitly revealed doctrine must be accepted on divine faith. For example, it is explicitly revealed that all the Apostles received the Holy Ghost on Pentecost; in this it is implicitly revealed that St. John received the Holy Ghost. It is explicitly revealed that all the popes are infallible, and in this it is implicitly revealed that Pius XII enjoys the gift of infallibility.

According to Catholic belief no new truths have been added to the deposit of public revelation since the death of the last Apostle. However, there has been development of this body of divine truth in the sense that, with the passing of the years, a clearer and deeper understanding of these divine truths has taken place. In other words, there has been a progress of the faithful in the faith, but not a progress of the faith in the faithful. This Catholic notion of the development of doctrine is entirely different from that championed by the so-called Modernists, who taught that an *objective* increase of revealed doctrine will go on until the end of the world.

There are three ways in which development of the material object of divine faith can take place, according to Catholic belief:

1. Scientific formulas and terms can be invented to express more clearly and technically truths held from the beginning in more popular and more indefinite terminology — e.g., hypostatic union, transubstantiation.

2. A truth held only implicitly, as contained in a more general truth, may become a matter of explicit belief in the course of time. Thus, in the original doctrine that Mary was a worthy mother of God was contained implicitly the doctrine of her immaculate conception, which became an article of explicit faith only after many centuries. Again, in the doctrine of the immaculate conception was contained implicitly the doctrine of Mary's bodily assumption.

3. A truth which from the beginning was believed and taught in a practical form may, in the course of time, be believed and taught in a speculative form. Thus, the practice of not repeating Baptism, Confirmation, and Holy Orders, which prevailed from the beginning, contained the revealed doctrine that an indelible character is impressed on the soul by these three sacraments.

When the Church, employing the fullness of her infallible teaching authority, proposes a doctrine of faith or morals as contained in revelation (either Scripture or divine Tradition), to be believed by all, the doctrine is said to be a matter of divine-catholic faith, or a dogma. There are two ways in which the Church can propose a truth infallibly — in the solemn manner or in the ordinary manner. The

Church teaches solemnly through the definition of an ecumenical council or of the Pope speaking *ex cathedra*. The ordinary manner of proposing a doctrine consists in this, that the bishops throughout the world unanimously (or practically unanimously) under the leadership of the Sovereign Pontiff teach a doctrine as contained in revelation. Because of this latter method there are certain truths of divine-catholic faith which have never been solemnly defined, but which nevertheless have the same doctrinal value as those solemnly defined by councils or popes. For example, it has never been solemnly defined that the Church is infallible, but it is certainly an article of divine-catholic faith from the ordinary and universal magisterium of the Church.

It should be noted that the infallibility of the Church in regard to truths not contained in revelation but connected with it is exercised in these same ways — by solemn definition or by the ordinary and universal magisterium. When a truth is thus proposed, it becomes an article of ecclesiastical faith.

4. *The Act of Faith*

The act of faith proceeds from the intellect, assenting to the truths revealed by God on account of the authority of God revealing. But it is commanded by the will, and aided by actual grace. Before a person can make an act of divine faith he must first make a judgment of credibility and credentity: "It is reasonable and obligatory to believe these doctrines as revealed by God." To make such a judgment, one must know with the light of natural reason certain facts, called the preambles of faith. These are: God exists; He is all-wise and all-truthful; He has revealed certain doctrines, imposing on all the obligation to believe them. The arguments by which one arrives at the judgment of credibility and credentity are called the *motives of credibility*. The chief motives of credibility for the Christian revelation are external signs, particularly miracles and prophecies.[3] However, children and uneducated persons can find sufficient motives of credibility in the testimony of persons whom they reasonably trust, such as their parents. But, as persons advance in age and intelligence, they should try to acquire more scientific and more cogent motives of credibility. Intrinsic arguments, such as the sublimity of the Christian revelation, should not be despised; but the extrinsic arguments of miracles and prophecies are the best, adapted to the intellectual needs of all persons.

It should be emphasized that the motives of *credibility* are not the same thing as the motive of *faith*. The motive of divine faith can be nothing else but the authority of God. But the motives of credibility leading to the judgment: "I can and should believe these doctrines on God's authority" are found in philosophy (theodicy) and in historical investigation (e.g., the Gospel account of Christ's life and miracles, taken as a purely historical record). When the intellect makes the judgment of credibility and credentity, the will (aided by actual grace) commands the intellect to elicit the act of faith. This command of the will is needed because the object of faith is not evident and therefore does not *compel* intellectual assent, even after the judgment of credibility. The motive impelling the will to give this command is the *goodness* and the duty of believing, just as the *credibility* of revelation assures a person that it is *reasonable* to believe. Hence, a person is physically free to believe or not to believe, even after the judgment of credibility, and hence when he does believe his act of faith is meritorious.

The act of faith is the first intrinsically supernatural act a person elicits. For there can be no intrinsically supernatural act of the will until the intellect has presented to the will the supernatural goodness and reasonableness of the act of believing, and the intellect has then believed in revelation. Hence, one cannot make acts of hope, charity, contrition, etc., unless he has first made an act of faith. For this reason the Council of Trent asserted that faith "is the beginning of human salvation, the foundation and root of all justification."[4]

5. *The Necessity of Faith*

We distinguish two kinds of necessity — necessity of means and necessity of precept. When a thing is necessary for the attainment of an end because it contains in itself something requisite for this purpose, we say that it is necessary by necessity of means. In such an event, if a person does not employ the means, even though it involves no fault on his part, *per se* he cannot attain the end. A thing is necessary by necessity of precept if a lawful superior commands its use; so that if it is inculpably omitted, the agent is not thereby impeded from attaining the end. For example, Baptism is necessary for salvation by necessity of means; the eucharistic fast is necessary for the lawful reception of Holy Communion by necessity of precept.

When we say that *per se* it is impossible to attain an end without something that is necessary by necessity of means, we imply that by

God's ordinance another means may supply in certain cases. Thus, baptism of desire and baptism of blood can supply the chief effects of the baptism of water in certain cases. In such an event, we say that the means in question is necessary by *relative* necessity of means, as distinct from the case when nothing will supply for the means (*absolute* necessity).

The *virtue* or *habit* of faith is necessary for salvation by absolute necessity of means. For no one can be saved unless he leaves this world in the state of sanctifying grace; and one who leaves this world in sanctifying grace always possesses the virtue of faith.

The *act* of faith, in the case of an adult (one who has attained the use of reason, which the Church presumes to come at the completion of the seventh year) is necessary by necessity of means for justification, and consequently for salvation. One who has the state of grace when he arrives at the age of reason must perform supernaturally good acts in order to remain in grace, and for these he needs an act of faith. The act of faith must extend, at least implicitly, to all that God has revealed. Explicitly, one must believe at least two truths — that God exists, and that He rewards or punishes in the future life according to one's deeds in the present life.[5] A few theologians once held that faith in the broad sense suffices — that is, the knowledge of God from the testimony of creatures — but this view has been condemned by the Church.[6] Accordingly, the recognition of God as existing and as remunerating must visualize Him as the author of the supernatural order, and hence must be derived from revelation. Even in the case of those peoples who seem cut off from supernatural revelation, theologians hold that each adult has the opportunity of learning enough about God as He has revealed Himself (whether by private revelation in the last hours, or by vestiges of primitive revelation still retained) so that he can make an act of faith and of divine charity and thus be saved, as long as he has not rendered himself unworthy of this favor by culpable violations of the natural law.

It is a matter of uncertainty whether or not explicit faith in the doctrines of the Holy Trinity and the Incarnation is also necessary for salvation by necessity of means. The negative opinion seems the more probable; but, since this is a case in which one may not use probabilism (since there is danger of a very grave evil not depending on conscience, the loss of salvation), the safer side must be followed and a person must be instructed in these truths also, even in the hour of death (if it is at all possible).

By necessity of grave precept the following truths must also be explicitly accepted: the Apostles' Creed (as regards its substance), the commandments of God and of the Church, the essential duties of one's state in life, the Our Father, the doctrines about the sacraments which one has received or intends to receive. (No special formula of these truths need be memorized, as far as grave obligation is concerned.) By necessity of light precept one is bound to know the exact words of the Creed, the Our Father and the Commandments, and also the Sign of the Cross and the Hail Mary.

A person is obliged to make an act of faith when the motives of credibility are sufficiently proposed to him, also sometimes in life (at least three or four times a year), and at the hour of death. A Catholic who leads a good life fulfills the obligation by his acts of devotion, such as attendance at Mass and the reception of the Sacraments.

6. *The Profession of Faith*

The obligation to profess the true faith is both negative and affirmative. As a negative commandment it forbids one ever to profess a false religion or to deny the true religion. Such acts are intrinsically wrong, grave sins, and even the fear of death will not justify a person in performing them. This principle extends also to an implicit denial of the faith, such as receiving the sacraments of a false religion. Even to wear the garb or insignia proper to a false religious sect would be gravely sinful when this dress or insignia would be equivalent to a profession of the *religion* itself. This would ordinarily apply to Masonic emblems and the garb of the Salvation Army. However, this would not be the case if the garb in question is primarily national or traditional (in a certain locality), even though ordinarily it is worn only by persons of one religious group. Thus, it would not be a denial of the faith to wear the fez in Turkey.

As an affirmative precept the obligation to profess the true faith binds a person (by God's law) as often as silence or ambiguity or his manner of acting would suggest an implicit denial of the faith, contempt of religion, an insult to God or scandal to one's neighbor. Thus, if a Catholic is present at a gathering in which the Catholic religion is being derided, he should ordinarily profess his faith and make some manner of protest. However, a person is not *always* bound to profess his faith, since there are times when silence, or even an ambiguous manner of acting would not involve any of the consequences just enumerated. In fact, at times a Catholic could perform an action which *in itself* is lawful, even though forbidden by Church law, with the realization that others will thus conclude that he is not a Catholic. For example, in time of persecution a Catholic could eat meat on Friday if otherwise he might be the object of suspicion. Again, a young person who enters the Church without the knowledge of his parents could stay away from Mass on Sundays when it would lead them to judge that he had become a Catholic and to punish him severely in consequence. It should be noted, however, that to abstain from professing the faith is not the same as denying the faith or professing a false religion, for such things are intrinsically evil. Thus, the young person in question would never be allowed to take active part in a false religion, however grave the inconveniences might be that the parents would inflict. Ordinarily ambiguities are to be avoided, and a Catholic must be willing to declare himself such. This is particularly true of a public personage. It is well to remember, however, that our American law does not require a statement of one's religious affiliation as a qualification for office — e.g., schoolteacher. Hence, if a person applying for such a job were asked his religion, he could refuse to answer.

By the law of the *Church* certain persons must profess the Catholic faith on particular occasions — for example, clerics before the reception of the subdiaconate, professors of theology at the beginning of each scholastic year or at least when they first enter on their office, university professors, etc.[7]

7. *The Sin of Infidelity*

Infidelity may be either negative or positive. Negative infidelity is the state of one who has not received sufficient knowledge of the Christian revelation to furnish him with convincing motives for its credibility. Such a person is not guilty of any formal sin in his unbelief. Positive infidelity is the state of one who refuses to accept the Christian revelation after it has been sufficiently proposed to him with the motives of credibility. This is a sinful attitude. It admits of various species. One who rejects the faith as soon as it is proposed is guilty of simple infidelity. One who has professed the Christian faith, and has received Baptism, but later rejects the Christian faith *entirely* is called an apostate. One who continues to regard himself as a Christian but rejects *some* of the truths to be believed with divine-catholic faith is a heretic. One who refuses to submit to the

Sovereign Pontiff or to communicate with the members of the Church subject to him is a schismatic.[8] Schism as such is not opposed to the virtue of divine faith, but is a sin against obedience and charity.

Since only *formal* sin expels sanctifying grace, a person who in good faith is in heresy can possess sanctifying grace and the theological virtues. Such a person is connected with the Catholic Church by *implicit desire*. All admit that one who is brought up in heresy can be in good faith. But the question arises: Can one who possesses the Catholic faith ever come to a state of mind in which in all sincerity — and consequently without formal guilt — he judges that the Catholic faith is erroneous and that it is his duty to leave the Catholic Church? This might be possible in the case of one who, though nominally a Catholic, is very poorly instructed, especially if he is placed in surroundings where there is very little opportunity to receive proper answers to his difficulties. But it would seem that one who has been properly instructed in the Catholic religion could not leave the Catholic Church without formal sin; for such a person knows his obligation to seek counsel when doubts arise, and when he receives such counsel (presuming it is correct and adequate) he will not act logically if he leaves the Church. Moreover, such a person knows of his obligation to pray in such circumstances, and through prayer he will receive light and help from God. Rarely, if ever, therefore, does a Catholic who has received proper Catholic instruction leave the Church without formal sin, for, as the Vatican Council says, "God does not desert a person unless He is first deserted."[9] It is to be noted, however, that the formal sin in question need not necessarily be a sin against faith. It may be a sin of another species (e.g., pride, impurity) whereby one renders himself unworthy of the special graces he needs in the crisis. Such a person, therefore, might retain the virtue of faith even after his defection from the Catholic Church.[10]

The sin of infidelity is *mortal from its entire nature,* in all its species, so that there cannot be a venial sin of infidelity as far as the matter involved is concerned. For, to deny or to doubt any revealed doctrine, however unimportant it may seem in itself, is *per se* a grave insult to the all-wise and all-truthful God.

8. *Religious Communication*

By religious communication we mean the association of Catholics with non-Catholics in religious functions. Formerly the Church was very strict regarding even civil communication of Catholics with non-

Catholics — for example, in business and social relations. But nowadays the Church forbids such communication only with one excommunicated *by name;* furthermore, this does not apply to spouse, parents, children, servants, and subjects. Other persons are allowed such communication with one excommunicated by name for a reasonable cause.[11]

Religious communication is twofold — non-Catholics with Catholics, and Catholics with non-Catholics. The former is generally forbidden when there is question of public or liturgical functions. Thus, non-Catholics may not be admitted to the sacraments *per se,* nor allowed to serve Mass, to take part in processions, nor receive the sacramentals publicly — that is, sacramentals given to individuals publicly, such as blessed ashes and palms. Non-Catholics should not be employed to sing in choir or to play the organ in a Catholic church. However, since these things are not intrinsically wrong, they can be permitted for a good reason. Thus, some non-Catholic singers could be allowed in certain circumstances; sacramentals can be given privately (especially blessings) to non-Catholics, the purpose being to obtain for them the light of faith.[12] For a good reason a non-Catholic could serve as witness at a Catholic wedding. But care must be taken in all these instances lest the impression be given that the Church will compromise on matters of faith or regard religious differences as unimportant. Furthermore, a non-Catholic may not serve validly as a godparent at a Catholic baptism,[13] although such a person might be allowed to act as a witness.

In the matter of communication of Catholics with non-Catholics in religious worship, we must first distinguish private from public worship. It is lawful for Catholics to participate with non-Catholics in *private* worship, provided the prayers, hymns, etc., contain nothing against the Catholic doctrine of faith or morals. Thus, Catholics could join non-Catholics in grace before meals; Catholics and non-Catholics in a dangerous wreck or accident could recite together the Our Father, although the Catholics should not recite the usual Protestant doxology: "For Thine, etc.," since this is regarded as a distinctively Protestant formula, although it contains nothing that is contrary to any doctrine of faith.

As regards the communication of Catholics with non-Catholics in public functions, the principle is that a Catholic is never allowed to participate *actively,* but *passive* assistance may be tolerated for a grave reason (the decision of the bishop is to be sought when there is doubt about the gravity of the reason), at marriages, funerals, etc., for the sake of a civil official or honor.[14]

From this we conclude that a Catholic may never join in the prayers or hymns at a non-Catholic public service. It should be noted that even when there is nothing erroneous expressed in these hymns or prayers, active participation is forbidden, because the basic reason why it is wrong to take part actively in such a service is the fact that the only religious body authorized by Christ to conduct public services is His one true Church. Hence, a Catholic would do something gravely wrong if he played the organ, sang, etc., at a public non-Catholic service, even though he were in extreme need of material support or even if he were commanded to take part by the officials of army or navy.

A Catholic is strictly forbidden to act as godparent at a non-Catholic baptism, although in certain circumstances a Catholic servant might hold the child. Neither may a Catholic act as bridesmaid or best man at a non-Catholic religious marriage, if the particular sect regards these functionaries as participants in the *religious* aspect of the ceremony. If they are regarded as merely attendants to the *bride* and *groom,* their participation would not be intrinsically wrong, though even in that case it would often be a cause of scandal for Catholics to take part in this way. Catholics may be allowed to take part as extra bridesmaids, ushers, etc., for a sufficiently good reason.

In extreme necessity a person may request the sacraments from a non-Catholic, which this latter is able to confer validly (e.g., a priest of the Oriental Orthodox Church), when these are necessary — that is, Baptism, Penance, and Extreme Unction (at least, when Penance cannot be received) in danger of death. But even in this event, the sacraments may not be sought under any circumstances if in the ceremony distinctively non-Catholic doctrines are expressed. (Although the general rule is that the Catholic sacraments may not be given to non-Catholics, there is a good theological view that allows this in the case of non-Catholics dying unconscious, at least if there is some reasonable presumption that they have a general will to receive whatever means God has ordained for their salvation.)

Catholics may never contract marriage before a non-Catholic clergyman acting as such, but in those instances in which they may contract marriage without a priest they might sometimes marry before such a person acting as a civil official or witness.[15]

As was stated previously, for good reasons a Catholic may assist passively at some public non-Catholic services, particularly funerals and marriages. By passive assistance is meant a courteous and respectful presence, without participation in the rites themselves. One could sit and stand with the congregation, but he should not kneel, even when the members of the congregation do so as a part of the ceremony. This is particularly true when they erroneously believe that their eucharist contains the Real Presence, as in the case of High Church Anglicans. It might be lawful to kneel at an Oriental Orthodox Mass, since their Holy Eucharist really contains the Real Presence. It should be remembered that a *grave* reason is required to justify the passive presence of a Catholic at a public non-Catholic religious function. The mere fact that one is a casual acquaintance does not justify attendance at this person's non-Catholic marriage. Moreover, if the marriage is invalid according to Catholic standards — e.g., if one party is a Catholic or a divorced person — it is hardly ever permissible to attend without giving grave scandal. This is particularly true in the case of the immediate family of a Catholic marrying outside the Church, such as the mother and father of the sinful Catholic.

Merely visiting a non-Catholic church when services are being conducted is not forbidden, provided no scandal is given. In a schismatic church a Catholic should adore the Blessed Sacrament privately when visiting; similarly, when the Holy Eucharist is being taken publicly to the sick a Catholic is supposed to adore, even though the priest is a schismatic. But a Catholic does not satisfy his obligation of Sunday Mass by hearing Mass in a schismatic rite, since the Church prescribes that one must hear Mass celebrated in any *Catholic* rite.[16] Active participation in a public non-Catholic service is a mortal sin from its entire nature; therefore, it admits of no parvity of matter. Passive participation can be a venial sin — e.g., when a person attends a single marriage without a grave reason, and no scandal or danger of perversion is present.

It is not permitted for Catholics to conduct disputes or conferences with non-Catholics, especially publicly, without the permission of the Holy See, or, if the case is urgent, of the local Ordinary.[17] There is frequently grave danger of giving encouragement to indifferentism through meetings on an equal footing with representatives of other religions. Nowadays, through special legislation of the Holy See, local Ordinaries can give permission for such meetings.

9. *The Prohibition of Books*

By the natural law a person is forbidden to read any book that
provides grave danger to his faith or morals (apart from a grave
reason, in which case he must strive to render the danger remote).
Hence, even if a person has received permission from the Church to
read a book forbidden by ecclesiastical law, he may not lawfully use
this permission if the book is actually a grave danger to him. The
Code states: "By permission, from whomsoever it is obtained, one is
not exempted from the prohibition of natural law to read books
which furnish him with proximate spiritual danger."[18] On the other
hand, if a book is forbidden by ecclesiastical law, a person may not
read it without permission, even though he is sure it would not cause
him any spiritual harm. For the laws of the Church in this matter
are directed against a common danger, and hence hold even in the
case of the individual who is not in such danger himself. It is similar
to the civil law prohibiting the citizens to carry deadly weapons without permission. A man may be sure that he would not do harm to
himself or others if he carried a revolver; but nevertheless the law
extends to him.

The ecclesiastical prohibition of books is twofold — general and
particular. By the general law of the Church certain types of books
are forbidden, even though they are not mentioned by name in the
Index. The general law is contained in Canon 1399. Under the
prohibition come:

Editions of Scripture or translations of the inspired writings if
they are published or translated or edited by non-Catholics; also
versions of Sacred Scripture unless they are published with the
approval of the Holy See or the bishops, and are provided with
suitable notes. However, the use of editions of Scripture edited by
non-Catholics or not provided with notes is allowed to students of
the Bible, as long as the books are faithfully and integrally edited
and the dogmas of the Catholic faith are not impugned in the preface
or in the notes.

Books which defend heresy or schism or strive to overthrow the
foundation of religion, or professedly attack religion or good morals.

Books of non-Catholics which professedly treat of religion, unless
it is evident that they contain nothing against the Catholic faith.

Books which narrate visions, miracles, etc., or propose new devotions
but have no ecclesiastical approval.

Books which deride Catholic dogmas, defend errors condemned by the Holy See, cast opprobrium on the hierarchy or the clerical or religious state.

Books of magic, superstition, etc., or which defend dueling, suicide, divorce, or uphold as good the Masonic Order or other such societies.

Books which professedly treat of obscene or lascivious subjects.

Editions of liturgical books in which there are changes from the authentic editions; also books in which indulgences not approved by the Holy See are published.

Printed pictures of our Lord, the Blessed Virgin, the angels or saints or servants of God which are not in conformity with the tradition and the decrees of the Church.

Under the heading of *books* in this ecclesiastical prohibition come pamphlets, newspapers, magazine articles, etc. A book that merely declares what is taught or believed in a non-Catholic denomination is not by that fact condemned, as long as it does not attempt to defend errors.

Church law forbids not only the reading but also the retaining, giving away, or translating of a forbidden book. However, this law admits of parvity of matter. To read three or four pages of a book that is very dangerous or about thirty pages of a book that is not very evil would seem to be sufficient matter to constitute a mortal sin.[19] Booksellers may not keep books that are professedly obscene; but other forbidden books they may keep privately for those who have permission to read them. However, they may not keep books of this kind publicly on sale, unless they have received permission from the Holy See.[20]

The *Index of Forbidden Books* contains a list of the books that have been condemned by name. Nowadays condemnations usually come from the Holy Office. A penalty of excommunication specially reserved to the Holy See falls on those who publish or edit books of apostates, heretics, or schismatics which defend apostasy, heresy, or schism, and also on those who knowingly read, defend, or retain such books or others forbidden by name through apostolic letters. Moreover, authors and editors who without proper permission print books of Holy Scripture or notes or commentaries on them fall into a nonreserved excommunication.[21]

If a book contains even selections from prohibited writings to a considerable amount the entire book must be regarded as condemned, unless the objectionable features are cut out. A librarian (e.g., in a public library) would not come under the condemnation, and he could hand out forbidden books to those who ask for them, unless he is sure that a particular person has no right to read a particular book. In this latter event, the principles of material co-operation, to be given later, apply.

Certain persons, such as cardinals, bishops, and the higher superiors of exempt clerical religious orders, are exempt from the ecclesiastical laws forbidding the reading of certain books. Other persons can obtain permission, for a good reason, either from the Holy See or from the bishop. The latter can grant permission for individual books in urgent cases.[22] By special privilege of the Holy See the bishops of the United States can grant a more general permission for a period of three years.

FOOTNOTES

1. *DB*, 1789.
2. Tob. 11:9.
3. *DB*, 1790; cf. 1812, 1813.
4. *DB*, 801.
5. Heb. 11:6.
6. *DB*, 1173.
7. Can. 1406.
8. Can. 1325, #2.
9. *DB*, 1794.
10. Cf. *DB*, 1815. Karl Adam, in *The Spirit of Catholicism*, Chapter 12, discusses this question and takes rather a broad view of the problem.
11. Can. 2267.
12. Can. 1149.
13. Can. 765.
14. Can. 1258, #2.
15. Can. 1098.
16. Can. 1249.
17. Can. 1325.
18. Can. 1405, # 1.
19. Pernicone, *Ecclesiastical Prohibition of Books* (Washington, D. C.: Catholic University Press, 1932), p. 234.
20. Can. 1404.
21. Can. 2318.
22. Can. 1402.

CHAPTER II . . . *HOPE*

1. *The Nature of Hope*

Natural hope, in the broad sense, includes even the sensitive passion that tends toward some good that is difficult of attainment. In the strict sense, hope is in the will, and indicates an efficacious desire for some good which is not yet possessed, but is possible of attainment. The love which is the basis of hope is called the love of concupiscence — love for an object as the good of the one loving. Thus, it is different from the love of benevolence, which tends to an object because it is good in itself.

As a supernatural, theological virtue, hope is the virtue which inclines us to expect with firm confidence eternal life and the means to attain it on account of the helping power of God. This definition includes the material and formal object of hope and the chief quality of the act (firm confidence).

2. *The Objects of Hope*

The primary material object of hope is eternal life, the possession of God through the beatific vision. The secondary material object is all the means, either necessary or useful, that contribute toward the attainment of this objective. In this category are included both natural and supernatural means.

Theologians are not in agreement as to the formal object of hope. Some place it in the omnipotence, mercy, and fidelity of God; others in His relative goodness (that is, in the goodness of God as our final end), etc. The more probable view is that the formal object of this virtue is the helping power of God — which means His power and His willingness to aid men to attain to eternal life. However, the other attributes of God just mentioned are presupposed. Thus, the reason why we know that He will help us is because He will be faithful to His promises; the reason why He is willing to help us is the fact that He is all-merciful.

The merits of Christ are not the formal object of the theological virtue of hope, for they belong to the created order, and the formal object of a theological virtue must be an attribute of the divine nature. However, the merits of our Lord (and this is true also of the intercession of our Lady and of the saints) are the *means* whereby the helping power of God is applied to us. These other factors can be considered as related to the virtue of hope somewhat as the infallible teaching authority of the Church is related to the virtue of faith.

3. *The Necessity of Hope*

The *habit* of hope is necessary for salvation, since no one is saved unless he departs from this world in the state of sanctifying grace, and whoever possesses the state of grace has the theological virtue of hope. For adults (those who have reached the age of reason) the *act* of hope is necessary, since no one can be justified or perform meritorious works unless he has hope that God will forgive his sins or reward his supernatural deeds.

There have been false systems of asceticism which denied the necessity of hope, or have taught that it is more perfect for a person to exclude from his love of God the hope of his own beatitude. This was the error of the Quietists, toward the end of the seventeenth century (led by Michael Molinos). They taught that "the soul must not think of reward or of punishment, or of heaven or of hell, or of death or of eternity,"[1] and that one who is resigned to God's will should not ask anything for himself from God.[2] A few years later Archbishop Fénelon held that "there is an habitual state of love of God which is pure charity without any admixture of personal interest. Neither the fear of punishment nor the desire of reward has any more part in it. God is no longer loved for the sake of merit or perfection, nor for the happiness in loving Him,"[3] and in this state of holy indifference "we no longer wish our salvation as our own salvation, as eternal liberation, as the reward of our merits, as our own supreme interest; but we wish it with our full will as the glory and pleasure of God, as a thing which He wills and which He wishes us to will for His sake." These ideas were condemned by the Church.[4]

According to Catholic principles, God wills that we strive for our own happiness, that we desire our happiness for our own sake as well as for the glory of God. Hence, even the purest act of love of God does not exclude at least an implicit desire of our own eternal happiness. As St. Thomas says: "Charity does not exclude, but even makes us keep our eye on the reward."[5]

Hope resides in the will, for its object is the supernatural *good*.

Hope can be present in this life in the soul of anyone. Probably hope is retained by the souls in purgatory. However, hope leaves the soul when it is admitted to the beatific vision, for the object of hope is a good not yet possessed, and the blessed in heaven possess God forever.

We say that hope is *certain,* and that we have firm confidence when we hope, in the sense that we are certain that *God* will give us the means necessary for eternal life. But from *our* standpoint hope is uncertain, in that we cannot be sure that we shall co-operate with God's graces.

Fear is one of the adjuncts of hope. The fear of God's punishments is in itself good, for God has imposed sanctions to urge us to obey His laws. However, there is a kind of fear known as *servilely servile fear,* which means that while a person is determined not to break God's law because he fears punishment, he has at the same time a positive desire to sin, and would sin in the event that there were no punishment. Such an attitude is sinful, not because of the withdrawal of the will from sin, but because of the (hypothetical) will to sin, in the supposition that there were no punishment.

4. *Sins Opposed to Hope*

The sins opposed to hope are two — despair (by defect) and presumption (by excess). A person is guilty of despair when he positively gives up the attempt to attain to eternal life because he judges the attainment of this goal impossible or too difficult for him. Sometimes despair includes a denial of the doctrine that God wills all men to be saved, and in this event, the person would be guilty of a sin against faith also. But, this does not necessarily happen, since, by a strange inconsistency, a person can continue to believe that God wills all to be saved, and yet judge that he himself cannot be saved. The sin of despair in the strict sense is mortal *from its entire nature,* and expels the virtue of hope from the soul. However, despair must not be confounded with discouragement, though people sometimes call this latter despair. Actually it is pusillanimity, and is usually not a grave sin. In fact, it may be only a temptation or a form of scrupulosity.

Presumption may be *against* hope or *beyond* hope. Presumption *beyond hope* does not expel the virtue of hope from the soul, since it consists merely in hoping for gifts of grace from God which He does sometimes give, though not indiscriminately. It may be either venial or mortal. Thus, it would ordinarily be a venial sin for a priest to undertake to preach a Sunday sermon with only slight preparation, hoping that God will help him to preach a very excellent sermon. It would be a mortal sin (against charity to oneself) if a person kept on sinning, year after year, with a firm confidence that God will give him the grace to repent when death is approaching.

Presumption *against hope* is twofold, for in God's plan man is to attain to eternal salvation *with the aid of divine grace* and *with his own co-operation.* Hence, a person commits a sin of presumption against hope when he tries to attain to salvation merely by his own efforts, without the aid of divine grace, or when he seeks to be saved only by the aid of divine grace without any co-operation on his part. The former is called Pelagian presumption, the latter Lutheran presumption. Both of these types of presumption are mortal sins by their entire nature, and expel the virtue of hope from the soul.

5. *The Precept of Hope*

A person is bound to make an act of hope when he first comes to the realization that he is destined to the supernatural possession of God; also (very probably) when he is in danger of death; and occasionally at least in the course of his lifetime (at least three or four times a year). However, as in the case of faith, one who leads a good Catholic life performs with sufficient frequency acts which implicitly include hope, as when he receives the sacraments, prays for grace to overcome temptation, etc.

FOOTNOTES

1. *DB*, 1227.
2. *DB*, 1234.
3. *DB*, 1327.
4. *DB*, 1332.
5. *III Dist.*, 29, a. 4.

CHAPTER III . . . *CHARITY*

1. *The Nature of Charity*

Charity is love of *benevolence* — that is, love for one because of his goodness considered in itself. From this standpoint it is very different from love of concupiscence, which is love for an object because of the benefit accruing to the one who loves. However, love of concupiscence naturally leads to love of benevolence, in that when a person hopes to secure some benefit from another he perceives goodness in that other and is thus drawn to love him for his own sake.[1]

As a theological virtue charity is defined: the theological virtue which inclines us to love God as the Author of the supernatural order, because of His absolute supernatural goodness, and ourselves and our neighbor because of their participation in this goodness of God.

A characteristic of charity, emphasized by our Lord,[2] is that it constitutes *friendship* between God and the soul. Genuine friendship exists only between those who in some manner share in the same state of life. In the friendship established by charity this element is found in the fact that through sanctifying grace man is made a sharer of the divine nature,[3] and thus, in a certain sense, is elevated to the state of God Himself.

Some of the older theologians taught that charity is actually the person of the Holy Ghost dwelling in the souls of the just; but the common teaching today is that charity, like the other theological virtues, is a created habit. Moreover, some theologians have taught that charity is identified with sanctifying grace, but again the common teaching inclines to the view that these two habits are distinct. Sanctifying grace is an *entitative* habit, perfecting the essence of the soul; charity is an *operative* habit, perfecting the will. As St. Paul tells us, charity is the greatest of the theological virtues,[4] the basic reason being that charity explicitly seeks God for His own sake, while faith and hope seek Him as benefiting man himself.

Charity is sometimes called the *form* of the other virtues. This means that charity directs the acts of the other virtues toward its own

85

end, God as He is in Himself, and thus renders them meritorious. In this same sense, charity is sometimes called the *queen* of the other virtues.

Charity resides in the *will*. It is given to the soul in proportion to the measure of a person's sanctifying grace. It increases in the soul in proportion to the increase of sanctifying grace. It is not diminished by venial sin, but is lost by every mortal sin.

2. *The Formal Object of Charity*

The formal object, or motive, of charity is the goodness of God — not His natural goodness, as perceived by reason from the works of creation, but His supernatural goodness, made known by revelation. Moreover, the object of charity is the *absolute* goodness of God, His goodness as He is in Himself, as distinct from His *relative* goodness, which is His goodness as the source of *our* supernatural happiness.

By the divine goodness, as the formal object of charity, is certainly meant at least the goodness of the divine essence in its entirety, comprising the divine nature and the three Divine Persons. Theologians dispute the question whether one divine attribute can be selected and made the formal object of our charity. Those who hold the affirmative point out that each of the divine attributes is actually identified with the divine nature. If this view be correct, we can love God for His benignity toward us, *considered as a divine perfection in God,* and thus makes an act of divine charity based on His goodness toward mankind. However, if our love is based on the *benefits conferred by His benignity,* we are making an act of gratitude, not charity, though gratitude easily leads to charity.

Charity does not exclude love based on God's benefits toward us (love of gratitude and of concupiscence) and His promised reward. Hence, a person can have at the same time perfect contrition (detestation of sin as offensive to God who is so good in Himself) and imperfect contrition (arising from the realization that sin excludes one from the happiness of heaven). The act of contrition in the Baltimore Catechism expresses both perfect and imperfect contrition.

Love for ourselves and for our neighbor is specifically the same virtue as love for God. For in both cases, the motive, or formal object, is the same — the divine goodness — though the material object is different. For when we love ourselves or our neighbor with true charity, the motive is the supernatural divine goodness which is

present, either actually or potentially, in the soul of the one we love —
namely, sanctifying grace, which is a participation of the divine nature.

3. The Material Object of Charity

The material object of divine charity is threefold — God, ourselves,
and our neighbor. God is the primary object; the others constitute
the secondary object. By our neighbor is meant everyone who is or
can be a partaker of the divine goodness through sanctifying grace —
the angels and saints, the souls in purgatory, all persons in the present
life — but not the devils or the lost souls.

By virtue of the charity which he owes himself, a person is bound
to seek what is necessary for his spiritual welfare, and particularly
to make provision that he dies in the state of grace. For this reason
a person who would deliberately choose to remain in sin for the
remainder of his life, merely because he hopes that God will grant
him the opportunity and the grace to receive the sacraments worthily
in the hour of death, would be guilty of a grave sin against charity
in regard to himself and would also commit a sin of presumption
beyond hope. Some theologians say that a person would sin gravely
in the matter of charity toward himself if he refuses to receive Extreme
Unction; others say that this would not be a grave sin, as long as he
receives the sacraments which are surely necessary for those in danger
of death — Penance (if there is any grave sin that must be confessed)
and the Holy Eucharist.[5]

Charity also obliges a person to employ *ordinary* means to preserve
his bodily health and bodily integrity. Hence, one who would exceed
the limits of Christian mortification and would thus impair his health
seriously would be guilty of a grave sin. However, moderate bodily
mortification is lawful, even if it may probably shorten one's life span
for a comparatively brief time, because of the spiritual benefits thus
gained by the practice of Christian asceticism. It should be noted that
only *ordinary* means toward the preservation of life are strictly
obligatory. For example, a person (especially one far advanced in
years) would not be obliged in conscience to undergo a very painful
and expensive operation in order to prolong his life a short time.
However, it would seem that the amputation of a limb when this is
a necessary means to preserve life would be of obligation, especially
in the case of a younger person.

Among our neighbors, whom we must love, are included our enemies, as was explicitly commanded by Christ.[6] In explaining this obligation, theologians distinguish two classes of signs of love — common and special. The common signs of love are those which are given normally to all other persons in the same status and circumstances as our enemies. For example, it is normal for those who are acquainted with one another to say "Good morning" when they meet in the morning. It is normal for the members of a religious community to speak to one another at table and recreation, to render one another help in common tasks, etc. These common signs of friendship must ordinarily be given even to enemies, and to deny them for a considerable time — for example, for two weeks in the case of those who meet frequently — would usually be a mortal sin because presumably it would be a manifestation of hatred. In very exceptional circumstances it would be permitted to deny these common signs of friendship for a time — for example, a mother whose daughter had been very ungrateful to her (for example, by marrying a divorced man) could refuse such signs until the daughter manifested repentance. Similarly, if one has tried several times to show charity toward an enemy and has been rudely repulsed, there is no obligation to do anything more until he shows a change of heart.

By special signs of friendship are meant those which we are accustomed to manifest toward our special friends — for example, to invite a person to dinner, to send him presents, to visit him in sickness, etc. There is ordinarily no obligation to manifest such signs toward an enemy. We say "ordinarily" because in certain circumstances such signs would be required — for example, to avoid scandal, or when an enemy is in grave or extreme necessity.

Since, in practice, wherever an enmity arises, each party thinks that the other is the guilty party, each is recommended to manifest signs of friendship. However, no one is obliged to give in to the "bully" type of person, and at times it is beneficial to such a person to have his victims treat him severely, at least by aloofness, so that he may know that he is acting unreasonably and uncharitably.

4. *The Order of Charity*

As is evident, God must be loved more than we love any creature — with our whole heart and soul, as our Lord expressed it. However, our love for God need not be sovereign in *intensity,* or fervor. It suffices that it be sovereign in *appreciation,* which means that we have the sincere intention to give God the preference over everything created, so that if we are faced with a choice between God and any creature, we shall give preference to Him. It renders the act of divine charity more perfect to have more fervor, but this is only an accidental, not an essential, perfection.

When a person compares himself to other human beings in the order of charity, he should *per se* love himself more than he loves anyone else. This principle is applicable particularly in reference to one's eternal salvation. Under no circumstances may a person deprive himself of sanctifying grace or means necessary for eternal salvation for the sake of another.

When there is question of helping a neighbor spiritually with some inconvenience to oneself in the material order, we must distinguish various types of necessity. If a fellow man is in *extreme* spiritual necessity — that is, if he is sure to be deprived of eternal salvation unless I help him — I am obliged even to give my life, if I am sure that I can give him the needed assistance. Thus, a person would be obliged to enter a burning building to baptize an infant who is trapped there, if the person is sure that he will be able to get to the child, even though he is equally sure that he will not be able to escape afterward. The same principle would apply to a priest who is called on to give Penance or Extreme Unction to a person who, it is morally certain, will otherwise lose his soul.

When a fellow man is in *grave* spiritual necessity (for example, one who is calling for the sacraments and will *probably* die, or one who needs the sacraments in the hour of death, but still has enough knowledge to make an act of perfect contrition, though with difficulty), a person who can help him is bound to put up with *great* inconvenience (for example, a long journey) but need not risk his life.

When a man is in *common* spiritual necessity (a man in mortal sin, but not in danger of death), one is bound to endure some light inconvenience to assist him. For example, a priest not having the care of souls should be willing to come down to the church to hear the man's confession; a lay person who has reason to believe that he can induce the man to go to confession should be willing to make the effort to see him and talk to him, as long as it is not very difficult to do so.

If a fellow man is in *extreme* temporal necessity (in imminent danger of death for lack of food, clothing, shelter, etc.), a person is bound to endure great temporal inconvenience to help him, though not to the extent of sacrificing his own life. Nor would even a very rich man be obliged to give a person a very large sum (e.g., $5,000) to save his life, since this would be an extraordinary means of preserving life.

When one is in *grave* temporal necessity (for example, the man who will lose his home by the foreclosure of a mortgage if he is not helped) another is obliged to endure a considerable amount of inconvenience to render assistance (e.g., a rich man would be bound to lend the man just described a few hundred dollars to tide him over the necessity if he is sure that it will be repaid). When one is in *common* temporal necessity (e.g., the man who needs a half dollar for a night's lodging) another is bound to help if the inconvenience and sacrifice are only light.

We are concerned now with the obligation of charity only; for in some instances there can be an additional obligation in justice to help a fellow man. Thus, a priest having the care of souls in a parish is bound in justice to give spiritual assistance to his people. A policeman is obliged in justice to help the citizens in their temporal necessities. As is evident, the obligation of justice binds one to endure greater inconvenience than does charity alone in giving help to others. Thus, the parish priest would be bound to risk his life to give the necessary sacraments to a person who is even in grave spiritual necessity. A policeman would be bound to risk his life to help his fellow citizens in their grave temporal necessity when aiding them in their necessity comes under the scope of his duty. Furthermore, there are times when it is commendable, even though not strictly obligatory, for a person to sacrifice or to risk his life or to endure great inconvenience for the sake of a fellow man in his spiritual or temporal wants.

In determining the order of charity among one's neighbors theologians lay down two norms — nearness to God and nearness to self. In practice the second has the greater influence. Thus, a religious should help his natural brother in preference to a religious brother, if both are in the same type and degree of necessity. However, one who is more remotely related should be given preference in the conferring of help if his need is greater or of a higher order. Thus, a stranger in *extreme* need of food should be given help in preference to a near relative who is only in *grave* need. Similarly, a stranger in extreme *spiritual* necessity is to be given the priority over a relative who is in extreme *temporal* necessity.

The order of charity in the case of a married man with children is as follows: wife, children, father, mother, brothers and sisters, other relatives. However, in *extreme* necessity one's parents are to be preferred to all others, because they gave one the great gift of life, so that they merit preference when their life is at stake.

5. *Almsgiving*

A person's temporal possessions can be divided into three classes: (1) Goods necessary to the *life* of oneself and one's dependents. (2) Goods necessary to maintain one's *state* in life. (3) Goods that are *superfluous,* not necessary to maintain even one's state in life.

If a fellow man is in extreme temporal necessity one must give him enough to relieve his necessity from one's possessions that are superfluous or necessary for the maintenance of state, but not from those necessary for the maintenance of one's own life or the lives of his dependents. However, even superfluous goods need not be given in a very great quantity — e.g., $5,000 from the very rich man to procure an operation necessary to save his poor neighbor's life.

If a fellow man is in grave necessity one must give of his superfluous wealth to assist him, but not from what is necessary for the maintenance of state, unless this can be done without much inconvenience. As regards those in common necessity the rule is that those who have superfluous wealth must give the poor some portion of this wealth. It is difficult to lay down a definite rule as to the amount that must be given, but it would seem that ordinarily about 5 per cent or 7 per cent of a person's superfluous wealth would suffice, as far as the strict *obligation* of charity is concerned. Moreover, the payment of a tax by which the needs of the poor are provided for diminishes a person's obligation of almsgiving, but does not entirely fulfill it, if the tax does not suffice for all the poor.[7]

Under the obligation of almsgiving is included the professional service which one can render to those in need of it. Thus, a doctor or a lawyer would be obliged in charity to give free service to a person in need, according to the norms just laid down.

Even one who has become poor through his own fault by debauchery or gambling has a right to receive alms as long as there is assurance that he will not squander them. Of course, a person who can work but refuses to do so has no right to live by alms.

6. *Fraternal Correction*

Fraternal correction can be regarded as spiritual almsgiving. Our

Lord spoke of it as an obligation;[8] and it follows logically from the very idea of charity that we must try to rescue our fellow men from spiritual evils (especially sin) just as we must try to rescue them from temporal evils. However, in order that a person be bound by a grave obligation to administer a fraternal correction, the following conditions must be fulfilled: (1) He must be sure that a mortal sin was committed or will probably be committed. (2) There must be at least a probability that the culprit will not amend on his own initiative or at the admonition of someone else. (3) There must be real probability that the correction will be beneficial. (4) It must be possible to make the correction without too great inconvenience or danger to oneself. For example, if there is danger that the culprit will seriously calumniate the corrector, there is no obligation of correction. (5) The circumstances of time, place, etc., must be favorable. Superiors have a graver obligation than others to correct those under their charge.

As our Lord pointed out, the general procedure of fraternal correction is to admonish the culprit privately before reporting his transgressions to public authority. However, if there is a greater probability that the correction will not be received properly, the superior may be informed at once — at least, when there is question of habitual sin which the superior will be able to check. On the other hand, if the culprit receives the correction properly and seems likely to amend, the superior should ordinarily not be informed about the matter.

7. Co-operation

We can co-operate with others in the performance of good deeds, and when we do this, we share in the merit. Ordinarily, however, when we speak of co-operation in moral theology we refer to participation in the sinful actions of others. Co-operation of this kind is either *formal* or *material*. Formal co-operation is committed when one actually takes part in the sin of another person. This may be either *through the end of the act and of the agent* or *through the end of the agent only*. The former takes place when one objectively shares in another's sin, even though he does so with a certain measure of reluctance. Thus, if a Catholic plays the organ for a non-Catholic religious service because he has not the moral courage to refuse, he participates formally through the end of the act and of the agent. One who commands or urges another to commit a sin is a formal co-operator, even though he does not physically participate. A person co-operates formally *through the end of the agent only* when he performs an indifferent act, which the principal agent utilizes toward his sinful objective, and the co-operator positively wills that his act shall aid toward the sin. An example of this is the renegade Catholic who helps to build an heretical church, positively willing that in this way non-Catholic worship will be promoted.

Material co-operation takes place when a person performs an act that is lawful in itself, though in this particular instance it will be used or directed by the principal agent to the accomplishment of his sinful end. Thus, the saloonkeeper co-operates materially toward the drunkenness of a patron when he sells him liquor with the realization that he will drink to excess. The truck driver who delivers magazines to various stores and knows that some of them are obscene is also a material co-operator toward the sins that will be committed by those who read these magazines.

Formal co-operation is always sinful, for by its very nature it is sharing in the sin of another, at least in intention. Material co-operation is sinful if it is performed without a sufficient reason, for it is *per se* against charity to aid another to commit sin, even though one's own action in itself is lawful. However, since charity does not bind with grave inconvenience, a person is permitted to co-operate materially in the sin of another for a sufficiently grave and proportionate reason. In evaluating the gravity of the reason required to justify material co-operation, two factors must be considered — the gravity of the sin involved and the degree of influence of one's co-operation toward the sinful action. In other words, the graver the sin, the greater must be the justifying reason; and the greater the influence one's action has, the greater must be the reason. These points will be more evident in the practical applications:

CO-OPERATION IN SINS AGAINST FAITH: It is not permitted for a Catholic to call a non-Catholic clergyman with the explicit request the he confer his sacraments to a sick person, for that would be formal co-operation. But it would be lawful to request that he come to visit the sick person (even though it is foreseen that he will administer false rites) provided there is sufficient reason, which would usually be present. In other words, there would be lawful material co-operation in this latter case.

Workmen, summoned to help in the erection of a non-Catholic church, are sufficiently justified in the fulfillment of this task by the fact that they need employment. But it would require a much greater reason to justify an architect or a builder, since these persons co-operate much more proximately than the workingmen. Indeed, it is a general principle that the more proximately a person co-operates, the greater reason is required to justify the co-operation.

To sell bread and wine to a non-Catholic clergyman would be permitted to a storekeeper, even though he foresees that they will be used for false religious rites, if otherwise he would be liable to lose his license. But to sell or to give altar breads, already made, especially to a minister who erroneously believes himself to be a priest and admits the doctrine of the Real Presence, could hardly ever be permitted, since that would be *proximate* co-operation toward a sin against religion — even idolatry — even though the ministers in question are most sincere in their belief.

To give money toward the erection of a church in which false doctrine is to be preached is material co-operation, but it is so proximate that only a very grave reason would justify it. The mere desire of retaining social contacts and friendships with non-Catholics would not seem to be sufficient. On the other hand, to give money to a non-Catholic organization for the help of the needy — e.g., the Salvation Army for their Christmas dinner to the poor — would be allowed, though a Catholic should ordinarily give preference to Catholic charities.

A Catholic would never be allowed to edit or to publish a book against the Catholic faith, for this would be proximate material co-operation, or perhaps even formal co-operation. But printers, typesetters, etc., in a firm that prints such literature occasionally would be acting lawfully, as long as they can get no other equally good job.

Public dealers in ecclesiastical goods can sell vestments to non-Catholic clergymen, since otherwise they would be liable to forfeit their license. But it would not be permissible for a community of religious to fill an order for a set of vestments for such a purpose, unless perhaps they were in extreme need. Apart from very extraordinary circumstances, it is impossible to justify a person who would make or sell insignia recognized as expressly anti-Catholic, such as Masonic pins and aprons.

CO-OPERATION ON THE PART OF TRADESMEN: If an article *can* be used for a good purpose, a tradesman may more easily sell it than if it is something which, for practical purposes, can be used only for a sinful objective. Thus, to sell liquor or firearms is not wrong, even though it is foreseen that *some* individuals will use these things for a sinful purpose. But if it is foreseen that a *particular* individual will abuse such things, a very good reason is required to justify one in selling them to him — a reason graver than the mere gaining of the profit derived from the sale. Thus, the owner of a saloon would ordinarily be bound to refuse liquor to a man who is evidently on the way to complete intoxication; whereas the waiter would be justified in serving it if otherwise he would lose his job.

When an article is not used for any other purpose than the commission of sin, a *clerk* would be allowed to sell it if otherwise he would lose his job without the hope of getting another. This would apply chiefly to the sale of contraceptives. But the *owner* of the store would be doing wrong if he kept such things in stock.

Those who keep paper stands would not be permitted to sell very obscene magazines, but they could sell those periodicals and newspapers which are ordinarily decent, though at times they carry something objectionable.

Nurses: The problems in co-operation that most frequently arise in the nursing profession are those that center about operations which, according to Catholic teaching, are opposed to the law of God, such as eugenic sterilizations and "therapeutic" abortions. A nurse could co-operate toward such operations *remotely,* if otherwise she would lose her job, be treated harshly, refused promotion, etc. By remote co-operation would be meant the care of the patient before the operation, the cleaning of the operating room, the sterilizing of the instruments, etc. But only for a most grave reason could a nurse co-operate *proximately* — e.g., by giving the anesthetic, by handing the instruments to the doctor, etc. Such a most grave reason would be the well-founded fear that she might be dismissed from the hospital and be barred from continuing her profession. However, ordinarily Catholic nurses should protest against being appointed to such operations, and in many cases their protests will be heeded. It stands to reason that the co-operation of a doctor in the actual performance of the operation would never be permissible, no matter what inconveniences he might otherwise suffer, for that would be formal co-operation — e.g., the young intern commanded by the surgeon in charge to perform a direct abortion.

8. *Scandal*

Scandal may be *active* or *passive*. Active scandal is an action (deed, word, or at times even an omission) which is either evil or has the appearance of an evil action, and is likely to furnish an occasion of sin to others. We say that even an action "which has the appearance of evil" may be active scandal, as in the case of a Catholic who has a dispensation to eat meat on Friday and does so in the presence of others who do not know of this dispensation and may be led to follow his example. Hence, scandal in the theological sense is not mere surprise or shock at the actions of others, nor is it uncharitable talk, although in common speech the word *scandal* is often used in these senses. The main feature of scandal, as the term is used in Catholic theology, is that it furnishes a bad example to someone, furnishing him with an occasion of sin.

Active scandal is *direct* when the scandalizer *intends* the sin of the other, as when a man leads others into drunkenness by his own example, either because he deliberately wishes them to commit sin as something pleasing to him in itself (diabolical scandal), or because he wishes it as a means to his advantage — for example, when he desires to rob them when they are drunk (simply direct scandal). Active scandal is *indirect* when the scandalizer *foresees* that his actions will lead others into sin, but does not intend this sin, as in the case of the man who drinks to excess and foresees that his son will follow his example; he prefers that this would not happen, but nevertheless continues to indulge his passion for drink.

Scandal is a sin against charity. For it is surely a violation of this virtue to furnish a fellow man the occasion to sin. If the sin is foreseen as certainly or probably mortal, the scandal-giver is *per se* guilty of mortal sin. If it is anticipated that several persons will be led astray the scandalizer commits as many sins as there are persons. Direct scandal, besides being a sin against charity, is also against the virtue which the other will be led to violate. Thus, in the example given above the man would be guilty of a sin against charity and a sin against temperance. It is possible that a person will be guilty of a mortal sin of scandal even though the sin he himself commits is venial — for example, the man who himself gets only slightly intoxicated, but foresees that in consequence of his bad example others will be guilty of complete intoxication. It is a disputed point among theologians whether indirect scandal is against charity only or also against the virtue involved.

Passive scandal is a sin occasioned by the action of another. If the action of the other is active scandal, it is called *given scandal* (*scandalum datum*). If the action which occasions the sin is a perfectly good action, the passive scandal is called *scandal received* (*scandalum acceptum*). An example of this latter would be the blasphemy which a man would utter because a priest refused to give him money for a drink. Scandal received is said to be *pharisaical scandal* when the sin is due to the malice of those scandalized, as when the Pharisees took the words of Christ as an occasion to commit sin; it is said to be *scandal of the little ones* when it is due to the spiritual weakness of those scandalized, as is the scandal of the bibulous sexton when the priest puts the altar wine in an unlocked cupboard.

At times it is permitted to perform an action that will be an occasion of sin to another. The principle of the double effect must be applied. The action of the one giving the occasion must be in itself fully lawful, and there must be sufficient reason to justify him in allowing the scandal to be taken by the others. A much lesser reason is required when the scandal taken is pharisaical scandal than when it is scandal of the little ones. At times a person would be bound to omit a good work — even a work that is obligatory by positive law — in order to avoid giving scandal. For example, if a Catholic convert knew that by abstaining from meat on Friday in the bosom of his family he would move his father to great wrath against the Catholic Church, he should eat the meat set on the table. Similarly, if a boy knows that by joining a religious order at the age of eighteen he will arouse his parents to bitterness against the Church, he should defer his entrance for several years.

On the other hand, a person would not be obliged to undergo very grave difficulties, temporal or spiritual, merely to ward off the occasions of sin from others, as long as his own actions are morally good. Thus, the young man in the case given above would not have to give up his desires of the religious life permanently in order to prevent his parents from becoming angry. If a man says to me: "Give me a dollar, or I will blaspheme," I am not obliged to give him a dollar, for this is a case of pharisaical scandal, and even the loss of a dollar is a sufficient reason to justify me in permitting the sin. A man who is a temperate drinker would not be bound to become a total abstainer merely because some of his friends find in his moderate drinking the occasion for intoxication.

EXAMPLES OF ACTIVE SCANDAL: Parents who neglect Mass and foresee that their children will do the same. Employers who refuse their employees a proper wage, and thereby stir them up to anger and hatred. Landlords who exclude families from their apartments merely because they have three or four children and thereby promote birth control. Girls who take part in "beauty contests" with scanty and immodest costumes.

According to many reliable theologians, it is permitted to induce a person to do a lesser evil deed, if this is the only way in which he can be prevented from doing a greater evil. For example, if a man who is determined to beat his wife can be prevented from doing this only by inducing him to get drunk, it is permissible to induce him to commit the sin of intoxication.

9. The Obligation of Making Acts of Charity

A person is obliged to make an act of divine charity when he comes to the knowledge of the infinite supernatural goodness of God; also at the end of life; and occasionally in the course of life — at least three or four times a year. It is most commendable to make an act of love for God at least once a day, offering Him all our thoughts, words, and deeds. An act of perfect contrition — which is sorrow for sin based on the realization that sin offends God who is all-good — immediately remits all mortal sin and restores a person to the state of grace, though he must have the intention of receiving the sacrament of Penance (if he is baptized) or Baptism (if he is not baptized). An implicit intention, contained in the general intention of fulfilling God's will, suffices for those who are unaware of the obligation to receive a sacrament. Catholics should be taught that it is not difficult to make an act of charity or of perfect contrition. It is important also to realize that an act of charity or of perfect contrition does not necessarily include the intention of avoiding all *venial* sins.

FOOTNOTES

1. St. Thomas, *Summa,* II–II, q. 62, a. 4.
2. Jn. 15:14, 15.
3. 2 Pet. 1:4.
4. 1 Cor. 13:13.
5. Cf. Can. 944.
6. Mt. 5:44.
7. Merkelbach, *Summa theologiae moralis,* I, n. 933.
8. Mt. 18:15.

1. *The Cardinal Virtues*

As was previously stated, the moral virtues are classified under the four cardinal virtues of prudence, justice, fortitude, and temperance. These four virtues are now to be considered separately. Since the virtue of justice involves many moral problems, and since this virtue has several related virtues of great importance, such as religion, several chapters will be devoted to the second of the cardinal virtues. One chapter will be devoted to each of the other three.

2. *The Nature of Prudence*

The cardinal virtue of prudence is defined by St. Thomas, following Aristotle, as *recta ratio agibilium,* which can be freely translated as "right reason applied to human conduct."[1] At greater length it can be defined as "the virtue which enlightens and inclines the intellect to choose the course of conduct that one should follow in order to reach one's ultimate end." Since this virtue perfects the intellect, it can be called an intellectual virtue; but since its direct purpose is to guide the possessor in the observance of the moral law, it is justly considered a moral virtue. The function of prudence is not to aid one to choose the proper end, for this is done by right reason (in the natural order) and by charity (in the supernatural order), but rather to assist one in determining how to attain the proper end, once it has been chosen. Since prudence directs the other moral virtues, it is the most excellent of the cardinal virtues.

Natural prudence dictates the course of conduct to be followed in order to attain to man's natural end, in conformity with reason; supernatural prudence dictates the course of conduct to be followed in order to attain to man's supernatural end (the eternal possession of God through the beatific vision), in conformity with revelation. Supernatural prudence, since it is based on a perception of truth through faith in a higher plane than natural knowledge, sometimes dictates a course of action that would not be recommended by natural prudence — for example, when it directs a young person to accept, as

99

the most perfect form of human life, the observance of the evangelical counsels in the religious life.

In the exercise of prudence a person *deliberates* on the proper means to be employed in order to reach his goal, *judges* which means are best adapted to attain this goal, and *is commanded* by his prudential judgment to follow this course of action. The act of *commanding* one to do the right thing is the chief function of prudence.[2]

3. *The Parts of Prudence*

According to St. Thomas, the integral parts of prudence (the conditions requisite for the practice of this virtue) are eight — memory of the past (since experience is a great help toward the practice of prudence), understanding of the present, docility (because a prudent person is always willing to learn from competent advisers), sagacity, the ability to reason well, prevision of future contingencies, circumspection, and caution.[3]

The subjective parts of prudence (the species into which it is divided) are *personal* prudence (by which a person regulates his own conduct) and *governing* prudence (by which one is guided in regulating the conduct of others subject to him). This latter admits of various subdivisions in as far as the group over which one is placed is a family, an army, a state, etc.[4] It is very evident that not everyone who is capable of properly regulating his own conduct is capable of properly regulating the conduct of others. However, the person who is able to choose the right course of action for himself is, generally speaking, better suited to govern others than is the man who does not properly regulate his own conduct.

The potential parts of prudence (virtues which bear some resemblance to the cardinal virtue, but do not contain all its essential features) are designated by St. Thomas as *eubulia* (the ability to deliberate properly in regard to details), *synesis* (common sense in regard to the ordinary happenings of life), and *gnome* (the ability to judge properly in regard to exceptional circumstances).[5]

There are many sins opposed to prudence, especially imprudence (lack of good judgment in regard to one's conduct), the prudence of the flesh (the habit of regulating one's conduct in accordance with the sensual desires of human nature), and excessive solicitude in seeking success in temporal affairs.[6]

The chief act of prudence is the right formation of conscience, which has been treated in Chapter IV of Part I.

FOOTNOTES

1. *Summa*, II–II, q. 47, a. 2.
2. *Ibid.*, a. 8.
3. *Ibid.*, q. 49.
4. *Ibid.*, q. 50.
5. *Ibid.*, q. 51.
6. *Ibid.*, q. 55.

CHAPTER V . . . *JUSTICE*

1. *General Notions*

The word *justice* is sometimes taken in a broad sense to signify the assemblage of all the virtues. Thus the state of supernatural and preternatural perfection in which our first parents were constituted before the fall is known as the state of *original justice.* The reason is that the possession of all these gifts rendered them *rightly ordered,* so that the lower faculties of their soul were subordinate to the higher, and the higher were subordinate to God. In the same sense, St. Joseph is called a just man,[1] and we speak of the reception of the supernatural life as *justification.*

In the strict sense, justice is a cardinal virtue, and is defined as "the moral virtue inclining the will to render to everyone his right, according to some measure of equality." The elements of *right* and *equality* must be present for the exercise of justice in the strict sense. Thus the virtues of gratitude and liberality, though potential parts of justice, are not ranked as justice in the strict sense, because what is rendered as a result of these virtues is not due to the recipient as his *right.* Similarly, the virtues of religion and penance are only potential parts of justice because man can never render to God homage or satisfaction that is equal to what is due to God. (A potential part of one of the cardinal virtues is a virtue possessing some but not all the essential factors of the respective cardinal virtue.)

Strict justice requires a distinction between the one having the obligation to give and the one having the right to receive. Consequently, a person cannot have an obligation of strict justice toward himself. Thus, one who squanders his own possessions or injures his health by excesses does not commit a sin of injustice toward himself, though he violates other virtues, especially *charity* due to himself. To constitute this distinction a diversity of *natures* suffices, even in the same *person,* as is evident from the Incarnation. In His *human* nature the Son of God made satisfaction in strict justice to the Holy Trinity, including Himself in His *divine* nature.

Under certain aspects two human beings can be so intimately

united that they are morally one, and in their dealings with each other under such an aspect there is no exercise of strict justice. For example, between a father and a child *as such* there is the exercise of piety, not of justice. Consequently, if a father neglects to provide his child with proper food and clothing, he sins, but he is not obliged later to make restitution because he has sinned against *piety,* not *justice.* On the other hand, outside of their specific sphere, such persons can act as distinct individuals, and then strict justice can be present. For example, a grown son who has a job in his father's store has a right in strict commutative justice to a proper wage.

2. *Divisions of Justice*

Justice is either *general* or *particular.* General justice is that which urges the individual to render to the *community* what is its due. Thus a citizen practices general justice when he obeys the laws of the state, when he pays his taxes, when he treats his fellow citizens in a peaceful and decent manner, etc. This is also called legal or social justice.

Particular justice is that which is concerned with rendering to individuals their rights. This again is twofold — *distributive* and *commutative* justice. Distributive justice binds the community to render to its members what is due to them, and its obligations rest on those who rule the community. For example, the civil authorities are bound by this virtue to apportion taxes according to the abilities and wealth of the citizens, to impose military service (where it exists) without consideration of personal friendship. Similarly, the superior of a religious community is bound to be fair toward the members, choosing for posts of authority and responsibility those whom he deems most capable. Commutative justice is that which concerns the rights and obligations of individuals toward each other. For example, when a man contracts to sell a house, he has an obligation to turn it over to the buyer and a right to receive a suitable price. The equality involved in distributive justice is a geometric equality (of proportion); that which is involved in commutative justice is an arithmetic equality.

It should be noted that when we speak of individuals as involved in commutative justice, we include also *moral* persons — for example, a business firm, a religious community. Thus two nations can have obligations of commutative justice toward each other, as in the sale of territory. A society can be bound in commutative justice toward an individual — namely, when he acts as one fully distinct from the society. For example, if the state hires one of its citizens to build a bridge, the state is bound by commutative justice to pay him. When legal or distributive justice is involved, there is not a *complete distinction* between the two parties; there is a relation of the part to the whole or of the whole to the part.

Violations of legal or distributive justice do not of themselves call for restitution; only the violations of commutative justice call for restitution. However, it frequently happens that a violation of distributive justice involves a violation of commutative justice. For example, if the law requires an official to distribute jobs according to marks given in a civil service examination, an official who would appoint a friend who did not earn a place would fail against commutative as well as distributive justice.

Marriage is intimately related to social justice, inasmuch as the primary purpose of marriage is the preservation and the upbuilding of society. Hence, violations of the natural law governing marriage, whether the use of the sexual powers outside marriage or the abuse of these powers by married persons through contraception, are sins against social justice.

3. *Right*

A *right* can be objective or subjective. An objective (or passive) right is a relation between things or actions demanding some equalization. Thus, when the house of Peter is transferred to the possession of John, there is an objective right established between the house and a sum of money demanding that the transaction be equalized by the transfer of the money of John to Peter.

A subjective (or active) right is a relation between a person and a thing, by virtue of which the person is allowed to possess and to use this object for his own utility. The basic reason for the possibility of a strict right is the dignity and the inviolability of the human person. Since the human person has an eternal destiny, he is far superior to all other earthly things, and may use them for his own utility. Moreover, since every human being is entitled not to be impeded by any others in his quest for eternal life, he may not be molested by them in the possession and use of earthly things necessary or useful for the attainment of his destiny.

Thus it is evident that the ultimate foundation of human right is God, who created man as a spiritual and immortal being with an eternal destiny. Consequently, a person who does not admit the existence of God and the spirituality and the immortality of the human soul cannot logically admit that there are any real human rights. The only source of right that such a person can acknowledge is the State; consequently, he must grant that whatever the State gives it can take away for its own benefit — e.g., private property, even life. This is actually the conclusion of totalitarian philosophy.

An animal can have no rights because it has no spiritual soul, no immortal destiny, no freedom of will to dispose of property. God has explicitly given man the right to use animals for his own benefit;[2] consequently, man is guilty of no injustice when he kills an animal or uses it in some other way for his own utility. Of course, one is guilty of injustice toward the owner of the animal if he injures it; moreover, unnecessary cruelty toward an animal is a sin because it is an inordinate use of a created thing, and because it often develops evil passions in the one who is guilty of it, but there is no injustice toward the animal itself. For a good reason, particularly in order to discover new remedies for the healing of human ailments, vivisection of animals is permissible, but unnecessary suffering should not be inflicted.

We are here considering only rights *in justice*. A person may at times have a right in charity. For example, a man in grave need has a right to receive help from one who can assist him without great inconvenience; but it is a right in charity only. The essential point of distinction is that justice is based on a relation between a person and an object to which he has a right; whereas charity is based on a relation of a person to God, inasmuch as he actually or potentially partakes of the divine goodness.

4. *Divisions of Right*

Subjective, or active, right is divided into the right *to* the thing (*jus ad rem*) and the right *in* the thing (*jus in re*). The former is the right of a person to acquire an object which is due to him in justice, but of which he has not yet taken possession — for example, the right of the workman to receive his salary at the end of the week. The latter is the right which belongs to a man who has already taken possession of the object in question — e.g., the right of the same workman after he has received his salary. This "right in the thing" is also called dominion, or ownership.

Dominion is perfect or complete if it includes both the right to possess a thing as one's own and the right to use it. Such, for example, is the dominion a man enjoys over his watch. Imperfect dominion includes only one of these two factors — either the right of possession without the right to use (the case of a religious with the simple vow of poverty), or the right to use something without the right of possession (the case of a man who has leased a house).

Examples of this second type of imperfect dominion are found in what is known as easements over the property of others. For example, a man may have an easement to pass through the property of his neighbor to the public road, or to draw water from his neighbor's well. It is interesting to note in this connection that a property owner has the right to dig a well on his own property, even though he thereby intercepts the water from his neighbor's well; but he has not the right to intercept the course of water flowing *over* his land to the detriment of his neighbors.[3] The civil law sometimes permits a man to extend his mine beneath the property of another, as far as the vein of coal extends, provided he does no damage to the property on the surface.

We can also distinguish *personal dominion* and *eminent domain*. The former is that which belongs to a person under ordinary circumstances, and which cannot be impugned even by public authority. The latter is the right of the State to dispose of private property, even against the owner's wishes, *when the common good demands it*. Thus, if a highway is very necessary which would run through a man's property, the State can require that he give it up, though ordinarily the State must make proper compensation. By the same right the public authority can dynamite a building in order to stop the spread of a fire.

5. *Some General Principles of Justice*

There are three principles pertaining to justice which have many applications in Catholic theology: *Res clamat domino* (an object cries for its owner). *Res fructificat domino* (an object fructifies for its owner). *Res perit domino* (an object perishes at the expense of its owner). The first principle means that if a person has a right (*jus in re*) to an object, he may claim it, whoever may actually be holding it, even though this latter is in good faith. Thus, if my neighbor is using my umbrella in a violent rainstorm, thinking it is his, I have a right to take it away from him, as far as justice is concerned. If I buy a watch from a dealer, thinking he has a perfect right to sell it, and it happens that the watch is actually stolen property, the owner may claim it from me without compensation, though I can put in a claim for the return of my money from the dealer.

The second principle means that the *natural* fruits of an object belong to the owner, even though another may have helped to produce them. Thus I prune and fertilize a tree at the edge of my property, thinking it is on my land. When the fruit is ripe, my neighbor proves that the tree is on his land, and consequently he has a right to the fruit, though I can put in a claim for my labor. (The case is different when there is question of *industrial* fruit, as will be seen below.)

The third principle means that when an article perishes from natural causes, the loss must be sustained by the owner, even though at the time the article was in the unjust possession of another. Thus, if *A* steals a horse from *B,* and a few days later the horse dies from natural causes which would have killed him even if he were still in *B's* possession, *A* is obliged to make restitution only for the loss which the owner sustained by the lack of the horse's service for those few days.

Catholic theology recognizes the authority of the civil law in the matter of justice, and in most instances as binding in conscience. Generally speaking, the acts of the civil law are reduced to two classes: First, the civil law can determine details which are left indefinite by the natural law. For example, the State can legislate for the formalities required for the validity of a contract or will. Second, the State can at times transfer the title of property from one to another, for the benefit of the common good. Thus, the State's law that an honest bankrupt need not pay his debts in full, even though he later acquires property, can be used in conscience. Again, the acquisition of property by prescription is an example of the State's power to transfer ownership from one to another.

6. *Objects of Dominion or Ownership*

The goods which can be the object of human ownership are classified under three headings — (*a*) internal (of soul or body); (*b*) external (money, lands, etc.); and (*c*) intermediate (reputation and honor).

a) God alone has direct dominion over man's soul and body; hence, these cannot be the object of any act of complete dominion on man's part. Thus a man may not directly kill himself. But a man has the right to the *actions* of his soul and body; he can even make these the object of a contract to hire out his services to another, as the employee does.

b) Man can have direct dominion over the external things of earth — land, minerals, animals, trees, fruits, etc. — for the possession and use of these things are useful to help man attain his destiny in time and eternity. Furthermore, God has explicitly constituted man the lord of the entire earth.[4] The things of earth can be possessed, not only by the human race as a whole but also by individuals. The right of private property is one of the important social teachings of the Catholic Church. The main arguments are: Man takes greater care of objects when they are his own than when they are common possessions; there is more peace and order when private property is in use; man is stimulated to labor more diligently when he realizes that the fruits of his labor can be transmitted to his own children.[5] Leo XIII adds that when a man labors to improve a piece of property, he puts the stamp of his own personality on it, and thus renders it, so to say, a part of himself, and something which can be lawfully transmitted to his heirs.[6]

Of course, there are limitations to the right of private property. One in extreme need may take what is necessary to relieve his present necessities from the private possession of anyone who has more than he actually needs himself. Moreover, no one may possess so much private property as to impede gravely the opportunities of his fellow men to preserve and to improve their economic status. For it must be emphasized that every human being has a natural right to procure all that is necessary to provide him with a decent sustenance.

c) Every man has a right to reputation and honor. However, under certain circumstances this right can be forfeited, e.g., when a person commits a public crime.

There are certain goods which though available for the common use of men are not to be made the object of private ownership, nor even the exclusive ownership of any one nation. For example, the open sea may not be possessed by any one people, though it is recognized that a nation has the right to exclusive possession of a certain portion of the ocean adjacent to its shores (e.g., three miles, the distance of a cannon shot in the old days). In practice nowadays there is a tendency to increase this distance.

7. Subjects of Dominion

Generally speaking, every human being has the right to possess and to use property, by reason of his dignity and inviolability as a person. The actual use of reason is not required. For example, an infant may own property, though the administration is exercised by its relatives. However, there are certain determinations of positive law in reference to certain classes, such as children, married women, etc.

If a minor (a person under 21) living at home works for his father, merely as a son helping his parent, he has no strict right to a salary; but if he is emancipated (for example, by marriage), he has the same right as an outsider. Similarly, if a boy living at home has a lucrative job outside the family circle, he is strictly obliged only to pay for his expenses, though filial piety would bind him to be more generous if his parents are in need. Goods given to a child which are consumable (e.g., candy, small sums of money) are supposed to be given him absolutely, so that he may dispose of them as he wishes; but other goods are given only for his use, and the direct dominion remains with the parents. Thus, a child may give away his pocket money and his candy; but he would fail in justice to his parents if he gave away his overcoat or his skates. A parent is not bound by the natural law to pay for damages done by his child possessing the use of reason, unless the parent urged the child to do this, or otherwise co-operated positively. Thus, if a boy of ten years breaks a window, the father is not obliged to pay for it, even though he knows the child is doing damage and neglects to stop him. The father in this case would be guilty of neglecting his *parental* duty, but the obligation of restitution rests with the child himself. But ordinarily the civil law requires that a parent pay in the case as presented, and this would bind in conscience after the sentence of the judge. If a parent does not stop a child below the age of reason from doing damage, when he can stop him, the parent is bound by the natural law to make restitution. A father is not bound to pay the debts contracted by his minor son unless he has authorized these debts.

A son or daughter of twenty-one years or more is an independent person, and has the disposal of his wages. If he lives at home, he must pay his expenses, and also when needed contribute his share of labor to the well-being of the family — for example, by shoveling snow, chopping wood. It should be noted that sons and daughters have obligations of piety toward their parents, over and above their obligations in justice. For example, a wealthy married man would fail gravely against piety (even though not against justice) if he refused to help his father in grave need.

A wife can use at her own discretion whatever she earns or inherits in her own name; and she has a right to proper support from the common funds of the family. But she has no right to use the common funds for excessive expenses against the will of her husband (a violation of justice). Still less has she the right to use the dowry (the money assigned to the use of her husband at the time of marriage) by her own authority. However, the dowry in the European sense is rare in the United States. We have what is known as the dower right — the right of a widow to receive a share (one-third) of the immovable goods of her husband.

By the natural law an author or inventor has the exclusive right to the products of his skill or genius. But once they have been made public, he can claim protection only by positive law. All nations have such laws, and it would be a violation of justice to transgress them — e.g., plagiarizing a story or a piece of music that has been published with a copyright.

Secular clerics have the right to use their money and other possessions in the same way as lay persons, with the exception of the fruits of their benefice. The benefice comprises the salary which a bishop or priest receives by reason of his office (not, therefore, what is received by the publication of books, lectures, teaching, or as stipends, gifts, etc.). Out of the fruits of his benefice the cleric may take enough for his decent sustenance; the remainder he is bound to expend for the poor or for pious causes.

The vow of poverty of a religious extends only to external goods which have a money value. Hence, a religious is not dependent upon the will of the superior for the giving of a blood transfusion (unless there is question of receiving money for it). Similarly, a religious can dispose of relics (spiritual goods) and manuscripts (the fruits of the mind), unless these last could be published and thus have a money value. After the death of a religious his will regarding relics, class notes, diary, etc., must be observed, whether these are for other members of the community or for outsiders. Religious with solemn vows renounce both the possession and the use of material goods; religious with simple vows renounce only the right to use property at their own will, not the right to possess it.

8. Modes of Acquiring Dominion

There are various modes of acquiring dominion over property. The most frequent is a contract, which will be considered subsequently. Other modes are occupancy, discovery, accession, and prescription.

a) Occupancy is an act whereby one takes possession of something which has no owner, with the intention of making it his own. This title is exercised particularly when a person captures a wild animal that is free — e.g., a bird from the air, a tiger from the jungle, a fish from the ocean. If such an animal has once been caught and then escapes to its natural habitat, anyone has the right to seize it, irrespective of the previous owner. But when such an animal, while enjoying a measure of freedom, is confined to a limited space — e.g., fish in a pond on a man's property, deer in an enclosed park — it belongs to the owner of the property. Animals that are naturally wild but have been tamed, so that they recognize their owner's property as their home — e.g., bees, pigeons — may not be seized by another, unless they have given up the habit of returning, and the owner no longer wills or is able to recover them. For example, a swarm of bees that has taken up its abode in a tree many miles away from the owner may be made the property of anyone who puts them in a hive. But domestic animals — e.g., dogs, cows, hens — remain the property of their owner, even though they have roamed away.

The civil laws regarding the times when one may hunt, a license for fishing, etc., are regarded by many theologians as purely penal, the violation of which does not constitute a sin, though one is bound to pay the penalty if brought to court. However, the violation of these laws is a sin if the common good is thereby greatly injured — e.g., if one kills female animals in the closed season so that the supply is greatly diminished, or if one catches lobsters under the size prescribed by law. A person who shoots and seizes game on another's property (that is, birds or animals that are not confined to the other's property) does not fail against justice in taking the game, though he may sin by trespassing.

A nation may occupy land which hitherto has no owner, e.g., in the Antarctic regions or in the South Pacific. However, by international law an army may not seize the private possessions of a conquered nation, though the army may take possession of the military supplies of the enemy.

b) Civil laws govern the ownership of treasure trove — treasure, once hidden, whose original owner can no longer be found. In the United States, generally, the finder may keep all, even though it is found on another's land — e.g., a workman tearing down a building and finding a chest of pirate gold. However, in Louisiana the owner of the property has a right to one half. In some places civil law gives the owner of the soil the right to the entire treasure if the finder is a trespasser.

When a person finds an article that has been lost he is obliged to make reasonable efforts, proportionate to the value of the article, to find the owner. If he neglects to seek the owner, and afterward realizes that he could have found him but now can no longer do so, he must give up the article to the poor or to pious causes, because he has become a possessor in bad faith. However, if at first he made all reasonable efforts to find the owner and was unsuccessful, he may use the article as his own after all prudent hope of discovering the owner has passed. Where the civil law lays down conditions as to the time that must elapse before one may use a found article, the law must be obeyed.

One who finds an abandoned article — one which the owner has voluntarily discarded or thrown away — may keep it. This applies to fruit left on a tree or on the ground after the harvest, a magazine left in a train, old clothing and furniture consigned to the city dump. But, if something is left in such an article which evidently the owner did not wish to abandon, such as a filled pocketbook in an abandoned coat, it must be treated as a *lost* (not an *abandoned*) article. Similarly, articles washed to shore from a sinking ship or found in a wrecked airplane are lost, not abandoned, and must be restored to the owner, if possible. Similarly, articles removed by an adventurous youth from a burning building or store must be returned to the owner.

c) Accession is natural, when it is produced by the forces of nature, and the principle must be applied: "An object fructifies for its owner." Thus, when a tree produces fruit or an animal gives birth to young, this belongs to the owner. But if a person uses property belonging to another to produce fruit by his own effort and skill, it is called industrial fruit, and it belongs to the one exercising the industry, even though the object has been taken unjustly. Thus, if a musician steals a violin and gives a concert, he has a right to the emolument, though he must restore the violin. If a man steals money and bets on a winning horse, he need restore only the original sum.

If a person sows seed on the soil of another, thinking it is his own land, the owner of the land has a right to the crops, though the other may demand payment for the seed and labor. If a woman makes a dress out of cloth she thought was her own, though actually it belongs to another woman, the dress belongs to the one who made it, though she must reimburse the other for the cloth. The norm for judging these things is that the one who has ownership of the *principal* element of the two that are now inseparably united, has a right to the whole, with the obligation to reimburse the owner of the other element. This is very evident in the case of the artist who paints a valuable picture on a piece of canvas belonging to another.

If the soil of one man's property is *gradually* carried over to another's property by the tide (alluvion), the latter by that very fact acquires the property. But if the transfer is *rapid* (e.g., by a tidal wave) the ownership of the man whose property was thus carried away (avulsion) goes with the soil.

d) Prescription is a mode of acquiring property or of being freed from a debt or obligation through long-continued and tranquil possession in good faith. This is a case of the exercise of the State's right to transfer property from one to another for the sake of the common good — because if a person could be deprived of an object even after he and his ancestors had held it in good faith for many years, there would be great uncertainty and contention on the part of property holders. The Church recognizes the right of prescription in regard to ecclesiastical property. However, some exceptions are made. Thus, certain things are not subject to prescription, such as Mass stipends and parish boundaries. Again, immovable and precious movable goods belonging to the Holy See are prescribed only by a period of one hundred years; if they belong to some other moral person, by a period of thirty years.

The good faith required for acquisitive possession (whereby something is acquired) consists in the sincere belief that the object belongs to oneself. Theologians teach that some species of title is necessary for valid prescription; but for practical purposes a presumed title, which is present when one has possessed the object in good faith for a long time, suffices.

In the United States prescription in the strict sense is recognized only in regard to incorporeal hereditaments (e.g., the right to pass through another's property, the right to fish in a certain pond), not in regard to land or immovables. However, there is recognized what is known as the right of adverse possession. In itself, this means merely that the real owner of an object may not take legal measures to recover property from the one in actual possession after a determined length of time — for example, twenty years. However, it is sufficiently probable that this can be used in conscience, as long as the requisite good faith is present, at least if a very long period of time has elapsed.

Liberative prescription is that by which one is freed from a debt. Usually the time prescribed by law for this is less than for acquisitive prescription. For example, in some of our states the established period is six years. This civil ruling is called the statute of limitations. It means that after this period, a creditor may not call on the law to enforce the payment of a debt. The question is: May a person in conscience use this statute? In other words, may he refuse to pay a debt without committing sin when the law will no longer support his creditor? It would seem that a debtor may do this in those cases in which it is understood that he need not pay until the creditor has sent the bill, if the bill was not sent within the required time. This is the case of the dentist's or doctor's bill, for a person does not ordinarily know how much he has to pay until he receives the bill. The same is true of suits for damage — that is, when a person without any moral fault has injured the property or person of another. In such cases, if the time for presenting the bill or claim has passed, and the creditor through negligence or some other fault has failed to send a bill, the debtor (it seems) can refuse to pay, as long as he did nothing to prevent the other from sending the bill or claim — e.g., by changing his address.

In the case of bills which are supposed to be paid even though a formal demand is not made — e.g., a personal loan from a friend — or in the event that the bill has been sent once, even though the creditor does not further press the matter, the statute of limitations may not be used in conscience as a form of liberative prescription. In other words, even though the law will not support the creditor's claim, the debtor is bound to pay in conscience. But there are times even in the case of such debts when acquisitive prescription may be used. This could happen in the case of an heir who did not know that his father had contracted a debt, which should have been paid out of the inheritance. If the heir continues in good faith for a long time — e.g., twenty years — it would seem that he no longer has the obligation to pay, even though the debt is then brought to his attention, if the law of adverse possession supports him. As is evident, good faith could hardly ever be in the one who contracted the debt, since ordinarily he would not be unaware of it for a long time.[7]

9. *Species of Injustice*

Since there are three types of justice — legal, distributive, and commutative — there are also three types of injustice respectively. When we speak of injustice, however, we ordinarily refer to a violation of commutative justice. This, in turn, has many species subordinate to itself, and in confession these specific distinctions must be declared. Thus the sin of robbing a man of his reputation is specifically different from the sin of stealing his watch, although both are violations of commutative justice.

It should be noted that it is not an act of injustice to take something from a person who knows this is being done and is willing to let it happen. For example, the small boy is not guilty of theft when he takes apples from his neighbor's tree (even though he has not explicitly asked permission) if the latter sees what is being done and makes no protest. On this same principle, workingmen are sometimes free from theft when they bring home for their own use pieces of board, screws, etc., with the knowledge and tacit consent of the owner. But this principle must not be extended too far. It is not the same thing to say that an owner does not protest because he *is willing that the article be taken* and to say that he does not protest *because he feels that a protest will do no good*. This latter is by no means the same as consent.

Moreover, injustice is not done to a person if his property is taken away when he is unreasonably unwilling. Thus there is no injustice done by the starving man who takes from his wealthy neighbor enough food for his present needs, even though the neighbor protests or even attempts to stop him. Again, the man who must get his child to a hospital as fast as possible may seize his neighbor's car for this purpose (if that is the only means available), even though the neighbor refuses permission.

10. *Obligations of Legal Justice*

Two duties particularly expected of citizens by virtue of legal justice are the payment of taxes and the waging of war. It is true, some theologians are of the opinion that laws demanding the payment of taxes are purely penal; but the view that should be followed is that they bind in conscience, out of legal justice.[8] However, it seems probable that one would not fail against this virtue if he used stratagem to diminish his tax bill *to some extent,* since the rates are based on the supposition that there will be some evasion on the part of many. Needless to say, this involves at least a falsehood, and is surely not to be recommended. But we are speaking of *justice.*

The Catholic Church teaches that the waging of war is not in itself unjust. However, certain conditions must be fulfilled before a nation may lawfully go to war. There must be a good reason, proportionate to the evils which can be anticipated. Thus the recovery of a large piece of stolen territory, and the ejection of unjust invaders, are just reasons. It is only when all peaceful measures are evidently unable to remedy the situation that a nation may have recourse to war. Furthermore, the rulers must be morally certain that they are in the right. Finally, a declaration must be made by the lawful authority — in the United States Congress. Only a defensive war can be justified. However, a nation that takes the initial step to war when it is *certain* that an enemy is about to attack *immediately,* can be said to be waging a defensive war.

In the waging of war, unjust means must be avoided. Means may be unjust because they are forbidden by the natural law (as would be the case of a direct attack on the civilian population), or by the positive law, such as the use of poisoned gas. However, if one belligerent violates a statute of positive law, the other is free to do the same.

As is evident, it is not possible for both sides to be objectively justified in a war. But it is possible for the citizens of both nations to be in good faith, and to be convinced that their cause is just. The individual citizen must take as his norm the general principle that he is obliged to obey his own rulers unless he is sure that what they command is unjust. Hence, he must go to war if commanded, unless he has the sincere conviction in his conscience that the war is unjust. It is rarely possible for the individual citizen nowadays to know enough about the working of his government to be sure that his side is unjust.

11. *Restitution as an Obligation of Commutative Justice*

Since the purpose of commutative justice is to establish the right order of things in such wise that each will possess that to which he has a real right, this virtue demands that when one person is in possession of something belonging to another, this article be given back to the owner. Similarly it demands that when one has been the guilty cause of another's loss, reparation be made, even though the guilty one is not in possession of anything more than he should have. It follows from this that one who has been guilty of a grave violation of commutative justice cannot receive the pardon of his sin (whether in a sacrament or by an act of perfect contrition) unless he has the intention of making restitution. This intention must be present, even though the person cannot make restitution immediately, and such an intention suffices in order that the sin may be forgiven. (Some Catholics erroneously believe that one who dies without having actually made restitution will not be admitted to heaven until the debt is paid. As is evident, the soul is not debarred from heaven as long as the person sincerely intended before death to make restitution or to have it made, as far as possible and necessary, by others after his death.) Furthermore, there are times when a confessor can leave a person in good faith about the obligation of restitution — one who is actually bound to make restitution, but is unaware of his obligation, and is now dying — if the confessor feels that it would be useless to urge it and the man would then be guilty of formal sin.

12. *Restitution Because of Damnification*

A person is bound to make restitution for damage done to another's property if the following three conditions are fulfilled:

a) The act of damnification was strictly *unjust*. Thus one has no obligation to restore if the damage was the result of a violation of charity. For example, if I see that my neighbor's barn is on fire, and I could easily call the firemen, but fail to do so because I am too indolent or because I dislike my neighbor, I am guilty of a grave sin against charity, but I am not bound to restitution. Again, if I get my enemy ousted from his job by persuading his employer that there is really no need of his services, I do not fail against justice. But if I use deceit for this purpose — for example, by calumniating my enemy — I fail against justice.

b) The act was effective — that is, it was the *cause* of the damage. Thus, if I set a bad example to others by breaking windows, I am guilty of no *injustice* with regard to the windows they break. I am bound to restitution only for those I broke. Again, if *A* commits a murder and *B* is convicted on circumstantial evidence, *A* is not bound in *justice* to make any attempt to rescue *B*, though he is bound in *charity* to try to get him vindicated, if he can do so without too great a risk to his own life and liberty. In such a case *A* is the *occasion,* not the *cause* of *B's* misfortune. Moreover, one who induces another to inflict damage is bound to restitution (in case the actual culprit fails to make it) only to the extent that he gave counsel. Thus, if I persuade a man to give my enemy a punch in the nose, I am not responsible if he also breaks his victim's leg on his own initiative.

c) The perpetrator was guilty in *conscience* — that is, he realized he was doing wrong, and voluntarily did it. Thus, if a boy drives a car carelessly and inflicts damage on someone's property, he is not obliged in justice to make restitution if he sincerely believes that he was not guilty in conscience, because he acted thoughtlessly, without realizing what might happen. However, in such a case, if the matter is brought to court and the sentence of the judge is that restitution be made, this is obligatory in conscience, even though there was no subjective guilt. For example, if I take due precautions to keep my dog on my property, but through some accident he gets loose and damages my neighbor's shrubs, I must pay if the court so decides. This is another example of the State's rights over private property for the benefit of the common welfare.

There is a grave obligation of making restitution only when the sin was both objectively and subjectively mortal. If the damage was objectively grave, but the person was guilty of only a venial sin because of lack of full advertence, there seems to be no obligation to restore anything. If the culprit had full advertence, but thought the damage was light, though actually it was grave, he is bound to restore only as much as he thought the damage would amount to. Thus, if I deliberately, for a joke, seize a friend's stickpin and throw it into the river because I am convinced that it is worth a quarter, though actually it contains a precious diamond, I am bound to give him only a quarter. However, he could justly bring me to court and force me to pay the entire amount.

If a person inflicts damages on a number of persons, each damage being light, he is guilty of that number of sins, not a mortal sin, even though the sum involved altogether is considerable. And he is not bound under pain of mortal sin to make restitution.

One who has deliberately done something which is now causing serious damage is bound in justice to attempt to stop it, even though he did not foresee the harmful consequences when he did it. If he fails to make such an attempt, he is bound to restitution for the amount of damage that occurs after he has positively neglected to do anything about the matter. For example, if a man thoughtlessly threw away his cigarette, and on going by the place an hour later saw that he had started a fire which was now endangering a house, he must call the fire department, or use some similar effective means to extinguish the fire. If he fails to do so, he must pay for the damage which results after this act of neglect. If he does what he can to stop the damage, but is unsuccessful, he is bound to no restitution, as far as the natural law is concerned. But if a person *culpably* started a fire, then repented and tried to stop it, but unsuccessfully, he must nevertheless make restitution for all the damage.

According to some theologians, if a person intends to inflict damage on the property of *A* but erroneously inflicts it on the property of *B*, he is bound to no restitution. At any rate, it is admitted by all that if a person is in a strict doubt whether or not he was the cause of damnification, he is not bound to restitution. For example, if it happened that two men shot at a neighbor's dog at the same time (without having entered into a plot to kill the animal) and only one bullet killed the dog, and it is impossible to determine whose shot took effect, neither is bound to restitution. But if several entered on a plot to do the damage, all must share the restitution, even though one only caused the damage.

If a person caused damage to another's person or property, and afterward is unable to find the individual (or his heirs) to make restitution, he is probably not bound to give anything to the poor or to pious causes, although this is fitting.

13. *Restitution by a Possessor in Good Faith*

A possessor in good faith is one who sincerely thinks an object belongs to him, or at least that he lawfully has the use of it. The principle governing his restitution is that he must restore to the true owner whatever of the object he has left when he finds out who is the owner, but not what has been disposed of, while he thought the object was his. Under the heading of "whatever of the object he has left" is included whatever remains *virtually* or *in value*. Thus, if a farmer thought that a certain cow belonged to his herd, and sold the milk for several weeks he would have to return the money to his neighbor, the real owner of the cow, because the milk's value remains. Even if he had butchered the cow, and he and his family had eaten it, he would still have to pay the value, if he had intended to butcher one of his cows in any event. But the man who finds a dish of ice cream in the refrigerator and thinks his loving wife has thoughtfully provided it for him and so eats it, is bound to no restitution when he finds out afterward that his wife was only keeping the ice cream for a neighbor whose refrigerator was out of order.

If a person in good faith sold what belonged to another, he is bound to restore (when he finds the true owner) only what he has left from the sale. If he gave it away, he is bound to nothing. However, if the real owner recovers the object from one to whom the man in question sold it, the buyer can sue the seller to get his money back, and if a court sentence so adjudicates the matter, it must be observed in conscience. On the other hand, if a man bought an article and afterward discovered that the seller had stolen it, he can return the object to the thief and demand his money back. In such an event he should in charity tell the real owner. But if the real owner demands the object back before the buyer can return the object to the thief, he must give it up, and then can try to get his money from the thief.

A person is not failing if he accepts gifts of money from a thief, as long as the gift does not render the thief incapable of making restitution. For example, the politician's wife, who knows that her husband is guilty of some dishonest transactions, can accept his presents as long as she believes that he still has enough honest money to make up for his dishonest dealings. However, if a gift renders the donor wholly or partially incapable of making restitution, it must be returned or given to those to whom restitution is due. It must be noted that we are speaking of a gift of money or some other *fungible* good; for if there is question of a stolen watch, fur coat, etc., the object may not be accepted, or if accepted must be returned to the real owner.

14. *Restitution by a Possessor in Bad Faith*

A possessor in bad faith is one who knows that a certain article belongs to someone else, and yet unjustly retains it. Ordinarily a possessor in bad faith is one who stole the object, but it can also be one who received it from the thief, knowing that it was stolen.

The principle governing this person is that he must restore the object or its value, even though it perished without any fault of his. Furthermore, he is bound to restore the losses sustained by the owner from the lack of the object, provided he foresaw them in some way when he committed the theft. Thus, the man who steals a taxi cab must restore, not only the vehicle, but also the money the owner would have earned during the time it was stolen.

In one case the thief does not have to make restitution for an object which perished when in his possession — namely, if it would have perished from the same natural cause, or some other natural cause, had it remained in the possession of the owner. For example, the stolen car which is burned in the thief's garage, but would have perished in the same fire had it remained in the possession of the owner. On the other hand, an object that is not so destroyed has to be restored by the thief, even though it would have perished had it remained in the possession of the owner.

15. *Restitution by Co-operators*

A person who co-operates in the unjust action of another is bound to make restitution in as far as his co-operation was unjust, effective, and culpable in conscience.[9] However, when the degree of co-operation on the part of several who took part in an act of injustice is unequal, the obligation of making the entire restitution rests on *individuals,* one after another, in suchwise that one further down in the scale of co-operation has the obligation only if those above fail to do so. For example, Peter, a gang leader, orders Paul, one of his henchmen, to rob a store. Paul commits the crime, aided by John, who helps him by driving a truck with the spoils, and by Henry, the watchman who for the sake of a bribe refrains from turning in an alarm. Then Paul turns the loot over to the care of James, who conceals it in his barn. The order of restitution is: James, Peter, Paul, John, Henry. In this sequence the obligation of making restitution falls on each, so that even the fifth is bound to pay all if those above him fail to do so. If two or more are in the same grade of co-operation, they divide the obligation. For example, if two gangsters beat up a man, they must share the expense of the doctor, etc. In all these cases, however, one must take the entire burden of restitution, as long as he shared in the commission of the entire crime, even though he received only a small portion of the spoils. Thus, if five robbers stole $10,000 from a bank, each receiving $2,000 and one of them later repents, he is bound to repay $10,000, if the other four refuse to do so. But, in practice, it is often advisable to leave such a person in good faith, because if told that he must restore the whole, he would probably do nothing and thus remain in sin, whereas at present he is sincerely convinced that he must restore only his share. Indeed, St. Alphonsus thinks that it may be presumed that the victim of the injustice will be quite satisfied to get back from this individual only his share of the booty, and will absolve him of the obligation of giving back the share of the others.

A person is not a *negative* co-operator to an act of injustice unless he neglects to perform an act which he was obliged in *justice* to perform. For example, if a man sees his neighbor's barn burning down and does nothing to stop it, he is guilty of an act against *charity*, not justice, and is bound to no restitution. But a policeman who would neglect to prevent a robbery (or a watchman, in reference to the building he is employed to watch) is bound to restitution, after the positive perpetrators and co-operators, for such an individual is bound to protect property in *justice*, since he is paid for this. A servant is bound in justice to prevent damage (as far as he reasonably can) to those goods of his master over which he has *special* charge (e.g., the chauffeur over the car, the gardener over the flowers) but not to the other goods of the master.

One can co-operate by merely giving counsel, even without physical participation — e.g., the bank clerk who informs the robbers just when the safe is unguarded. However, a person may co-operate toward a robbery if his own life is threatened. In that event he is using the principle that one may use the goods of another to save his own life in extreme necessity.

16. *Circumstances of Restitution*

Restitution must be made, in the first place, to the one whose right was violated. If he is dead, restitution for injustice in external goods is to be made to his heirs. If the possessor in bad faith is unable to find the victim or his heirs, he must make restitution to the poor or to pious causes — e.g., the foreign missions. In the event that he has done this last, after sufficiently seeking the true owner, he is not obliged to make restitution again to this latter if he unexpectedly appears.

Restitution to the federal government can be made by buying postage stamps and burning them. Sometimes a debt of this kind can be paid by donations to the poor — e.g., in a place where the government is patently negligent in providing for the poor. If a person is very poor himself, he can make restitution to himself, but this principle must be used very cautiously.

A person can make restitution in the form of a gift, unless this will draw a gift from the other party in return. One who is bound to make restitution to the poor can count the donations he made to the poor since the obligation began as portions of this restitution.

Restitution should not be deferred too long; but at times, especially when restitution is to be made to the poor, a person can put it off until after his death — that is, by leaving it in his will to some charitable cause.

17. Causes Excusing From Restitution

If a person has nothing with which to make restitution, of course he is excused *for the time being,* though he should have the intention to restore when he can. Neither is a person forced to give up a justly acquired place in society in order to make restitution, but he should curtail his expenses as much as possible. Nor is a person obliged to sacrifice his good name in order to make restitution. For example, if a widow, knowing that one of her children was conceived of an adulterous union, could rectify the matter of the inheritance only by revealing her sin (that is, in such wise that only the legitimate children would get the inheritance of her deceased husband) she would not be obliged to make such a revelation.

If a person goes into bankruptcy honestly — that is, if he does his best to keep his business going but fails, and then declares all his assets — it seems quite probable that afterward he is not obliged to make up for the debts he could not then pay, even though he acquires another fortune. The basis seems to be that the State exercises its power over private property to transfer to his credit the amount he cannot pay, and also the general understanding among businessmen that they will condone the debt of an unfortunate colleague, expecting the same favor from him in like circumstances. As is very evident, these principles do not apply to the dishonest bankrupt, the man who declares bankruptcy when he is able to keep his business going, and who conceals a large sum.

18. Injustice in Reference to Internal Goods

By internal goods are meant the cultivation of the intellect, spiritual benefits, life, and bodily integrity. Since it is a violation of justice to deceive another, a person who leads others into error which is liable to be harmful is bound to correct this error. If his act was inculpable, he is not bound to go to the same lengths as if it were culpable. Of course, the greater the harm that may ensue, the graver the obligation to correct it. Thus, a professor in a medical school who discovers that, because of his neglect in preparing his lectures, he has suggested the use of a very harmful drug as a remedy, must make very great efforts to correct this error, and is even bound to reparation for harm that has been done as a result of this error in the meantime. Similarly, a priest who (through culpable neglect) gives a wrong decision about the obligation of restitution must endeavor to correct it, and may even be bound to make the restitution himself.

The superiors or consultors of a religious order who refuse to admit a novice to profession through merely personal animosity, when the novice is really worthy and desires to become a member, also sin against justice, because in admitting a novice an order makes an implicit contract to accept him as a member if he is found worthy.

Suicide is an act of injustice against society and against God, for every human being is a member of society and the creature of God. The suicide also fails in the charity he owes to himself. We are speaking here of *direct* suicide, when death results from an action which has for its only immediate effect the death of the person concerned. On the principle of double effect, one may, for a sufficiently grave reason, perform an action from which his death results as one effect, there being also an equally immediate good effect, which will sufficiently compensate for his death. For example, the pilot who crashes his plane into an enemy ship, or the man who jumps into the water to lighten the weight of the lifeboat, or the man who goes into a burning building to baptize a baby, etc., is acting lawfully. Moreover, it is a probable view that a convicted criminal may be given by the authority that convicted him the right to inflict death on himself.

A person is obliged to use ordinary means to preserve his life, but not extraordinary means, such as a very expensive operation, the procuring of an "iron lung" for permanent need, the continued and frequent use of blood transfusions. Moreover, a remedy for easing pain may be given to a person, even though it may shorten his life somewhat. But one who is not prepared spiritually for death should not be given a remedy that will render him unconscious when he is dying, as long as there is any hope of getting him to make his peace with God. Of course, it is never permitted to accelerate a person's death, *directly intending this,* by a drug. Such an act is murder, no matter how much he is suffering or how hopeless his case may seem.

The direct killing of an innocent person is a sin of injustice against him, society, and God. However, in virtue of the divine authority communicated to the State, civil rulers may put to death those guilty of serious crime; and they may authorize their citizens to kill the enemy in a just war. This last right also includes the execution of members of the enemy forces (or even civilians) found guilty by just trial of crimes, such as barbarism. The indirect killing of innocent persons can sometimes be justified on the principle of the double effect — for example, civilians near a fort which is being attacked, an operation for a cancerous uterus on a pregnant woman resulting in the death of the child.

A person can kill one who is unjustly attacking him (or some innocent person) with a view to murder or to rob (provided a considerable sum is at stake), to mutilate or to violate sexually. However, this must be understood with certain qualifications. If sufficient protection can be obtained by merely maiming the assailant or by running away, this should be done. The death (or wounding) of the assailant is permitted only on the principle of double effect, the good effect being the preservation of life or of some precious possession. A girl could not kill a man only because he was guilty of indecent touches on her, but she could physically resist by kicking, striking, etc. Moreover, a girl who has been raped may not subsequently kill the assailant, since it is only the right to protection, not to vindication, that she possesses.

A person who has been unjustly sentenced to death or to prison may attempt to escape, even to the extent of striking or disarming the guards, but not to the extent of killing them. One who is justly sentenced is not *per se* justified in escaping, unless the sentence is very severe — e.g., death or life imprisonment in severe conditions. But even in that case he may not inflict physical harm on the guards.

A duel, in which two persons, by previous agreement, fight each other with deadly weapons, is forbidden by the divine law and is gravely penalized by the Church.[10] Even if neither has the intention of killing the other, or even if precautions are taken against grave injuries, the penalties are inflicted.

A prize fight is not a duel, because deadly weapons are not used. Nevertheless, it is difficult to see how prize fighting can be excused from sin, since the direct purpose of each is to inflict serious (even though not lasting) injury on the other. But boxing, for the purpose of developing skill in self-defense, would not be sinful, if proper safeguards are used — e.g., large padded gloves, light blows, short rounds — even though accidentally one may be hurt at times.

A person may mutilate, or have mutilated, a part of his own body when this is necessary for the good of the whole body. For example, a diseased limb can be amputated. If the purpose is to render the body more beautiful, a limited measure of mutilation is allowed — e.g., face lifting, the perforation of the ears for earrings. Even if the particular part of the body is not diseased, it is permitted to mutilate it if the physical good of the whole requires it — for example, if a man's hand is caught in a trap, he may amputate it if otherwise he cannot escape. It seems probable, also, that one can authorize the mutilation of his own body for the physical benefit of another — for example, giving the cornea of one's eye to a blind person.[11] Certainly, blood transfusions are lawful. The right to mutilate the body is derived from the principle that man is the administrator of his own body, under God, the Lord of life and death, and a prudent administrator may dispose of a portion of what is committed to him to save the whole.

However, it is unlawful to mutilate the body for other reasons — e.g., to excite pity and thus receive alms, to escape military service, to render oneself unattractive and thus to avoid proposals of marriage. Above all, we know from the clear teaching of the Church, mutilation of the human body for the direct purpose of rendering a person sterile (e.g., the married woman who wishes to have no more children, the eugenic sterilization of morons) is forbidden by the law of God, as tampering of the human body for the purpose that is not *per se* for the benefit of the whole. It seems probable, however, that sterilization may be inflicted as a penalty, just as death may be inflicted. But from the practical standpoint, it is not an adequate punishment, at least as it is generally performed in the United States, since it does not render a person incapable of sexual gratification.

If a person is guilty of killing or wounding another unjustly, he is bound to make restitution for the temporal loss sustained by the family from the death or the disablement of this person — that is, as far as the assailant foresaw this when he committed the crime. *Per se* this obligation remains even in case the murderer has been sentenced to death, for his death will not repair the temporal harm done by his crime.

A man who attacked a girl and rendered her pregnant is bound to make restitution for any temporal harm he caused her (e.g., infection) and also to provide for the support of the child. When a man and woman voluntarily have sexual relations outside of wedlock and a child is born, both are bound to share the expenses of bringing up the child. However, ordinarily such parents may put the child in a foundling asylum, because such institutions have been established for this purpose, and the state (or private funds) provide for such contingencies. It is to be noted that there is no obligation by the natural law for a man to marry a girl when he has rendered her pregnant, and it is not advisable for him to do so, unless both sincerely wish it. Usually the evils consequent on an unhappy marriage are greater than the evil of illegitimacy.

If a child is born of a married woman from an adulterous union, the child has no right to an inheritance from the woman's husband. If he thinks the child his, and his wife feels that great harm would come if she revealed the truth, she can keep silent; but she is bound, if she has means, to make up the deficit of the inheritance to the legitimate children.

19. *Injustice in Reference to External Goods*

Theft is the unjust taking of something belonging to another with the intention of keeping it. Strictly speaking, theft is committed by stealth, without the knowledge of the owner. If violence is used, the crime is robbery. Theft is a crime against both the individual and society. Consequently, in determining the gravity of a sin of theft from the standpoint of the amount, there is a twofold norm — the *relative* norm and the *absolute* norm. The former is based on the harm done to the individual who has suffered, the latter on the harm done to society. Generally speaking, when the victim of a theft is one who supports himself and his family by a daily wage, the relative sum for a grave sin of theft is the amount of one day's salary. Thus it would be a mortal sin to steal $5 from a very poor person (on relief), $10 from a laborer, $20 from a person of the middle class, $30 from a person in comfortable circumstances, $50 from a rich person (e.g., $20,000 annual income), $75 from a millionaire. This last sum would give what seems to be a reasonable absolute sum — namely, a sum which is so large that society would suffer much if it could be stolen without grave sin even from the richest or from a wealthy corporation. The amount would vary with changes in the value of money.

If a person steals small amounts, they may coalesce if he keeps the money until he accumulates a large sum, or if they are so close together that morally they make one act. For example, if a man steals $2 every week from his place of business, there would be a moral coalescence. However, if a person steals at intervals, it takes more to constitute a grave sin — perhaps one and a half times as much — than if he committed only one act. Similarly, if one stole small amounts from different persons, it would take more — perhaps one and a half times as much — to make a grave sin.

Thefts by children or by a wife are not grave unless about twice the amount for this particular family is taken. Moreover, in the case of the thefts by children of fruit, cakes, etc., the parents are considered to be unwilling regarding the mode rather than the actual taking of the articles, and so restitution is not required. The same is true in regard to small thefts of money by children — that is, restitution need not be demanded, on the principle that the parents will condone this obligation.

Thefts by religious from the common fund are violations of both justice and poverty. The gravity of the sin against justice is measured by the financial condition of the religious house; the gravity of the sin against poverty is measured (it seems) by the economic status that the particular order professes. Thus, such a theft might be a grave act of injustice and a light transgression of the vow of poverty, or vice versa.

A person in extreme necessity of the means of life (that is, in danger of death from starvation, lack of necessary clothing, etc.) may take from another what he needs to relieve the present crisis. However, if the other is in the same extreme necessity, he is not to be deprived of what he possesses. If the one in need has funds or means in some other place, he can take what he needs from another only with the intention of repaying. But if he has nothing of his own, he can seize the necessities of life and make them his own, without any obligation of recompense, even though later he acquires wealth.

The possessor of the necessary goods sins against justice if he *prevents* the needy person from taking what he needs; but he sins only against charity if he *refuses to give them* to the needy person himself. In other words, the right which the needy person has is the right *to seize* what he needs, not (in justice) the right to the goods themselves before he has taken possession of them. He gets the title to ownership only by taking them (occupancy).

At times a person can recover what is due to him by occult compensation. This means that if another owes him a debt, and it cannot be collected in the normal way, the creditor can secretly take from the debtor what is due to him. In such an event, the creditor should let the debtor know in some way that the debt no longer holds — e.g., by saying: "Don't worry about that debt any more; we can consider it canceled."

Employees may not use occult compensation to raise their salary to what they think they deserve, as long as they have freely contracted for a certain amount, even though it is actually below the living wage. However, if they are practically forced to take a job to escape starvation, and the employer who can pay more refuses to do so, because he knows he has them at his mercy, they may compensate themselves occultly. Moreover, if the employer demands extra service and gives no extra wages, they can use this same method of making compensation. But they must be careful not to over-work this principle.[12]

20. *Injustice in Reference to Intermediate Goods*

Reputation, or good name, is the common esteem of a person's excellence; honor is the external acknowledgment of this excellence. Everyone has a right to reputation as long as he has done no public evil. This is true even of the man who is privately leading a wicked life, for if it were permitted to divulge a person's private vices, society would suffer much, the good relatives of the person would be disgraced, etc. However, on the principle of the double effect, a person's private vices may be revealed for the sake of the common good. For example, the fact that a young man is leading an immoral life secretly can be revealed to a good girl who is planning to marry him. Similarly, if a person knows that a candidate for Holy Orders is unworthy because of some secret sins, he should reveal the matter to ecclesiastical authorities, since the common good of the Church is at stake.

A rash judgment — that is, a *certain* judgment that a person is guilty of some wrong, based on insufficient grounds, is a sin against justice. However, a grave sin is not committed if there is good circumstantial evidence to support the judgment, or if it is a mere *suspicion* of the person's guilt.

Detraction is the injuring of the reputation of one who is absent. If what is said is true (that is, the revelation of secret sins), the sin is simple detraction; if it is false, the sin is calumny. Both are violations of justice. The gravity of the sin is measured, not by the gravity of the crime narrated, but by the injury that is done to the person's good name. Thus, if it is publicly known that a man is a drunkard, his reputation is injured little more if one states that he also quarrels with his wife. On the other hand, to say of a man of high reputation that he is addicted to little falsehoods could be a grave sin.

It is not injustice to manifest a person's crimes if they are now public — that is, when many know them, and it is impossible for them to be hidden much longer, even though the individual who is now hearing of them was previously unaware of them. It would seem that it is not against justice to tell the recent evil deeds of a man in one place, if they were committed and are publicly known in another place. But when a person's evil deeds have been forgotten and he is now leading a good life, it would seem to be against justice to bring them up now.[13] Sometimes, although it may not be against justice to reveal something, it is against charity, e.g., when a person who was convicted of a crime years ago has recovered his good standing in the community.

One who listens to detraction or calumny and does not encourage it does not fail against justice, unless he has the obligation officially to correct the detractor (e.g., a pastor or religious superior). Often it is better not to make any explicit protest against detraction (e.g., (gossip) but rather to try to change the conversation. One who encourages detraction is a co-operator in the sin.

Contumely is the act of taking away from a person the honor he deserves. It can be a grave sin, when it is very insulting. It is committed in the presence of the person, at least in the sense that his image is present, as when the college president is hanged in effigy by the students. Its gravity is measured by the dignity of the person dishonored and the authority of the one who commits it. Thus, if the Pope is dishonored it is worse than if it is a simple priest; an act of insult proceeding from a person in high office is worse than one committed by a person of low rank. For this reason the insults passed back and forth by the patrons of a barroom are generally not grave sins, even though they may be very opprobrious.

There is an obligation of repairing calumny and detraction, grave or light in accordance with the measure of harm that has been done. In the case of calumny, the guilty person does not have to admit that he told a lie, if he can repair the harm by saying that he was mistaken. When there is question of simple detraction, since the truth was told, a person may not deny it, but he can attempt to make up by bringing out the good qualities of the one injured. When a person has been guilty of calumny or detraction in the public press, he should use this same means to make reparation. If it took place by word of mouth, and the guilty person has reason to believe that those to whom he spoke have repeated the story to others, he should ask them to pass along the reparation also.

At times the obligation of repairing the detraction or calumny ceases — namely, when there is good reason to believe that the matter is now generally forgotten, and it might do more harm to bring the subject up again, or when it is very likely that the hearers regarded the story as groundless gossip and consequently no great harm was done.

One who has dishonored another is also bound to make reparation. This need not take the form of an explicit apology; at times it suffices to show the person a special honor — e.g., inviting him to dinner. But, at any rate, such reparation should be made known to those who witnessed the act of contumely.

FOOTNOTES

1. Mt. 1:19.
2. Gen. 1:28.
3. Kent, *Commentary in American Law*, III, 439.
4. Gen. 1:28.
5. Cf. St. Thomas, *Summa*, II–II, q. 66, a. 2.
6. Encyclical *Rerum Novarum*, cf. *Five Great Encyclicals*, p. 4.
7. Cf. Martin, *Adverse Possession, Prescription and Limitation of Action* (Washington, D. C.: Catholic University Press, 1944).
8. Cf. Crowe, *The Moral Obligation of Paying Just Taxes* (Washington, D. C.: Catholic University Press, 1944).
9. Cf. n. 12.
10. Can. 2351, § 1.
11. Cf. Cunningham, *The Morality of Organic Transplantation* (Washington, D. C.: Catholic University Press, 1945).
12. Cf. *DB*, 1187.
13. Moore, *The Sin of Detraction* (Washington, D. C.: Catholic University Press, 1950).

1. The Nature of a Contract

A contract is an act of consent, externally manifested, whereby two or more persons agree on the doing of something which involves an obligation on at least one party. A contract is *unilateral* when the obligation rests on one party only (as when a person binds himself in justice to present a gift to another, and this other accepts). A contract is *bilateral* when there are obligations on both sides (e.g., the contract of buying and selling). A contract becomes binding only when both parties have externally manifested their consent. Merely internal consent is not sufficient, since a contract involves the mutual agreement of human beings, and human beings can inform one another of their internal consent only by external signs. These signs can be words, writing, gestures — at times even a deliberate silence, when it is reasonably presumed that the person would object if he did not agree. Consent can be expressed by a representative or proxy, even in the case of the important contract of marriage.[1]

A *substantial* error or an *accidental* error can be present in one who enters a contract. A substantial error is one that is concerned with the very nature of the object of the contract (e.g., when a person buys a piece of glass thinking it is a diamond), or with the nature of the contract itself (e.g., when a person accepts something as a gift, whereas the other intends to sell it to him), or with the primary purpose of the contract (e.g., if a Catholic promises funds to a missionary society which he thinks is Catholic, whereas it is under non-Catholic auspices), or with some quality of the object which is regarded by him as an essential feature (e.g., when a Latin priest buys hosts for Mass, thinking they are made of unleavened bread, whereas they are leavened). An error as to the identity of the other person is substantial in some contracts, especially the contract of marriage — e.g., if John goes through the marriage ceremony with Mary, thinking it is her twin sister Jane. A substantial error in one or both of the parties to a contract renders the contract null and void.

An accidental error is one that is concerned with some secondary feature on which the consent of the parties is reasonably presumed not to depend, as when I give an alms to a poor man, thinking he is very virtuous, whereas in reality he is a drunkard, or when a girl marries a man whom she thinks to be very rich, whereas in reality he is poor. An accidental error ordinarily does not invalidate a contract, unless one of the parties expressly stipulated that he is giving consent only on condition that this particular feature is present, and actually it is not present, as would be the case if the girl in question explicitly asserted that she intends to contract marriage with this man only on condition that he is as rich as he claims to be. It should be noted that to enter marriage with an intention of this kind, rendering the contract doubtfully valid, would be a serious sin, unless the parties agree to abstain from conjugal relations until the marriage is proved to be certainly valid. An accidental error caused by fraud would render a contract rescindable at the choice of the victim.

A contract binds in justice, either under penalty of grave sin or of light sin, in accordance with the importance of the matter involved and the intention of those who make the contract. Thus, even if grave matter is involved the contracting parties can bind each other with only a light obligation, if they wish. When a contract is confirmed by a promissory oath, there is an added obligation from the virtue of religion.

Grave fear unjustly imposed on a person to get him to make a contract does not invalidate a contract in general, but it renders it rescindable at the will of the victim. It does, however, render invalid a gratuitous contract — one which is for the benefit of one side — such as the promise of the father to pay a sum to kidnapers for the return of his son. Furthermore, by the law of the Church, grave fear exerted by another person to induce a person to marry, when the fear is unjustly inflicted, renders the marriage invalid.[2]

If two persons enter into a contract whereby one agrees to perform a sinful deed, the contract is null and void, and any recompense that has been paid must be given back before the deed is done. But, if the deed has been performed, the money may be kept, in virtue of the probable opinion that the risk incurred in performing the deed has become the object of a legitimate contract. On the other

hand, since there is also a probable view to the contrary, the one
who agreed to pay for the deed is not obliged in strict justice to pay.
Thus, if John agreed by contract with Peter to kill James for $500
(and the money is handed over), John is bound to abstain from
the deed and hand back the money to Peter. But, if John has
committed the murder, he may keep the money. On the other hand,
if Peter has not paid, he is not obliged to do so after the murder
has been committed.

People may use in conscience the rights the civil law grants
them regarding the making of contracts. For example, if a minor
contracts debts on his own authority, he can sometimes use the
benefit of the law and repudiate them when he comes of age. This
would not hold, however, if he pretended to be over twenty-one
when he contracted the debts. Businessmen are supposed to be
familiar with this law, and not run any chances by entering into
a contract with a minor.

One who unjustly violates a contract must make up for all the
damages caused to the other, in as far as he foresaw them and
was guilty in violating the contract. For example, the man who is
bringing back to his neighbor the money he borrowed and loses
it on the way is not responsible for the fact that his neighbor was
unable to pay his mortgage and thereby lost his house. But, if he
deliberately refuses to pay when the debt falls due, foreseeing in
a general way that his neighbor may suffer loss from his delinquency,
he is bound to make up for the damages.

If one party of a contract fails substantially to fulfill his part, the
other, generally speaking, is free from his obligations. But that does
not mean that the *state* brought about by the contract is dissolved.
Thus, if a man is guilty of adultery, his wife is not obliged afterward
to give him conjugal relations; but that does not mean that their
marriage is dissolved.[3]

2. *Wills*

A will is a contract of donation, whereby a person determines who
shall receive his property after his death. The right to make a will
is found basically in the natural law, though the details have to
be made by positive legislation. All countries have laws for the
making of wills — e.g., the number of witnesses, the age of the
person who can make a will, etc.

It is a disputed question among theologians whether or not a will devoid of the formalities prescribed by law is valid. Since each side is probable, one may use either opinion to his advantage, though not in respect to the same will. Accordingly, the natural heir (e.g., the wife or son of the deceased) may refuse to pay legacies found in a will devoid of some formality (e.g., signed by only one witness), even though he knew the deceased really wished these legacies to be paid; but, on the other hand, one who has got possession of a legacy from a will devoid of the formalities may keep it until legally dispossessed. Thus, if a friend is present at a deathbed, and the dying man says: "I want you to have my watch after my death," the friend may take possession after the man's death, even though the written will contains nothing about such a gift. On the other hand, the heir may sue for the recovery of the watch. However, there is one exception — in the case of pious legacies — which are to be given, even if they are expressed by the deceased in a will devoid of the legal formalities — e.g., by mere word of mouth — provided the heir is sure this was the will of the deceased.[4]

Religious and priests should follow exactly the prescriptions of Canon Law as to the making of wills,[5] and be sure that all the prescriptions required by the particular State are fulfilled.

3. *Buying and Selling*

This contract, so common in present-day life, is made when a commodity is transferred for money. It differs, therefore, from barter (commodity for commodity) and exchange (money for money).

There are three species of price — legal, common, and conventional. The legal price is that which is set by civil law. *Per se,* this must be observed: however, if a merchant would have to sustain a great loss unless he demanded more for his goods, he would be justified in demanding more. Similarly, if a person could not obtain the ordinary goods of life unless he paid more than the "ceiling" price, he could do this in conscience. But to conduct a "black market" business just because of the profits it brings is surely a violation of legal justice.

The common price is that which is set by the common estimate of men. This admits usually of a variation. For example, the common price of eggs in a certain locality might vary from 60 to 75 cents a dozen. The general principle is that it is lawful to buy and sell within these limits, when there is no legal price. Hence, if a buyer charged more than the highest common price, he must restore.

There can be at times reasons for going above or below — for example, the fact that cash is paid immediately, or the fact that the buyer is buying really out of charity for the seller, will justify a cutting down of the price below the lowest common price; the fact that the seller is allowing credit until the end of the month will justify a raising of the prices above the maximum. But the fact that the buyer is in great need of a commodity at present does not justify a great increase in price. For example, the fact that the country storekeeper knows that the village painter is hired to begin painting a house tomorrow and can get a paint brush only from his store does not justify him in raising the price of the brush from $2 to $20.

The seller is bound to reveal the substantial hidden defects of his product, if they are not perceived by the buyer, and also to tell any accidental defects he is asked about. Thus, to sell an auto with a defective engine (at least when the car is supposed to be in good condition) is a violation of justice, if the buyer is unaware of it. In certain sales, such as auction sales and horse-trading, it is understood that the seller will reveal nothing, and the buyer must judge for himself, according to the adage *Caveat emptor* ("Let the buyer beware"). But even then positive deception on the part of the seller is wrong.

The buyer is bound to give a fair price, even though the seller is ignorant of the true value of the object. For example, if a man familiar with books offered $5 to an ignorant countryman for a first edition of Shakespeare which the latter found in his garrett, he would be guilty of injustice, and the contract would be null and void because of a substantial error. But in buying at auction sales or secondhand bookshops or pawn shops or antique shops, the buyer need not reveal the true value of the object which he can get at a very low price.

Salesmen may praise their wares and it is expected that in advertising, etc., there is some exaggeration. But downright falsehoods, such as we find in many ads today, are utterly unjust. For example, to claim for a patent medicine (which is only water and a few herbs) that it will cure all diseases, so that simple people buy it in great numbers, is undoubtedly a grave sin of injustice. The radio ads of the present day are sometimes as deceptive as such crude methods.

4. *Hiring and Renting*

A person may rent to another an article, such as a house or car, and this contract obliges him to deliver the article in usable condition. The one who hires the object must care for it properly and return it at the time agreed on. If the article is lost or injured without any fault of the latter, he has no obligation in conscience to replace or repair it, unless this was stipulated in the contract. This last is usually done nowadays, at least to include damage or destruction done by human agents whom the one who hires can and should supervise. Thus, if a man rents a house and his friends come for a party, and even without any fault on his part, damage the apartment, he can be held to repayment.

This form of contract also constitutes the relation of employer and employee. A man can hire out to another the abilities whereby God wills that he earn the necessities of life for himself and those depending on him. This is the basis of the obligation of an employer to pay a living wage — the fact that he is getting the advantage of that work whereby the employee could provide for his own needs and those of his wife and children. This argument shows that a living wage should be a living *family* wage, since every man has a right to have and to support a family; and this is a basic human right. However, some theologians still doubt if an employer is bound in commutative justice to pay a *family* wage. At any rate, such a wage is obligatory at least in social justice, and sometimes also in charity.

There are reasons which will justify an employer in paying less — if the worker is not competent, or is a youth, or if he cannot pay such a wage but the worker freely contracted for less.

At times, the workingman is justified in going on a strike. A strike is a form of economic warfare, and the same principles that are used to justify a war are used in this connection. All other means must first be used to settle the matter peacefully, and there must be good reason to believe that the evils resulting from the strike will not be so great as to outweigh the good that is hoped for. For example, if the public will suffer widely from an attempt of workers to get a slight raise in wages, there is no justification for the strike. It must be remembered that a strike in which the public is the chief victim is as unjust as a war against the civilians of a nation.

Only just means may be used. It would seem that the strongest measure of a physical nature that might be taken would be to prevent the "scabs" from entering the shop — e.g., forming a group outside the door — but it would be wrong to inflict physical injury on strikebreakers except in self-defense, or to damage property. The sit-down strike cannot be justified apart from very exceptional circumstances. Again, the slowdown strike cannot be justified if the workers are receiving pay for full-time work.

The same general principles can be applied to the lockout on the part of the employers. It is hard to see how a strike on the part of such government employees as the police force (and to a somewhat lesser measure the sanitary division and schoolteachers) can be justified, apart from the most extreme cases of injustice.

It is the wish of the Pope that Catholic workers should have organizations in which they will learn and exemplify the principles of the Church on labor. In fact, the ideal condition would be Catholic labor unions. In our country, this seems impossible; but Catholic men who go into labor unions should try to animate them with correct principles.

5. Loans and Interest

If an article that is borrowed perishes without any fault on the part of the one who borrowed it, the borrower has no obligation in conscience to repay unless such an obligation is included in the contract. However, ordinarily this is included in the contract, especially if the article is of any great value; and the lender could ordinarily get recompense by taking the matter to court, even if there was no recompense agreed on (e.g., the high hat borrowed by A from B to attend a party, which is ruined by a bottle thrown by one of the guests).

Much controversy has been centered about the matter of interest-taking, and the Church has been charged with changing its doctrine in this matter. The truth is this: when a person lends money, he has no right to any more than the original sum, if we consider only the money in itself. For money is a mere medium of exchange, and if he demands more than he lent, there is an inequality established. He gets more than he himself originally possessed, and there is no intrinsic reason for this.

However, there can be — and today there generally are — extrinsic titles for interest. Such are the temporary loss of the chance on the part of the lender to use his money, or the danger that it may not be returned. On this account, a person is not blamed by the Church nowadays if he demands interest within the limit of civil law. Indeed, as far back as the Lateran Council (A.D. 1215) the Church approved of "Mounts of Piety" which were banks for lending people money, and in return they paid a sum over and above the loan for the support of these places of business.

6. Aleatory Contracts

An aleatory contract is one in which an uncertain good is sought or an uncertain evil is avoided for a determined price. The latter type, in which an uncertain evil is avoided, is found in the contract of insurance.

It is evident that certain practices in the matter of insurance render the contract null and void and oblige to restitution. For example, if a person burns down a building to get the insurance, he must restore what he has gained; or if one insures a man who is actually dead, the contract is invalid. The difficult problems concern the matter of deception regarding age, previous condition of health, etc., in the taking out of a life insurance policy. It would seem that a slight falsification does not invalidate the contract — for example, if a man stated that he was 40 years old when in reality he was 42. Furthermore, if the concealed fact did not actually contribute to a person's death, the insurance could be accepted. For example, if a man concealed the fact that he had had several heart attacks and got an insurance policy, his relatives could accept the money if his death was caused by an auto accident. But, even in this case, the relatives would have to pay the difference between what he paid in policies and what he would have had to pay if the truth had been told.

If the insurance company's doctor examines a person and finds no trace of disease, the person need have no scruples in taking the policy, even though he himself believes that he has some hidden malady. In that case, the company is supposed to take the word of the doctor, and the other need make no statement.

Gambling is also an aleatory contract, in which the uncertainty is on both sides. Gambling is not in itself sinful, though it may lead to many sins, such as injustice, hatred, excessive love of gain, drunkenness, etc. Civil laws forbidding organized gambling are binding in conscience.

That a game of chance be lawful, it is required: (1) that each stake something that belongs to himself. (2) That each play willingly. (3) That a reasonable proportion be observed between what is bet and what may be gained and that each have a fair chance to win. (4) That the rules of honesty be observed in the play. Thus, it would render the game null and void if one had cards concealed, if false dice were used, or if a slot machine were "doctored." On the other hand, it is not forbidden to look at an opponent's hand if he carelessly exposes it or to observe any marks that may be by chance on the back of the cards.

If a person gambles with money belonging to another, *per se* he may keep the gains, because they constitute industrial fruits. But if he has nothing to restore in case he loses, and no hope of getting any means of restoring, the game is null and void from the beginning (and the winnings must be restored to the other player), because he actually bet nothing that his opponent could lawfully win.

A person cannot gamble justly if he is *sure* of the results. For example, if a man privately knows that one of the horses in the race is sick and cannot finish, he may not bet against this horse with a person who knows nothing of the animal's ailment.

7. Some Items Relative to Legal and Distributive Justice

A superior is obliged in distributive justice to choose the most suitable persons for office. This may bind under pain of mortal sin, when the common good is gravely at stake. The sin of violating this obligation is called acceptance of persons.

The obligation of giving military service when lawfully called is one in legal justice, and a person who unjustly gets out of this obligation (e.g., by bribing the doctor) is guilty of a grave sin. On the other hand, universal conscription in peacetime is to be regarded, generally speaking, as an evil, against which the popes have spoken. Of course, even in peacetime, when a hostile nation is threatening, a nation may maintain a strong military force by universal conscription.

A judge is obliged to render a just sentence, and is strictly forbidden to take bribes. If he takes a bribe for rendering a just sentence, he is obliged to restore it, for he has taken a double price for his service, since his salary already obliges him to give a just decision. If he takes it to render an unjust decision, he must make recompense to the persons wronged, if the person who won the suit will not do this.

A person accused of crime in a criminal suit must be considered innocent until he is proved guilty. Moral certainty of guilt is sufficient, and this at times can be obtained from circumstantial evidence. A judge may not convict a man whom he privately knows to be guilty, unless the evidence points to this. If the evidence points to guilt, but the judge knows the man to be innocent, he should try to arrange matters, so that his innocence may be manifested — e.g., by calling the witnesses again, by trying to get another trial, etc. If this does not succeed, it is disputed whether or not the judge may pronounce sentence of guilt. Some say that he may do this if only a fine or a slight jail term is involved, but not in the case of a death sentence or a long term in jail.

FOOTNOTES

1. Can. 1089.
2. Can. 1087.
3. Can. 1129.
4. Can. 1513, § 2.
5. Can. 569, 583, 1301.

CHAPTER VII . . . *RELIGION*

1. *Religion in General*

Religion can be understood either objectively or subjectively. Objectively, religion is the system of truths and duties by which man is *bound* (*re-ligare*) to God. In this sense we speak of the Mosaic religion, the Catholic religion. Subjectively, religion is the virtue whereby man believes the truths and fulfills the obligations by which he is bound to God, and thus gives God worship or cult. Religion is a moral, not a theological, virtue, because its immediate object is not God, but the *cult* due to God.

Cult, which is the object of religion, can be given to God or even to creatures in as far as they show forth the perfections of God. In the Catholic religion we distinguish a threefold cult — *dulia,* which is given to the saints; *hyperdulia,* which is given to the Blessed Virgin; and *latria,* which is given to God. Each of these can be either *absolute* or *relative.* Absolute is that which is given to the person in question; relative is that which is given to an object connected with that person. For example, we give absolute cult of dulia to St. John Vianney, relative dulia to the cassock which he wore; absolute hyperdulia to the Blessed Virgin, relative hyperdulia to a statue of our Lady; absolute latria to our Lord in the Blessed Sacrament, relative latria to a relic of the true cross. It should be emphasized that in giving relative cult to a material object, we intend primarily to give absolute cult to the person with whom the object is connected. The Catholic Church does not worship or venerate pictures or statues in the sense ascribed to it by the enemies of the Church. The cult of such material objects is analogous to that which patriotic Americans give to the books or the clothing used by George Washington.

2. *Prayer*

Prayer is one of the chief acts of religion. Prayer, in a broad sense, is any movement of the soul toward God, e.g., an act of faith. In a stricter sense, it is an act proceeding from the virtue of religion and directed to any or several of four ends — adoration, thanksgiving, propitiation, petition. But in the strictest sense, prayer is an act of petition. It is this type to which our Lord has affixed the promise of infallible efficacy.[1] This promise refers only to prayer for oneself; moreover, it is to be understood of prayer with the proper dispositions (humility, perseverance, etc.) and directed to an object that will be advantageous to our eternal salvation. For adults prayer is necessary as a means to salvation in the sense that ordinarily only those who pray will obtain the graces they need for the attainment of eternal life.

We can pray to God directly or to our Lady or the saints asking that they present our prayers to God. It is a disputed point whether the souls in purgatory can pray for us or for themselves. St. Thomas denies that they can pray.[2] The Church never prays *to* the suffering souls in her liturgy, though we are not forbidden to do this privately. Of course, we can pray *for* the souls in purgatory, as the Church does in public acts of cult.

To pray in such wise that a law of the Church commanding prayer is fulfilled (e.g., the recitation of the Divine Office, assistance at Mass) one must have the intention of praying, and also at least *external* attention. This is present if one merely avoids actions which by their nature are incompatible with internal attention. Whether one must also have some *internal* attention (for the fulfillment of the ecclesiastical precept) is a disputed point, but the negative is sufficiently probable to be accepted. Needless to say, one who would limit himself to external attention in the act of prayer and would voluntarily admit distractions would be guilty of sin; but ordinarily it would be a venial, not a mortal, sin.

3. Sanctification of Feasts

In the Old Law, by God's decree, there were certain feast days for the special exercise of religion, such as the Sabbath, the Pasch, etc. In the New Law every Sunday is a feast. Some have held that the selection of Sunday is by divine law, at least in the sense that God commands one day in seven to be sanctified; but the better opinion is that this law is entirely ecclesiastical. The divine law merely commands that *some* time be given to God's worship, but leaves further determination to the Church. At any rate, the holydays of obligation are of merely ecclesiastical origin. By general law, there are ten holydays: Christmas, the Circumcision, the Ascension, the

Immaculate Conception, the Assumption, All Saints, Corpus Christi, the Epiphany, St. Joseph, SS. Peter and Paul.[3] In the United States we are dispensed from the observance of the last four.

There are two obligations imposed by the Church for the proper sanctification of Sundays and holydays — abstention from servile work and attendance at Mass. It is not easy to define exactly what is servile work, though, generally speaking, it is that which is done with the hands, and with a certain amount of hard labor, such as farm work, carpentry, tailoring, and sewing, etc. It is to be noted that even when one wishes to perform such labor as a means of recreation, it does not justify the performance. On the other hand, *liberal* works (e.g., writing, embroidery work, painting a picture, typing, photography) and mixed works (driving a car, athletic sports, hunting, fishing with a rod and line) are allowed. If a person devoted about two and one half hours or more to servile work (three hours if it is light, such as tending a garden) without a sufficient reason, he would be guilty of mortal sin. Even if one is paid for liberal and mixed works, he is allowed to perform them.

The law of the Church also forbids on Sundays and holydays of obligation forensic works (conducting court), public markets, and bazaars, buying and selling in a public fashion.[4]

Causes which excuse one from this obligation are custom (e.g., ice-cream and soda stands in the United States), a reason of piety (e.g., ringing church bells, laying out and putting away vestments), public necessity (e.g., shoveling snow), one's own or a neighbor's necessity (e.g., cooking, taking in hay to protect it from a storm, work that will enable a poor man to get considerable extra pay on Sunday). But work that can be put off should not be done on Sunday or a holyday (e.g., washing windows, fixing the car, etc.). Generally speaking there is a tendency nowadays to forget this law of the Church among Catholics, and a return to better observance is desirable.

A pastor can dispense individuals or individual families of his parish (and even visitors when they are actually in the parish) from this law, and a bishop has the same power in his diocese.[5] The superior of an exempt clerical religious order has the same power in respect to those under his jurisdiction, as also the rector of a seminary with respect to all who live in the seminary.[6] But other religious superiors have no such ordinary power of dispensing.

The other obligation for Sundays and holydays is the duty of attending Mass. To fulfill this obligation, the following must be observed:

1. One must hear the whole Mass, so that the culpable omission of even a small portion is at least a venial sin. One satisfies substantially if he is present from the beginning of the Offertory to the end — also, from the beginning of the Epistle through the priest's Communion. To miss a small portion within the Mass (by going out and returning) is also venial matter. For example, if one missed only the Offertory, or a small part of the Canon, he would satisfy substantially. To miss the Consecration alone, however, would seem grave, and some would say the same of the priest's Communion.

A person substantially satisfies his obligation by hearing portions of two (or more) Masses *successively* which make up the whole, provided the Consecration and priest's Communion are heard in one and the same Mass.

2. A person must be present corporally. It is not sufficient to hear Mass over the radio or television or to be so far off that it can be followed only with a telescope. It suffices to be able to follow the Holy Sacrifice by sight (normal) or hearing, or even to be joined to an overflow crowd outside the church, as long as one is not too far away from these who make up the crowd. One can assist from the sacristy, and it would seem from a window in an adjoining house, if he can see the priest.

3. One must have the intention of hearing Mass, and at least external attention. Hence, a person who is entirely distracted, but in his outward demeanor acts with some attention to the sacred function, satisfies the Church's law. Those who serve or sing, the ushers (if they at least keep some attention on the Mass), one who recites the rosary or reads a spiritual book, a cleric saying the Office — all these satisfy. On the contrary, one who is fast asleep for all or most of the Mass, one who talks continually, or one who is present merely to hear the music, does not fulfill his obligation.

4. One must hear Mass celebrated in the Catholic rite, and either in a church, a public or semipublic oratory, a private chapel *in a cemetery* or that of a bishop or cardinal, or in the open air.[7] If this be taken literally, one could not satisfy his obligation at a Mass celebrated by a priest in a hall or a dwelling house, even though the priest had the privilege of a portable altar. However, some theologians interpret this law of the Church in the sense that one can satisfy his obligations anywhere save in a strictly private domestic chapel. In

such a chapel only those can satisfy to whom permission is granted in the indult. A bishop can grant a priest permission to celebrate Mass in an extraordinary case outside of a church or oratory, but in a decent place (e.g., in a school hall), and in that event he can also permit the faithful to satisfy their obligation in that place.[8]

It must be noted that there is a difference between hearing Mass and satisfying one's Sunday or holyday obligation. A person certainly hears Mass when it is celebrated in a private chapel, but — apart from those included in the indult, and the priest and the server — he does not satisfy his obligation, on a Sunday or feast day.

Causes excusing one from hearing Mass are physical weakness or sickness (e.g., the woman who is pregnant and liable to get sick), necessity of taking care of the sick or infants, when no one else can be procured, distance (more than three miles each way if one must walk — more than thirty miles, if one can easily get a car and the roads are good), even the fact that one has no decent clothing and there is no early Mass which one could attend without embarrassment. A pastor or bishop has the same power of dispensing, as in the law regarding servile work.

A man of limited means who could earn a good sum for working on Sunday and thus missing Mass, could do this, at least occasionally, but not always. Again, a man who could get a well-earned vacation or relaxation only in circumstances such that he misses Mass on one or another day of obligation in the course of the year, would be justified in doing this.

4. Vows

A vow is a deliberate and free promise made to God out of the virtue of religion, obliging one at least under pain of venial sin. To make a vow validly a person must have the intention of making it, must understand substantially what he is promising and what is the nature of a vow, and must be free to do so. A vow made under the influence of unjust and grave fear is invalid by Church law.[9] However, fear coming from some intrinsic cause, such as the fear of hell arising from one's belief in this doctrine, does not invalidate a vow.

The matter of a vow must be something possible, good, and better than the opposite. Thus, a person could not vow to avoid even semi-deliberate venial sins, because that is impossible apart from a special privilege of divine grace. A person could not per se vow to get married, since to marry is not per se better than the opposite, but he could make such a vow in particular circumstances, when it would be better to marry — for example, to legitimate a child.

To vow to commit a sin is a sin; it is a mortal sin to make such a vow when what is vowed is a mortal sin, and very probably a mortal sin even though the thing that is vowed is only a venial sin. On the other hand, to vow something that is good, though not better than the opposite, is a venial sin.

A vow is public if it is accepted by the legitimate superiors of the Church in the name of the Church; otherwise it is private. A public vow is solemn or simple, according as the Church has determined for different religious institutes. By ecclesiastical law there are different effects for these. Thus, a simple vow of chastity renders marriage prohibited, but not invalid; a solemn vow is an invalidating impediment. A simple vow of poverty excludes only the disposition of property; a solemn vow excludes also the ownership.

The deliberate breaking of a vow is a sin against religion. It is a grave sin if the violation is considered grave matter, venial if the matter concerned was light. In the case of a private vow (not therefore the vows in a religious institute) a person can bind himself even to grave matter under light obligation.

If a person doubts whether or not he made a vow to perform an action, he may consider himself free from any obligation by vow to perform the act. A personal vow (e.g., to make a pilgrimage, to say a rosary every day) binds only the person himself; but a real vow (e.g., to give a sum of money to the Church) passes on to one's heirs.[10]

The obligation of a vow can cease, in the first place, intrinsically by a substantial change of circumstances, e.g., if a man who had made a vow to give $10 to the Church every month became very poor, or if the reason for the vow passes away (e.g., if a girl made a vow to recite the rosary every day for the health of her father, the vow no longer holds if he dies).

The vow can also cease through an extrinsic cause. This can take place by annulment (*irritatio*). A direct annulment can be given by one who possesses dominative power over the will of the one who made the vow, such as a father over the vows of his children before the age of puberty or a religious superior (including local superiors and superioresses even of nonexempt communities) over the vows of subjects made after they came under this dominative power by religious profession. Of course, in the case of religious superiors, this power does not extend to the very vows of religion or to the vow to enter a stricter order. When a vow is annulled directly, it ceases permanently. The basis of this direct annulment is the fact that one under another's dominative authority is not supposed to make a vow except with the condition that the one with this authority accedes to it, since dominative authority extends over the will of the subject.

An indirect annulment is given by one who has authority over the *matter* of the vow, even though he may not have authority over the *will* of the person. Thus, a husband can indirectly annul the vow of chastity made by his wife, to the extent of demanding his conjugal rights. A farmer could annul in this way a vow to fast made by one of his farm hands, when he realizes that the man cannot properly do his work. Similarly, religious superiors can indirectly annul the vows of the religious and those of novices prejudicial to the life of the community. By the law of the Church vows made before religious profession are suspended as long as the individual who made them remains in religion.[11] An indirect annulment by its nature is only temporary, and when the exercise of authority ceases, the vow revives.

A dispensation from a vow can be given by the Church for a good reason. The Pope can dispense from any vows (though ordinarily not those in favor of a third person giving him a real right); bishops can dispense their subjects and also visitors in their dioceses from all but the reserved vows (with the same exception as for the Pope). Religious superiors in exempt clerical orders have this authority toward those subject to them. A pastor as such cannot dispense from a vow, though in many dioceses all priests have this power by delegation from the bishop. But this does not extend to the two reserved vows — that is, the vow to observe perfect and perpetual chastity, made after the eighteenth birthday, and the vow to enter a religious order with solemn vows, made after the same date, which can be dispensed only by the Holy See.[12]

One who can dispense from a vow can commute the matter into something else. Indeed, apart from the reserved vows, a person can commute his own vows into something equal or more perfect.[13] It is to be noted that a reason is required to dispense from a vow, even when the Pope does so; but the reason need not be so great as to be an excusing cause. In a doubt whether or not there was a sufficient reason for the dispensation from a vow, the dispensation is to be regarded as valid.

5. *Oaths*

An oath is the calling on God to witness the truth of a statement. To make an oath validly, a person must have the intention of doing so, and use some manner of formula — e.g., "So help me God," the kissing of the Bible, etc. The statement: "God knows I am speaking the truth," is not a sufficient formula.

An oath is *assertive* if it is intended to confirm the truthfulness of a statement regarding the past or the present — e.g., an oath taken by a witness at a trial. An oath is *promissory* if it is intended to confirm the truthfulness of a promise to do something in the future. It should be noted that such an oath does not directly regard the fulfillment of the deed that is promised, but the sincerity of the promise *at present*.

Three conditions are required for the lawfulness of an oath — truthfulness, prudence, and justice. The first means that the person sincerely believes in the truth of what he is asserting or is sincere in his intention of doing what is promised. If this condition is lacking, a person is guilty of a grave sin of perjury, even though the falsehood is of little consequence. Prudence means that there is sufficient reason for taking an oath. One who would take an oath regarding a matter of little or no consequence would sin by irreverence; but it would be a venial sin only, if he is speaking the truth. The third quality means that a person has a right to say what he is declaring under oath. For example, it would be a sin to confirm detraction by an oath. But, again, the lack of this quality (presuming the statement to be true) is usually only a venial sin against religion, even though the detraction itself is gravely wrong as an act of injustice.

A person may confirm a mental restriction by an oath, when there is sufficient reason for doing so; but a graver reason is required than when one makes such a statement without an oath. Even in a trial, one could do this if the judge exceeded his authority in asking a question — for example, regarding the seal of the confessional.

A person who fails to fulfill a promissory oath sins, either gravely or lightly, in accordance with the gravity of the matter involved. The violation of such an oath is not perjury (which regards only the *truthfulness* of the statement when the oath was made) but is a sin against religion. An oath to do something sinful is invalid, and it is sinful to make such an oath. If the thing promised is gravely sinful, it is a mortal sin to take the oath; if it is venially sinful, it is disputed by theologians whether the oath is a mortal or a venial sin.

The obligation of an oath ceases in the same ways as that of a vow — either intrinsically (by a substantial change of circumstances), or extrinsically by annulment, dispensation, or commutation. The same persons who can annul or dispense from a vow have the same power regarding a promissory oath; but if the dispensation would tend to the prejudice of others who refuse to remit the obligation, only the Holy See can dispense from the oath on account of the necessity or utility of the Church.[14]

6. Superstition

Superstition literally signifies a sin of excess. With respect to religion it means the sin whereby a person gives cult to the true God, but in a manner that is excessive, or gives to another the cult that is due only to God.

A person could sin mortally in giving cult even to the true God — for example, if the excess lay in the fact that the cult was based on a serious falsehood. Thus, one who would worship God with the ceremonies of the Old Law, which imply that the Redeemer has not yet come, would sin mortally. On the other hand, one would sin venially by giving God cult which is excessive only in its manner — for example, if a priest would add genuflections and bows in the sacred rites over and above those prescribed by the Church.

Superstition of the other type — cult due to God alone but given to another — can be either idolatry, divination, or vain observance. Idolatry is the worship of an image of a false god, and it is a most grave sin. Under this would come also worship of the sun or an animal, etc.

Divination is the undue quest for knowledge of secret things by the aid of the devil. If it involves an express petition to the devil, it is, of course, a most wicked insult to God. But, it may be tacit; and actually this takes place when a person tries to "read" the cards or tea leaves or a crystal ball. He is implicitly calling on the devil, for these things of themselves cannot furnish the information; God or good spirits will not use these means of communicating knowledge, and so the only source remaining is the evil spirits. Hence, divination is a mortal sin *from its whole nature,* admitting no lightness of matter. However, it frequently happens that those who practice it are excused from grave sin through ignorance or thoughtlessness, or because they engage in it merely in jest. But often, even in such circumstances, there is danger that scandal will be given and that the participants will be led to more serious occult practices.

The ouija board is a form of divination. Spiritism particularly is a grave form of this sin, and for this reason the Church explicitly forbids Catholics to take any part in spiritistic seances, even merely passive assistance. Much of the spiritism practiced today is fraud; but since the danger of diabolical intervention is always present, it is a serious sin of superstition.

Astrology, as it exists with us, is also largely chicanery. But if one strives to obtain from the stars knowledge of the future, in as far as this is dependent on men's free acts, this too is superstition. At most one could hold that the heavenly bodies exert an influence on the sensitive factors of human nature, and thus indirectly and fallibly influence men's conduct. Such a doctrine has little to support it scientifically, but it would be free from the sin of superstition.

To believe that one can obtain knowledge of occult things through dreams is usually a sin of superstition. God at times makes use of dreams to communicate knowledge,[15] but in this event He also gives the recipient assurance that it is He who has spoken. To go to a fortuneteller on one occasion as a joke, without ascribing to her any occult powers, might be only a venial sin; but it would be dangerous, and those who do this habitually are guilty of mortal sin.

The sin of vain observance consists in the attempt to obtain through the use of some creature an effect which is above its nature — e.g., a rabbit's foot or a lucky coin to secure protection from harm. This too is an implicit seeking of help from the devil, in as far as any special power which the creature may possess cannot come from God or a good spirit, and hence must have its source in the devil. But, as in the case of divination, often those who perform acts of vain observance give no heed to any diabolical intervention and are in good faith — hence, can be excused from mortal sin. Hence, it is better to treat such customs as knocking on wood or avoiding thirteen at table as foolish rather than sinful.

If it is doubtful whether or not a certain object is able to produce the desired effects naturally, it is permissible to use it, especially if the user protests that he has no intention of calling on the devil. Thus the use of the divining rod for finding water or metal is allowed.

Even sacred objects, such as medals or pictures, would be used wrongly if a person believed that these things *in themselves* possess special power, or if he regarded them as *infallible* means of obtaining some temporal effect. Catholics should be on their guard against using sacred things as if they were charms or "lucky pieces."

7. Sacrilege

Sacrilege is the abusive treatment of a sacred person, place, or thing. It is a mortal sin *from its nature,* not from its *whole nature,* and hence can be a venial sin — namely, when the matter involved is slight, such as the careless use of a blessed medal. There are three species of sacrilege — personal, local, and real.

A *personal* sacrilege is committed when a sacred person is involved. For example, when one physically mistreats a sacred person (a cleric or a religious, even a novice) it is a sacrilege, punished by censure if it is grave. It is also a personal sacrilege to bring a cleric to court or to force him into military service. A personal sacrilege is also committed when a sacred person (professed religious or cleric in major orders) either commits or is the object of a sin of impurity, even merely internal. It is disputed whether it is a sacrilege to make as the object of such a sin a person with a private vow of chastity, but one who has made such a vow sins against religion if he violates it.

A *local* sacrilege is committed when something is done in a sacred place that is degrading to its sacred character. A sacred place is a church, public or semipublic oratory, or a consecrated cemetery. For example, an external sin of impurity committed in such a place is a sin of local sacrilege. Certain actions committed in a church or a cemetery bring about the violation of the sacred place, so that it needs reconciliation before it may again be used for sacred purposes. These acts are: homicide, the unjust and grave shedding of blood, impious or sordid uses (e.g., if a church is used as a stable), and the burial therein of an infidel or of one excommunicated by declaratory or condemnatory sentence.[16] These acts must be notorious and certain in order that canonical violation be incurred. It is disputed whether or not a theft is a sacrilege from the fact that it is committed in a church.

A *real* sacrilege is the abusive treatment of a sacred thing. Such, particularly, is the unworthy reception of a sacrament. It is also committed by irreverence toward the sacramentals, Sacred Scripture, chalices, relics, etc. It is to be noted that a blessed object loses its blessing when it is substantially modified — e.g., if a blessed candle is burned, the remaining wax is not blessed; if a chalice is melted, the metal is not consecrated. Similarly, a vestment loses its blessing if it is cut up. But even in that event, it should not be used for a sordid purpose (e.g., as a dust rag), though it can be used for a profane purpose (e.g., as a drapery).[17]

The most grievous of unworthy receptions of the sacraments is the unworthy reception of Holy Communion. However, it must not be thought or said that this is the greatest of all possible sins. A sin of blasphemy is more grievous *per se*. Furthermore, there is a great difference in gravity between an unworthy reception of Holy Communion through fear or loss of reputation and one motivated by malice, though both are mortal sins.

8. *Simony*

Simony[18] consists in buying spiritual things for a temporal price. There are two types — simony of divine law and simony of ecclesiastical law. Simony of divine law, or simony in the strict sense, is that which has been defined, an exchange of something of a spiritual nature (such as a sacrament, an ecclesiastical office, an indulgence) for some temporal benefit, such as money or a car or a house. Simony of ecclesiastical law is committed when something is done that is forbidden only by the Church — not by divine law — because it involves a danger of irreverence toward spiritual things, or is likely to lead to simony of divine law (e.g., if a priest demanded a higher stipend than that stipulated by ecclesiastical authority for certain functions).

It is not simony to accept money *on the occasion* of some spiritual service because of an extrinsic title, such as the support of the priest, or some extrinsic service connected with the spiritual function. Thus, if a priest would say Mass for a sum of money, intending to make the spiritual fruits of the Holy Sacrifice the *object of a contract,* he would be guilty of simony of divine law. However, he may accept a stipend *as an offering for his support on the occasion of the Mass.* But if he would demand more than the stipend stipulated by ecclesiastical authority, he would sin, though probably not by ecclesiastical simony.[19] If, however, some special circumstance gave him another extrinsic title — e.g., if he said Mass at a very late hour — he could ask some remuneration for this.

Simony of divine law is a mortal sin *from its entire nature* — in other words, however small the amount involved, it is a mortal sin, when something spiritual is actually sold for something temporal. Simony of ecclesiastical law is a mortal sin *from its nature* — in other words, it is only a venial sin when small matter is involved.

By ecclesiastical law any benefice, office, or dignity obtained through simony is null and void.[20] However, Church law decrees that if a man were elected Pope through simony, the election, though gravely sinful, would be valid, lest the validity of a pope's authority be challenged.[21]

Indulgences attached to rosaries or other objects are lost if the objects are substantially changed, as by being broken up, or if they are sold.[22] However, it would not be *sinful* to sell a blessed object, provided the price is asked only for the object itself, not for the blessing. For example, if a priest sold a brother priest a chalice he could charge a just price for the chalice itself, but not for the consecration which is on it (and which remains after the sale). A blessed or consecrated object loses its blessing or consecration when it is exposed to *public* sale.[23]

FOOTNOTES

1. Jn. 16:24.
2. *Summa*, II–II, q. 83, a. 11, ad 3.
3. Can. 1247.
4. Can. 1248.
5. Can. 1245.
6. Can. 1368.
7. Can. 1249.
8. Can. 822. The Holy See has now decreed that this permission is granted to the congregation whenever a priest celebrates Mass outside a regular place by virtue of this Canon (*Acta Apostolicae Sedis*, 1952, p. 497).
9. Can. 1307, #3.
10. Can. 1310, #2.
11. Can. 1315.
12. Can. 1309.
13. Can. 1314.
14. Can. 1320.
15. Mt. 1:20; 2:19.
16. Can. 1172.
17. Can. 1510.
18. From Simon Magus, who offered money for the power to give the Holy Ghost (Acts 8:18).
19. Can. 831, #1.
20. Can. 729.
21. *Doc. I in Codice*, n. 79.
22. Can. 924.
23. Can. 1305.

CHAPTER VIII

OTHER POTENTIAL PARTS OF JUSTICE

1. *Piety*

Piety is the virtue whereby we give honor and service to those to whom we owe our being — our parents and, more remotely, our country. In this second sense piety would correspond to our idea of patriotism.

Children are bound to give their parents love, honor, obedience, and assistance. For example, ordinarily a son or daughter would sin grievously by striking a parent, even though only lightly. (We say *ordinarily* because there could be an exception in the case of a drunken parent, or one who is out of his mind and is misbehaving.) The obedience due to parents, strictly speaking, ends with the attainment of majority (twenty-one years) or emancipation (e.g., by marriage), but even then, if a son or daughter lives at home, obedience must be given in matters relating to domestic order (e.g., they must be in the house at a reasonable time, they may not have rowdy friends visiting them). But such older children are not bound to the same detailed obedience as younger children — e.g., they could not be kept at home regularly every night, they would not have to render an account of all their correspondence and social doings.

Children, even minors, are not obliged to obey their parents as regards a state of life. Hence, a girl has the right to choose the religious life even against the will of her parents. Often, however, it is not prudent for her to execute her plan until she comes of age. Similarly, there is no obligation to follow the directions of their parents regarding marriage itself, or marriage with a particular person, though young folks should ordinarily consult their parents on these matters. The Church decrees that a pastor shall not assist at the marriage of minors, when the parents do not know about it or are reasonably unwilling, until he has first consulted the bishop.[1]

Children, even after majority, are bound to assist their parents in grave or extreme necessity. Indeed, a child would not be allowed to enter religion if his parents were in grave necessity and could not otherwise be helped; and one already professed as a religious would be obliged to leave the convent or monastery to help parents in extreme necessity, if that is the only way in which their necessity can be relieved.

2. *Duties of Parents*

Parents are bound to show their children special love. It is wrong if they favor certain of their children more than the others without reasonable cause. Second, they must provide them with proper bringing up (*educatio*), bodily, mental, and spiritual. The spiritual care begins with the obligation to have the child baptized as soon as possible after birth.[2] It is difficult to interpret "as soon as possible" as more than three weeks, though some theologians stretch it to a month. When the child grows older the parents are bound to provide it with a truly religious (Catholic) education, and the Church forbids Catholic children to be sent to non-Catholic or nonreligious schools or colleges unless the bishop judges this can be tolerated.[3]

Parents must also provide their children with a means of making their way in life. Ordinarily this means that they must give them a start in some profession or trade. But parents should not force a particular type of work on a child. They should not try to force a boy to become a doctor when his heart is set on owning a garage.

3. *Obedience*

Obedience can be taken in a general sense, or as a special virtue. In a general sense obedience is found in the observance of every precept; but in a special sense it is exercised only when a person observes a command precisely because the superior possesses the authority to command. This latter is also called *formal* obedience.

Similarly we can distinguish between two types of disobedience. In a general sense, a person commits a sin of disobedience whenever he transgresses a law or a precept; actually, he does not sin against the virtue of obedience as such, but rather against the virtue which motivated the command. Thus, one who misses Mass commits a sin against religion; one who eats meat on Friday, a sin against temperance; a religious who fails to rise for the community meditation, a sin against charity (toward himself, and perhaps toward others by scandal).

A sin of formal disobedience is committed when one refuses to fulfill a command precisely because he despises the command as such or the one who gives the command (not merely as an individual but in his position of authority). This sin is mortal from its nature, but admits of light matter in respect to disdain for the command.

Ecclesiastical or religious superiors who have the right to issue a formal command should not do this unless some grave matter is at stake, and they have first attempted all normal means of procuring obedience from the subject or subjects involved.

4. *Veracity*

Veracity is that virtue (potential part of justice) which inclines one to manifest the truth in word and in deed. It can be violated by excess, when one manifests a secret without sufficient reason, or by defect, when one tells a lie.

A secret may be natural, promised, or committed. A natural secret is one which is such by the very nature of things (e.g., the hidden faults of my neighbor). A promised secret is one which must be kept because a person promised to do so after he became aware of the secret. A committed secret is one which arises from a contract, either express or tacit, made before the manifestation of the secret. The most usual form of the committed secret is the professional secret (the doctor, the lawyer, the priest, etc., in reference to those matters coming within their professional scope), since everyone who practices a profession implicitly agrees to observe this manner of secrecy with respect to his clients.

It is *per se* a sin to divulge another's secret against his will, since a man has as much right to his own secrets as he has to his property. The natural and the committed secret bind out of justice, the promised secret out of fidelity (though often this is also a natural secret and in that event binds also in justice). The sin committed by the violation of a secret is either mortal or venial, in accordance with the gravity of the harm that is done. The harm done by the transgression of the professional secret is not limited to the particular case, but includes the general lessening of confidence on the part of the public that can be one of the consequences.

If there is probability that a person regards some secret knowledge as very important, it would be a mortal sin to strive to get at it — e.g., by listening at the keyhole, by piecing together a torn letter. On the other hand, if a person has good reason to believe that his own great good is involved, he may read another's letter. Parents have the right to supervise the mail of their younger children, and even of the older ones, if they think some serious harm may thus be averted. Religious superiors have the rights given by the rule, but they should be mindful of the letters which Canon Law allows religious to send and to receive without any inspection.[4]

A secret may be divulged if the consent of the interested party can be at least reasonably presumed, or if the matter has become public in some other way, or if the common good or the good of some individual requires it — provided that the good is sufficient to outweigh the evil that may come from the manifestation of the secret, particularly the professional secret. (It should be remembered that no reason, however important, will justify the manifestation of confessional knowledge.) An example of lawful manifestation of a professional secret is the case of the doctor who knows that a young man, infected with a social disease, is preparing to marry a girl who knows nothing of his condition. The doctor could warn the girl if the young man will not do so himself.

A lie is a statement contrary to what a person believes to be true. It may be in word, in writing, or in deed. It is forbidden explicitly in Sacred Scripture,[5] and also by the natural law. Some theologians base their argument on the fact that the purpose of speech is to manifest what one believes to be true; and hence it is against the primary purpose of this faculty to tell a lie. Other theologians argue that the primary purpose of the faculty of speech is to promote the welfare of mankind by mutual communication of ideas, so that a lie is wrong because it tends to disrupt the spirit of trust and confidence among human beings. However, they say, when a person is unjustly trying to force me to reveal a truth which I have a right to conceal, I do not sin if I say something to the contrary. In that event I am telling a falsehood, but not a lie. This opinion is truly probable, but those who accept it must be very careful not to abuse it.

Theologians distinguish three types of lies — helpful, jocose, and harmful. The first is that which is intended to render some helpful service to oneself or another, the second is that which is intended as a joke, the third is that which is aimed at causing harm. Generally speaking, the first two are venial sins, the third is mortal or venial sin in accordance with the measure of harm that is wrought.

To tell a lie is not the same as to conceal the truth. This latter is permitted at times, even by the use of what is known as mental restrictions. By a mental restriction is meant a statement which *can* be understood in a true sense, either from the words actually used or from custom, even though in the present instance it probably will be understood in another sense. One may not use a mental restriction unless there is a good reason for concealing the truth. For example, if one is asked regarding a sick person: "How is he doing?" and should answer: "He is doing very well" or "His health is much improved," signifying that the person has received the sacraments, so that his spiritual condition is much better, he would be making use of a mental restriction, which would be perfectly lawful, when there is good reason for concealing the truth from the questioner. Again, if the servant tells the visitor: "Mrs. Smith is not at home," when Mrs. Smith actually is at home, but does not wish to receive callers, the servant's words are a legitimate mental restriction, because this phrase is commonly understood to include such a case. Even in the case of one who inquires directly of a person: "Were you guilty of such a crime?" the answer can be "No," unless the questioner has the right to know, such as the priest in the sacrament of Penance. For a categorical negative in the case of an accused person, even though he is being charged with a crime in court, is to be understood as meaning: "I have no obligation to confess my guilt to you; therefore, if I am guilty, it is your task to prove it." Under this comes the case of a woman accused by her husband of marital infidelity, when she is really guilty. Even in that case she can say: "No." Those theologians who teach that a falsehood is a justifiable means of defense against an unjust attempt to force information from a person would say that in such instances this theory is applicable. Those who do not admit this theory regard such a denial as a justifiable mental restriction.

FOOTNOTES

1. Can. 1034.
2. Can. 770.
3. Can. 1374.
4. Can. 611.
5. Col. 3:9; Jn. 8:44.

Fortitude, the third of the cardinal virtues, is that virtue which inclines a person to be courageous in dangers (particularly the danger of death) so that he is not thereby deterred from doing good. The sins against this virtue are the two extremes of *timidity* (by defect) and *audacity* (by excess). An example of the former is the excessive fear of death which the materialism of the present day fosters, as if death were the greatest of evils, and which shows itself in the reluctance of so many (even Catholic) families to inform one of the members who is dying of his true condition. An example of the latter is the daredevil spirit of some of our youth today toward reckless driving, which endangers their own lives and the lives of others.

The supreme act of the virtue of fortitude is martyrdom. As theologians understand it, martyrdom is the willing and nonresisting acceptance of death or of physical injuries capable of causing death, which are inflicted out of hatred for Christ or for some Christian virtue. From the objective standpoint, the conditions required for martyrdom are: (1) That the sufferings which one endures be *physical,* affecting the body, not merely mental. (2) That these sufferings cause death, or at least be such as would naturally cause death (in some instances a person affected with sufferings which would naturally cause death was miraculously preserved from death, but did not thereby lose the merit of martyrdom). (3) That those who inflict the sufferings act out of hatred for Christ or for some Christian virtue. For example, when a man attacks a girl with the idea of violating her, his attack is directed against her chastity, so that if he kills her in consequence of her refusal to give in to his demands, he is slaying her through hatred of a Christian virtue, as was the case with St. Maria Goretti.

These conditions suffice for the martyrdom of an infant, but in order that an adult may be truly a martyr, certain subjective conditions are required; namely — (1) That the person have the supernatural intention of accepting death for Christ or for the preservation

of some Christian virtue. (2) That the person make no positive resistance — that is, by fighting back. (On this account, soldiers are
not martyrs if they are killed in battle, even though it is in defense
of the faith.)[1]

Martyrdom derives its efficacy from the fact that it is an imitation
of the Passion of Christ, who did not resist, but accepted death from
a supernatural motive, inflicted by those who hated Him. Consequently, martyrdom is a kind of sacrament, and for that reason can
confer the state of grace on an infant who is in original sin. When
an adult suffers martyrdom, all the temporal punishment due to his
sins is remitted, and he is admitted to heaven immediately after death.

Among the virtues subordinate to fortitude are magnanimity (the
virtue which inclines one to perform great deeds) and magnificence
(which inclines one to make great things externally, such as a great
and beautiful church). Other virtues classified under fortitude are
patience, long-suffering, perseverance, and constancy.

FOOTNOTE

1. However, a girl who resists an attack on her chastity does not thereby lose the merit
of martyrdom, since her resistance is directed to the preservation of her virginity
rather than of her life.

CHAPTER X . . . TEMPERANCE

1. General Notions of Temperance

Temperance, the fourth of the cardinal virtues, is the virtue which moderates man's desires for the pleasures of sense. The principal pleasures of this nature are those connected with food and drink and those connected with the use of the generative or sexual faculties. To the use of the digestive and generative faculties God has attached pleasure so that human beings may be led to use them, and thus provide adequately both for the preservation of themselves as individuals and for the preservation of the human race.

The sins against temperance are insensibility and intemperance. The former is a sin of excess. It would be committed by a person who would abstain from nourishment to such a degree that he would injure his health, or by a married woman who would show herself so opposed to normal marriage relations as to alienate her husband. The sin of intemperance is committed when one fails by defect to observe the proper norm in seeking sensible pleasures.

The species of temperance are abstinence (with reference to food and drink), sobriety (with reference to intoxicating drink), chastity (with reference to the use of the sexual faculties), and modesty (with reference to secondary acts related to sexual matters). The sins by defect against these virtues respectively are gluttony, drunkenness, impurity, and immodesty.

Among the potential parts of temperance are humility, studiousness, and eutrapelia.

2. The Virtue of Abstinence

Abstinence is that virtue which moderates man's use of food and drink. A person would fail against this virtue by excess if he would not take enough nourishment to support his health and strength; he would fail by defect if he took so much as to injure or inconvenience himself. Ordinarily a person is guilty of only a venial sin if he eats too much; but it would be a mortal sin if he rendered himself seriously ill or unable to fulfill his grave obligations.

That fasting is a virtuous act is evident both from the example of

Christ and from the traditional teaching of the Church. It is an effective means of strengthening the will against temptation and of doing penance for past sins. The Church has made laws prescribing certain forms of fasting at certain times. These are classified under two headings, known respectively as fast and abstinence. (It should be noted that in this connection the words "fast" and "abstinence" are taken in a restricted and technical sense, differing from the sense used above).

The essential feature of a fast day of the Church is that only one full meal is allowed. The essential feature of a day of abstinence is that one must abstain from flesh meat. Some days are days of both fast and abstinence, others are days of fast alone, others days of abstinence alone. There can also be days of partial abstinence, on which a person may eat meat only *once*.

The days on which both fast and abstinence are prescribed by the general law of the Church are twenty-eight and one half in number: Ash Wednesday, the Fridays and Saturdays of Lent (Holy Saturday until noon only), the Ember Days, and the vigils of Pentecost, the Assumption, All Saints, and Christmas. Days of fast alone are all other weekdays of Lent; days of abstinence alone are all other Fridays throughout the year.

Outside of Lent, if a Sunday or a holyday of obligation coincides with a day of fast or abstinence or both, the fast or abstinence or both cease. A vigil is not anticipated, as far as fast and abstinence are concerned, even though the Mass and Office are anticipated (e.g., when All Saints falls on a Monday).[1] A bishop has the right to impose days of fast and abstinence on the people of his diocese in particular instances.[2] The obligations of fast and abstinence imposed by religious rules bind under sin or not, as is laid down in the rule.

The single full meal allowed on a day of fast is supposed to be taken either at noon or in the evening; nevertheless, it would seem that it would not be a grave violation of the law to take it any time in the course of the day. At any rate, 11 a.m. is considered to be morally noon, as far as this law is concerned. As far as the law of the Church is concerned, there is no limitation to the quantity of food that may be taken at this meal, but the natural law of temperance would have to be observed. The meal is not supposed to be protracted more than two hours; however, a slight interruption would not break the unity, as in the event that a person had finished his meal, and shortly afterward a box of candy was produced.

The Church fast is not broken by liquids, however copious, as long as they are not too nourishing. For example, water, ginger ale, tea, and coffee (even prepared with milk and sugar), milk, fruit juices, wine, and beer are allowed between meals as well as at meals. On the other hand, soup, cream, etc., are forbidden between meals.

Besides the full meal, a small breakfast and a small supper (or midday lunch) are allowed. The quality and quantity of these are to be determined by custom prevailing in the particular place.³ Custom does not allow flesh meat at these minor refections, even on a day of mere fast. Custom in the United States until recently allowed a morning refection of bread, crackers, etc., to the extent of only about two ounces, without butter, and an evening refection of about eight ounces.

The rule allowing the breakfast and lunch (or supper) to consist of two and eight ounces respectively is called the *absolute norm*. There is another norm for determining the amount that may be taken at these two smaller meals, called the *relative norm*. According to this standard a person may eat a sufficient amount at the breakfast and lunch (or supper) to enable him to perform his daily tasks without too great inconvenience, but in such wise that he eats somewhat less than usual, and these two smaller meals together do not equal the amount of one full meal for this particular individual. Thus, the amount of food a person may take on a fast day is dependent, to some degree, on his particular needs and appetite. For example, a person who would normally eat twenty-four ounces for his principal meal might take six ounces for breakfast and twelve ounces for lunch (or supper) and yet be truly fasting. However, he may eat meat at his full meal only, and may not eat solid food outside his three meals. Many bishops of the United States have accepted this standard of fasting, beginning with Lent, 1952.

If a person, either advertently or inadvertently, has taken two full meals, the fast is broken irreparably, and he no longer is obliged to observe it.

The law of Church abstinence forbids flesh meat. In general, flesh meat is that which comes from warm-blooded animals. On the other hand, the flesh of snails, frogs, or snakes is allowed because they are cold blooded though they live on land. Custom in some places permits the use of what is actually flesh meat — e.g., wild duck in Louisiana. Custom also seems to justify the eating of a warm-blooded animal that lives in the water, such as whale.

Soup made from flesh meat is also forbidden, but the Church law allows condiments, even those made from the fat of animals.[4] Thus, lard and drippings from fat may be eaten or used for cooking on a day of abstinence.

Nowadays, there is no longer a law forbidding the eating of meat and fish at the same meal, when meat is allowed.

3. Subjects of Church Law of Fast and Abstinence

The law of Church abstinence binds all who have completed their seventh year, provided they have also reached the use of reason. It begins to bind on the day after their seventh birthday. A child below this age, even though he has the use of reason, or one over this age if he has not reached the use of reason is free from the law.

The law of Church fast binds all who have completed their twenty-first year (beginning the day after their twenty-first birthday) up to the beginning of their sixtieth year. (Hence the law ceases the day after their fifty-ninth birthday.)

It is a disputed point whether or not non-Catholics (baptized) are bound by the Church laws of fast and abstinence. The better opinion is the affirmative; but, in actual practice, they cannot be bound because of the probable view to the contrary. Hence, a boardinghouse keeper could give meat to the Protestant boarders on Friday. The better course, however, would be to obtain a dispensation from the bishop or the pastor.

4. Excusing Causes

A person who cannot observe the Church laws of fast or abstinence without grave inconvenience is excused from them. From fasting, therefore, are excused laboring men, those in weak health, and women who are pregnant or nursing infants. Those who have a "white-collar job," such as teachers, students, lawyers, stenographers, barbers, etc., which requires a full day of hard work, are ordinarily excused where the absolute norm (two and eight ounces for the smaller meals) prevails, but ordinarily such persons are bound to fast where the relative norm is in use, as in the United States at the present day. Catholics should consult a priest if they are in doubt on this matter.

A greater reason is required to be excused from abstinence than from fasting. However, a man who works at a very laborious job, such as a steel-mill worker, might be excused on this score. Besides physical necessity, moral necessity is to be considered an excusing cause from abstinence. Thus a child of non-Catholic parents who will provide only meat as substantial food on Friday is excused. The question is discussed by theologians whether a Catholic is excused if he is invited to dinner on a day of abstinence and meat is served. Some say that if the host would be gravely offended by a refusal, the guest may eat the meat. But this solution is rarely applicable in the United States, at least on Friday. Non-Catholic hosts should know the laws of the Church on this matter; and if they serve meat on Friday, they should realize that what they have done is offensive to their Catholic guests. Indeed, at times their purpose is to make the situation embarrassing for Catholics, and they consider it a great victory if they get them to eat meat on Friday. It is ordinarily the duty of a good Catholic in such a situation to refuse courteously but firmly to eat the meat.

5. Dispensation

The Pope can dispense from the laws of fast and abstinence throughout the entire Church. Bishops and pastors, in individual cases and for a just cause, can dispense individuals and individual families subject to them, even outside their territory, and within their territory visitors also. Because of a great gathering of people or for the sake of public health, bishops can dispense the whole diocese or a portion of it from the laws of fast and abstinence. In an exempt clerical religious order the superiors have the same power as a pastor in relation to those subject to them.[5] However, the superiors of non-exempt orders and the superiors of nuns have no power to dispense, though at times they may declare that an excusing cause is present. Confessors as such have no power to dispense, though often they receive this power by delegation from the bishop.

The following are to be noted in reference to the United States:

1. Our bishops can dispense from fast and abstinence on civil holidays.

2. Our soldiers and sailors are dispensed from the law of fast and abstinence on all days of the year except the vigil of Christmas, Ash Wednesday, Good Friday, and Holy Saturday up to noon. This dispensation embraces the family of a Catholic soldier or sailor *when he is living with them habitually,* and also civilians living in military reservations, and religious and nurses attached to the military hospitals. (It is to be noted that by the family of a soldier or sailor is meant wife, children, relatives, and servants. Habitual residence is

requisite; when a soldier is home merely on leave of absence or furlough, the family does not enjoy the privilege.) A soldier or sailor, as well as the others to whom this dispensation extends, can use it, not only when in camp or on board ship, but also in a restaurant, etc.

3. Beginning with the Lent of 1952, the bishops of the United States promulgated the following rules regarding fast and abstinence.

Regulations on Fast and Abstinence

To foster the spirit of penance and of reparation for sin, to encourage self-denial and mortification, and to guide her children in the footsteps of Our Divine Savior, Holy Mother Church imposes by law the observance of fast and abstinence.

In accordance with the provisions of Common Law, as modified through the use of special faculties granted by the Holy See, we herewith publish the following regulations:

On Abstinence

Everyone over 7 years of age is bound to observe the law of abstinence.

Complete abstinence is to be observed on Fridays, Ash Wednesday, the Vigils of the Assumption and Christmas, and on Holy Saturday morning. On days of complete abstinence meat and soup or gravy made from meat may not be used at all. Partial abstinence is to be observed on Ember Wednesdays and Saturdays and on the Vigils of Pentecost and All Saints. On days of partial abstinence meat and soup or gravy made from meat may be taken only once a day at the principal meal.

On Fast

Everyone over 21 and under 59 years of age is also bound to observe the law of fast.

The days of fast are the weekdays of Lent, Ember Days, the Vigils of Pentecost, the Assumption, All Saints, and Christmas.

On days of fast only one full meal is allowed. Two other meatless meals, sufficient to maintain strength, may be taken according to each one's needs; but together they should not equal another full meal. Meat may be taken at the principal meal on a day of fast except on Fridays, Ash Wednesday, and the Vigils of the Assumption and Christmas. Eating between meals is not permitted; but liquids, including milk and fruit juices, are allowed.

When health or ability to work would be seriously affected, the law does not oblige. In doubt concerning fast or abstinence, a parish priest or confessor should be consulted.

Those taking advantage of these mitigations should compensate by prayer, the more frequent reception of the sacraments, etc.

6. Violation of Ecclesiastical Law of Fast or Abstinence

Generally speaking, a quantity of four ounces suffices to commit a mortal sin against the law of Church fast where the absolute norm is in use. Where the relative norm is used a greater quantity is required for grave matter — e.g., one fourth of a full meal. For the violation of abstinence two ounces of flesh meat suffices to constitute a mortal sin. The law of abstinence is divisible — in other words, a person would commit several distinct sins on a day of abstinence by eating meat on several occasions. But the law of fast is indivisible — that is, one sin would be committed if a person ate several times on a fast day over and above what is permitted. Small amounts of food taken several times in a day can coalesce to grave matter.

One can sin by co-operation in respect to these laws. For example, a wife who gives her Catholic husband meat on a Friday just because otherwise he will be somewhat cranky is sinning. But for a grave reason — if he would beat her or get into a furious temper, she could give him the meat, on the principle that material co-operation in another's sin is permitted for a sufficiently grave reason.

7. Sobriety and Drunkenness

Drunkenness, a sin against sobriety, is the inordinate and voluntary use of intoxicating liquor for the sake of pleasure. It is complete if the use of reason is taken away; it is incomplete if it does not go to this extent, but nevertheless lessens the control one has on himself. Ordinarily complete drunkenness is a mortal sin, incomplete drunkenness is a venial sin. The malice of drunkenness consists in the fact that, without a sufficient reason, a person in a violent way deprives himself of the use of the noblest of his faculties.

It is difficult to distinguish in practice between complete and incomplete drunkenness. It is not requisite for complete drunkenness that one be rendered utterly stupid and helpless. The essential factor seems to be that one does things that are inordinate which otherwise he would not do — e.g., blasphemy, wild driving, uncontrolled temper, etc. In other words, "he is not himself." A person is guilty of imperfect drunkenness when his speech becomes somewhat thick, when he gets excessively humorous, when he repeats the same jokes over and over again, etc. It should be noted that a person may be guilty of grave scandal even by venially culpable drunkenness.

The basic malice in drunkenness is not that one deprives himself of the use of reason, but that he does so in a violent manner and merely for the sake of pleasure. Consequently, it is not a sin when a person deprives himself of the use of reason by the use of a drug when he has to undergo an operation. Indeed, if no other anesthetic were available, one could render himself insensible by alcoholic liquor to mitigate great physical pain or to undergo an operation.

The use of narcotics, such as opium, etc., is to be judged by the same norms as the use of alcoholic liquor. Such drugs should not be used when a person is dying, except in as far as is necessary to mitigate great pain, because the last hours should be spent in acquiring merit. However, if a person is in great agony, a drug could be given him to relieve him, even though he would die unconscious — provided he has been prepared spiritually for death.

A person who deliberately becomes intoxicated, foreseeing that in that condition he will commit certain sins — e.g., blasphemy, impurity — is guilty *in cause* of those sins. For this prevision certainty is not required. It suffices that one judge with good probability that this will occur. On the other hand, a merely remote probability that one will commit some serious sin will not add another sin to the sin of drunkenness.

8. *Chastity*

Chastity is the virtue which moderates the inclinations of the sex appetite according to right reason. Besides perfect chastity, which consists in the permanent abstention from all deliberate sexual actions, there is what is known as *juvenile* chastity, the abstention until marriage; and also *conjugal* chastity, which means the exclusion in marriage of anything against the law of God, while admitting the due use of conjugal rights.

The vice opposed to chastity is impurity, which is the inordinate use of the sexual functions either outside of marriage or in marriage. To understand the nature and the gravity of this sin we must realize that the principal purpose of the sexual function, according to God's law, is the procreation of offspring so that the human race may be preserved and propagated. Now, the only way in which the human race can be properly preserved and propagated is by sexual relations, performed in the normal way, between a man and a woman who are united by the bonds of a permanent marriage. For, if the sexual powers are not used in the normal way between a man and a woman, there will be no conception; if the man and woman are not united in marriage, the offspring cannot be properly brought up. Consequently, any act of impurity is a violation of the common good of mankind, a sin against social justice (at least). Moreover, every sin of this nature is grave, because of the great good, the common good of mankind, that is at stake. This is true, not only of the completed sin of action, but even of incipient acts of impurity or even internal sins. For, these imperfect acts by their nature tend to the completed act, and on account of this close connection share its gravity.

It is to be noted that there is reference to sins of *impurity* — that is, those in which sexual pleasure is involved, at least in intention — not to sins of *immodesty*. There can be lightness of matter, venial sin, in these latter, such as indecent talk, looks, and touches which do not bring about a proximate danger of sexual pleasure. It is not correct, therefore, to say that there can be no venial sin against the *sixth commandment*. There can be no fully *deliberate* sin of *impurity* which is not mortal; but there can be fully deliberate sins of *immodesty* which are only venial sins.

Furthermore, it is to be noted that sexual emotions of a physical nature can be *permitted* at times without sin, outside of marriage. This occurs when a person does something which *as a remote cause* produces such emotions, presupposing that there is no grave danger of the consent of the will to these sensations. In such an event, it is a venial sin to place such a cause without sufficient reason, no sin to do so if there is a sufficient reason. For example, if the reading of an ordinary love story, decently narrated, has this effect on a particular person, he could consider that the recreational value of the story sufficiently justifies him in allowing this to happen provided there is little or no danger of consent. The same principles would apply to a movie containing some scenes of an emotional nature. But if a person did something which is a *proximate* cause of sensual emotions — such as the reading of a very obscene story — a grave sin would be committed, unless there is a very grave reason for doing so. The same is true if one places a remote cause and is in grave danger of consenting to the effects.

9. *Sins of Impurity*

The following are the different classes of sins against purity:

1. Fornication, which is the sexual union of an unmarried man and an unmarried woman, voluntarily performed by both. Its sinfulness is evident not only from revelation, but also from the fact that a

child born of such a union could not be properly reared, and thus society would suffer.

2. Rape, which is an attack by a man on a woman who is unwilling. If a girl feared that some great evil would ensue if she resisted — e.g., she would be beaten or even killed — she would be allowed to abstain from resistance and accept the attack passively. Furthermore, if a woman is attacked, she may subsequently use a douche to prevent conception from occurring. But she could not do anything that even probably would produce an abortion, in the event that conception has taken place.

3. Adultery is committed when one (at least) of the parties is married. This adds the malice of a sin against commutative justice, which the married person owes to his or her partner. If both parties are married, it is double adultery.

4. Incest is committed when the parties are related, either by blood or by affinity, or by spiritual relationship, in any of the degrees which the Church decrees as prohibited for marriage. Such a sin would be committed if the parties were second cousins, or brother-in-law and sister-in-law, or godparent and godchild.

5. Sacrilege, which is committed when one (at least) of the parties is bound by religious vow or has received at least the major order of subdiaconate. It is also a sacrilege when a sacred person is the object of even a desire (impure) on the part of another, or when a sacred person is guilty of a sin of impurity, whether in thought or desire, in word or in deed.

A local sin of sacrilege is committed when an impure action is committed in a sacred place — that is, a church, a public or semi-public oratory, or a cemetery. Merely internal sins of impurity in a sacred place do not constitute a sacrilege.

A sin of sacrilege would also be committed if a person violated chastity immediately after receiving Holy Communion, or used a sacred object, such as a crucifix, as an instrument for an impure action.

6. Masturbation or self-abuse is the inordinate use of the sexual faculties by oneself. Young folks who have contracted such a habit are to be treated kindly, and assured that they can overcome it by the use of natural and supernatural means. The natural means are to keep busy and avoid idleness, to avoid occasions of sin, such as dangerous movies or books. The supernatural means are especially prayer in time of temptation and the frequent reception of the sacraments.

7. Sodomy is a sin of coition between persons of the same sex. A base mode of coition between man and woman is also called sodomy.

8. Bestiality is a sin of impurity with an animal.

9. Onanism or contraception is the sin of a married couple who take positive means of avoiding conception, while participating in marital relations. It is a very grave violation of the married state, and has been condemned severely by Pius XI in his encyclical on Christian marriage. The main argument of the Church against this vice, so common today, is that it is a frustration of the principal end of marriage, as intended by the Creator. No reason ever justifies a couple in the commission of this sin, although in some circumstances the fault is on one side, and the other party, after endeavoring to correct the erring partner, may submit.

At times, however, married persons are allowed to make use of periodic abstinence (the Rhythm), which means that they have relations only at that period of the month when conception is unlikely. To do this without any serious reason — e.g., merely to be able to avoid the inconvenience of having children — is wrong, and if kept up for a long time (e.g., several years) might be a mortal sin. However, when a married couple have a good reason, they may make use of Rhythm. Such a reason could be the weakened condition of the wife, financial straits, or the fact that they know by experience that any children they may have will probably be diseased or crippled. Pius XII explained the morality of the Rhythm in an address to the Union of Italian Midwives on October 29, 1951.

10. *Modesty and Immodesty*

Actions which are generally called immodest are those which are not in themselves impure, but are calculated to arouse impurity. Such are looks, touches, reading, talk, etc., when the object is something of a sexual nature. It should be emphasized that these things *in themselves* are not sinful, and under certain circumstances such actions can be perfectly lawful. For example, the doctor in his professional duties may find it necessary to see and touch the bodies of his patients in suchwise as to constitute a temptation; yet, there is a sufficient reason for this, and he may lawfully do it as long as he uses the proper precautions not to sin. The same principle is applicable to the man who is called on to censor movies.

Such actions, therefore, become sinful when the *purpose* of the one who performs them is wrong. Such purposes may be the arousing of sexual passion (mortal sin) or mere curiosity (venial sin). Again, they may be wrong because they exert a strong impetus to sins of impurity and there is no sufficient reason for performing them. Finally, they may be sinful because they give scandal. Such, for example, might be a slight act of immodesty on the part of a priest or religious.

In the development of the virtue of modesty in boys and girls, two extremes must be avoided. On one hand, those things which provoke the passions and can be avoided must be avoided. For example, movies which present even a few scenes which are plainly dangerous to purity (e.g., some Class B pictures) should be forbidden to our youth. The liberties between young folks known as "petting" or "necking" must be regarded, generally speaking, as mortal sins, since they either comprise downright acts of impurity or are a proximate occasion of impurity. The custom of "steady company-keeping" between boys and girls of high school age without any idea of marrying for at least several years must be reprobated, for it is generally a moral danger, and it should be remembered that steady company-keeping is allowed only when a couple is planning to be married soon.

On the other hand, it is not good to develop a prudish attitude or to give young folks the impression that things which in themselves are lawful are sinful. For example, a certain measure of friendliness between boys and girls of high school age, such as is developed by decent dances and parties, going together to the movies occasionally, etc., is perfectly lawful and should even be encouraged.

Girls should not be expected to dress as their grandmothers did. Styles are largely arbitrary, and a form of dress which offers no danger to the average person beholding it is to be regarded as permissible. For example, girls should not be reproved for wearing the present-day bathing costumes recognized as the usual garb for the beach. Evidently this does not refer to costumes which are intended to be daring and provocative. No decent girl would wear such dress, nor would a decent girl participate in a "bathing-beauty contest." We should not be severe toward girls who wish to use lipstick and paint their fingernails nor imply that they have a bad motive.

A proper training in regard to sex matters is an essential part of Christian education. The persons who normally should give this are the parents. However, in certain circumstances teachers are to give this — e.g., in the case of children in an orphan asylum conducted by religious or in a boarding school. In the case of older girls — e.g., in college — some frank talks about sex and marriage are called for, particularly when they are about to be graduated. Sometimes, it is advisable to call in a Catholic doctor or nurse to give some lectures on these subjects. Religious teachers must remember that most of their pupils will enter the married state, and hence should not treat their students as if they were all prospective religious.

11. *Potential Parts of Temperance*

Humility is one of the potential parts of temperance. It is the virtue which refrains the inordinate desire of one's own excellence. It is not opposed to the virtue of magnanimity. On the contrary, a talented person can regard all his abilities as the gifts of God and use them in a magnanimous way while he also humbly acknowledges his own defects. The sin opposed to humility is pride.

Studiousness is the virtue which moderates a person's curiosity in the pursuit of knowledge and impels him to study those things which are adapted to his particular state and needs. Its opposite vice is negligence.

Eutrapelia is the virtue which moderates a person's recreational activities. A certain measure of gaiety and sport should be cultivated lest one become too serious and morose. This virtue inclines us to take enough, but not too much, recreation.

FOOTNOTES

1. Can. 1252.
2. Can. 1244, § 2.
3. Can. 1251.
4. Can. 1250.
5. Can. 1245.

PART III:

THE SACRAMENTS

INTRODUCTION

The purpose of this part is to explain the doctrinal and moral aspects of sacramental theology. The method will be both speculative and practical. The speculative factor will consist in the presentation and the development of the basic theological principles regarding the sacraments. The practical factor will be the application of these principles to the special needs of Catholics today in living the sacramental life, which is a very vital phase of the Catholic life, and the explanation of the rules regarding the administration and the reception of the sacraments, laid down by divine or ecclesiastical law. Action presupposes understanding, and one of the necessary requisites for Catholic Action is that the participants understand these potent means of grace in the Church which are called sacraments.

1. *The Nature of a Sacrament*

A *sacrament,* in general, is a sign of something sacred. In early Christian days the word *sacrament* was used in a very broad sense, which included certain religious doctrines, the ceremonies that accompanied Baptism, exorcisms, etc. But in the twelfth century the word was restricted to a definite type of rites conferred in the Catholic Church; namely, to those which not only signify but also effect, as the instruments of divine power, the sanctification of men. In this sense we can define a sacrament as a sensible sign, instituted by Christ for permanent use in the Church, to signify and to confer on men supernatural sanctity.

The specific characteristic of a Christian sacrament is found in the special way in which it confers sanctity or grace. That is, it contains *in itself,* as an instrumental cause, the efficacy to give supernatural holiness to those who receive it without any impediments — though always with subordination to the power of God, the principal cause of grace. From this standpoint the Christian sacraments are quite different from those rites of the Old Law, such as circumcision, purifications, etc., which did not have in themselves the power to confer grace, but only aroused in the recipients the dispositions of faith, repentance, etc., through which they merited grace.

That God should sanctify men through sacraments is most fitting. For man is made up of body and soul, with an intimate union and interaction between them. Man's ideas and inspirations naturally come to his soul through the things he perceives with his senses; and consequently, it is most fitting that God should make use of signs which appeal to a man's senses as means of conferring on him internal holiness or supernatural grace.

The sacraments are the *arteries* of the Mystical Body, the Church. Just as in the natural human body the arteries transmit the life-giving blood to the various members, so the sacraments transmit the graces from Christ, the Head, to the various members of the Body. It is well to recall that the reception of a sacrament, though it gives its grace directly only to the individual who receives it, is a social act, beneficial also to the other members of the Church, insofar as the spiritual development of any individual member of the Mystical Body profits the entire Body.

2. *The Number of the Sacraments*

The Catholic Church holds as an article of faith, defined by the Council of Trent,[1] that there are seven sacraments — Baptism, Confirmation, Holy Eucharist, Penance, Extreme Unction, Holy Orders, and Matrimony. It was only in the twelfth century that the Church explicitly taught that there are seven sacraments, for it was only then that the word *sacrament* began to have the definite and exclusive meaning of a rite which was established by Christ for permanent use in the Church and which signifies and effectively confers grace. But, from the fact that it was then universally acknowledged without any dissension that there are seven sacraments, and also from the fact that the Oriental Churches, although separated from the Catholic Church, acknowledge this same doctrine, we conclude that it was implicitly recognized from the beginning. That is, all Christians from the earliest days knew that certain rites were effective signs of grace and were instituted by Christ, so that when a common term was proposed for such rites, there was no difficulty in acknowledging that the number of such rites was seven.

St. Thomas[2] argues to the fitness of seven sacraments from the analogy with the principal needs and stages of man's natural human life. For, in the natural order, man (1) is born, (2) comes to maturity, (3) needs nourishment, (4) is healed from sickness if he becomes unwell, (5) convalesces to perfect health. Thus far man is considered as an individual. In the social order, men (6) receive power to govern others and (7) through marriage as an institution of nature receive the duty of propagating society. To supply the needs or phases of the supernatural life corresponding to these seven needs or phases of the natural life Christ has instituted: (1) Baptism, (2) Confirmation, (3) Holy Eucharist, (4) Penance, (5) Extreme Unction, (6) Holy Orders, and (7) Matrimony as a sacrament.

It is true, this argument from fitness is not intended as a proof that Christ had to institute seven sacraments. But, given the institution of these seven, we can perceive how congruous they are toward helping man in the main necessities and crises of the spiritual life.

3. *Constitution of the Sacraments*

Every sacrament is made up of things and words. Theologians and the Church in its official documents call the *things* in the sacraments the *matter* and the *words* the *form*. By things are meant material objects, such as water and oil, or human actions such as the imposing of hands. Matter which exists before the administration of a sacrament (such as the water used in Baptism) is called *remote* matter; the application or use of this remote matter (such as the pouring of the water) is called *proximate* matter.

Since both matter and form make up the essence of a sacrament, both are necessary for the validity of the sacrament. Thus, if wine were used instead of water for Baptism, the sacrament would not be conferred. Again, if a person baptizing said, "I baptize thee in the name of the Holy Trinity," instead of, "I baptize thee in the name of the Father, etc.," the sacrament would be at least very doubtful. On the other hand, an accidental change of matter or form would not invalidate the sacrament — e.g., if a small amount of salt were added to the water for Baptism, or a person added to the baptismal form the words, "and of the Blessed Virgin," meaning merely to invoke our Lady's protection on the child.

The matter and form must be sufficiently united. For example, if a person poured the water and only after several minutes said: "I baptize thee, etc.," there would be no sacrament. However, different union suffices for different sacraments. Thus, the form of Penance (absolution) could be given validly an hour after the person had finished his confession and expressed his contrition, which are the proximate matter of this sacrament.

The chief division of the sacraments is into sacraments of the dead and sacraments of the living. The former are those which have for their principal purpose the conferring of the life of grace on the soul dead in sin — Baptism and Penance. The sacraments of the living are those whose principal purpose is to increase the life of grace in the soul already possessing it — the other five.

The sacraments are not all equal in dignity. The noblest is the Holy Eucharist, since it contains Christ Himself, while the others contain only the grace of Christ. The order of dignity after this is: Holy Orders, Confirmation, Baptism, Extreme Unction, Penance, Matrimony. However, in the order of necessity Baptism comes first.

4. *Institution of the Sacraments*

Only God, by the operation of His divine nature, can be the *principal* cause of the sacraments, for the sacraments give grace, which is the participation of the divine nature; and only God Himself through the operation of His divine nature can grant a participation of the divine nature. As an *instrumental* cause of the institution of the sacraments God could have chosen a mere man; but actually only Christ, the God-Man, has been empowered in the present order of the New Law to institute sacraments, as the primary instrumental cause. We know explicitly from Scripture that certain sacraments were instituted by Christ during His life on earth — Baptism, the Holy Eucharist, and Penance. But we have the testimony of tradition that all the sacraments were instituted by our Lord while He dwelt on earth. It was fitting that He alone should be empowered to do this, for the sacraments dispense grace, and it was Christ as Man who, by His Passion and death, merited all the graces that are given to men.

Although our Lord instituted all the sacraments, it is a disputed point whether He determined the matter and form of all the sacraments *specifically*. In regard to some of the sacraments, especially Confirmation and Holy Orders, it is possible that He determined what was to be the purpose of these sacraments and left it to the Church to choose matter and form suitable to this effect. This is called *generic* determination of the matter and form.

5. *The Minister of the Sacraments*

Christ explicitly deputed the Apostles to confer certain of the sacraments — Baptism,[3] the Holy Eucharist,[4] and Penance.[5] And since He wished that the sacraments should be in use in the Church until the end of time, He evidently willed that men should continue to administer them until the consummation of the world.

Five sacraments can be given only by a consecrated or ordained minister — Holy Eucharist (the *consecration* of this sacrament), Confirmation, Penance, Extreme Unction, and Holy Orders. Two can be administered by a person not possessing sacred power — Baptism and Matrimony. Moreover, the mere *conferring* of the Holy Eucharist does not require any special sacred power.

The minister of a sacrament, since he acts in the name and by the authority of Christ, must have the intention of doing what Christ did, or what the Church does, in conferring the sacred rite. The intention need not be explicit, nor need the person who gives the sacrament necessarily believe in its efficacy, as long as he wishes to do what the Church does or what Christians do by this rite. Thus, an unbeliever can give the sacrament of Baptism if he goes through the ceremony properly and wishes to do thereby what Christians do by this rite.

The *intention* must not be confused with *attention*. Intention is in the *will,* attention in the *intellect.* A person may be entirely distracted when he gives the sacrament, yet if he intends to give it by virtue of an intention previously elicited and in some way influencing the present act, he has what is called a virtual intention which suffices for validity.

The minister of a sacrament, since he is performing a very sacred act, would be guilty of grave irreverence, a mortal sin, if he administered a sacrament in mortal sin, at least when he is an ordained minister administering the sacrament with the solemn ceremonies. It is not certain if a lay person in mortal sin, who baptizes, in case of necessity, commits a mortal sin, or even if a priest in mortal sin is guilty of grave sin if he administers a sacrament without the solemn ceremonies in urgent need.

Catholics should all be instructed in the manner in which Baptism is to be given, and be prepared to give it in case of emergency. If a person in mortal sin is called on to give this sacrament, he should make an act of perfect contrition. Of course, a person in mortal sin who confers the sacrament of Matrimony on the one he is marrying would himself be guilty of mortal sin by receiving the sacrament unworthily. Catholics preparing for marriage should realize the great privilege they have of conferring as well as receiving a sacrament.

6. *The Subject of the Sacraments*

The subject, or recipient, of the sacraments is necessarily a living person. For only in the course of his mortal life can one receive grace. It is true, the sacraments (particularly Baptism, Penance, and Extreme Unction) are sometimes conferred on those who are apparently dead; but the reason is that it seems quite probable that the soul remains in the body for some time after all signs of life are gone; and hence the Church allows this opinion to be applied by the priest for the benefit of one who has apparently died two or three hours before.

We know from the practice of the Church that one who has reached the use of reason must have an intention of receiving a sacrament in order to receive it validly, for God expects those who are able to exercise their free will to co-operate toward their own sanctification. For most of the sacraments it is sufficient to have an habitual intention, that is, an intention once made and not retracted, which consequently remains in the will even when a person has lost consciousness. Furthermore, an *implicit* intention, contained in a more general intention, is sufficient. Thus, a person may be leading a practical Catholic life without ever making an explicit intention of receiving Extreme Unction in the event he becomes dangerously ill. He is suddenly injured seriously and is rendered totally unconscious. He could be given Extreme Unction validly, for in his general intention of living and dying as a Catholic was certainly implicitly contained the intention of receiving the sacrament destined for those in danger of death. Two of the sacraments — Penance and Matrimony — require more than an habitual intention in the recipient. For in Penance, the subject himself performs the acts that constitute the proximate matter: confession, contrition, and satisfaction; and in Matrimony, each party furnishes the proximate matter (the giving of conjugal consent) and also confers the sacrament on the other by expressing the form (the acceptance of the other's consent). Hence, in these two sacraments the recipient must have the same degree of intention that is required of a minister — either virtual or actual.

We must carefully distinguish between the *valid* and the *fruitful* reception of a sacrament. A sacrament is received validly when the subject actually obtains the spiritual reality which is *able* to give him grace, even though because of his lack of dispositions no grace is given. It is received fruitfully also when the grace too is conferred. A sacrament can be valid without being fruitful, but not vice versa. Thus, if a person receives Confirmation without the required disposition, the character is imprinted on his soul, but he receives no grace.

Faith is not required for the *valid* reception of a sacrament. Thus, we could imagine the case of a person who wishes to be baptized for a merely worldly reason — e.g., because he wishes to marry a Catholic girl, and thinks he has a better chance to win her by externally embracing the Catholic faith, even though he does not believe it in his soul. If he received Baptism he would have the character on his soul, and would be bound to obey the Church's laws, but he would not have received the grace of Baptism. On the contrary, he would have committed a grave sacrilege.

For the fruitful reception of the sacraments of the dead, the required dispositions on the part of an adult (one who has reached the age of reason) are an act of faith and an act of contrition. For the fruitful reception of a sacrament of the living, one must have the state of grace. This is the general rule, though (as will be explained later) a person in mortal sin can sometimes receive the state of grace from a sacrament of the living. The more fervent one's actual dispositions are, the more grace he receives.

Those who have never reached the use of reason can receive validly and fruitfully the sacraments of Baptism. Confirmation, and Holy Eucharist, even though they cannot have any intention to receive them. This we know especially from the tradition and practice of the Church. Our Lord decreed to give these little ones the benefit of these sacraments without demanding any co-operation on their part because they are incapable of performing human acts. In the Latin Church those who do not possess sufficient use of reason to have at least a general notion of what the Holy Eucharist contains are never given Holy Communion, but in some Oriental rites children receive the Blessed Sacrament (under the species of wine) after they are baptized. If a male infant is given Holy Orders, the sacrament is conferred validly, but a bishop would never be allowed to give Holy Orders licitly to an infant.

7. *Efficacy and Effects of the Sacraments*

It was one of the basic doctrines of sixteenth-century Protestantism that the sacraments do not give grace of their own power, but merely arouse in the recipients dispositions through which faith (trust in God) is elicited, and thus man is justified. The Catholic Church teaches that the sacraments confer grace *ex opere operato* on those who place no impediment.

The phrase *ex opere operato* means that grace is given to the soul by the very objective power of the sacramental rite, acting as the instrument of God (the principal cause of grace), not by virtue of the dispositions of the recipient. It is true, the more perfect the recipient's dispositions, the more grace will be given, but the reason is not that the dispositions add anything to the efficacy of the sacrament. They perfect the *receptivity* of the subject, just as the dryness

of wood that is being burned does not add anything to the efficacy
of the fire but renders the wood more susceptible to the action of the
fire. In order to indicate that the dispositions add nothing to the
efficacy of the sacraments, we speak of them negatively in referring
to the causality of the sacraments, saying that the sacraments give
grace to those *who place no impediment.* It is to be noted that we
are speaking of an impediment to the *fruitfulness* of the sacrament,
not an impediment to its *validity.*

The efficacy of the sacraments is clearly indicated in the New
Testament. For example, our Lord said, in reference to Baptism:
"Unless a man be born again of water and the Spirit . . ."[6] The word
of in this text — *ex* in Latin and Greek — indicates causality, and in
this instance is applied both to God (Spirit), the principal cause, and
to the water, the instrumental cause. A similar argument can be
drawn from the words of St. Paul: "I admonish thee to stir up the
grace of God which is in thee *by* the laying on of my hands."[7]

The sacraments of the Old Law gave their graces by moving
the recipients to good acts, through which they merited divine favors.
However, circumcision given to infants was an *occasion* of grace, in
the sense that God had determined to give grace to any infant to
whom it was applied. This was different, however, from the *causality*
exercised by the sacraments of the New Law.

Every sacrament gives sanctifying grace. The sacraments of the
dead are intended primarily to give *first grace* — that is, grace to a
soul that was previously deprived of it. However, accidentally, these
sacraments can give *second* grace — that is, an increase of grace to
a soul that already possesses it. Thus, when a person in sanctifying
grace goes to confession he receives more grace. The sacraments of
the living are intended primarily to give *second* grace. That is, Christ
intended them primarily for persons already living the life of grace.
But accidentally they can give *first* grace. That is, if a person in
mortal sin receives one of these sacraments of the living, he is put in
the state of grace provided two conditions are present; first, he is
in good faith (that is, he is unconscious of his unworthiness); and,
second, he has elicited an act of imperfect contrition. For example, a
Catholic in mortal sin is stricken unconscious and is dying in that
condition. Before he lost consciousness he made an act of contrition
based on the fear of hell (imperfect contrition). If he is then given
Extreme Unction he regains the state of grace. This doctrine is certain

with respect to Extreme Unction,[8] and is very probable with respect to the other sacraments of the living.

Besides sanctifying grace, each sacrament gives a special *sacramental* grace. For, if each gave nothing more than sanctifying grace, there would be no need of *seven* sacraments. It is commonly held that sacramental grace is identical with sanctifying grace with an adaptation toward the effectiveness of the particular sacrament. Thus, the sacramental grace of Baptism is the sanctifying grace it bestows, adapted toward the living of the Christian life; the sacramental grace of Extreme Unction is its sanctifying grace, adapted toward imparting strength to one in the sufferings that accompany danger of death from sickness.

Included in the sacramental grace of each sacrament is the right to receive the actual graces needed to fulfill the duties imposed on those who have received it. Thus, the sacramental grace of Matrimony gives a right to the actual graces which the couple will later need to live up to the duties of the married state.

The measure of the grace bestowed by a sacrament corresponds to the dispositions, in the case of an adult. In the case of those below the age of reason it is the more common view that there is a measure of grace determined by Almighty God, which is the same for all children receiving the same sacrament.

The practical Catholic will be mindful of the fact that certain sacraments which he has received — particularly Baptism and Confirmation — have given him a claim to God's special assistance in all the needs of the Christian life, and he should invoke the grace of God by virtue of these sacraments in times of special need, particularly in the hour of grave temptation.

8. *Revival of a Sacrament*

By the revival of a sacrament we mean that, after having been received validly but unfruitfully, it subsequently confers its grace, the impediment to its fruitfulness having been removed.

It is certain that Baptism can revive. That is, an adult who has received this sacrament without the requisite dispositions for its fruitfulness can afterward receive its graces, if he supplies what is necessary. If this were not the case, one who had received Baptism unworthily could never be justified, since he could not repeat this sacrament, and the sins committed before its reception can be taken away only by the power of this sacrament. It is also commonly held that Confirmation and Holy Orders revive; and it is quite probable that the same is true of Extreme Unction (for the period of the danger of death), and Matrimony (as long as the marital union lasts). There can be no revival of the Holy Eucharist (at least, after the sacramental species have ceased to exist); and, for practical purposes, Penance cannot revive, since there is hardly any possibility that this sacrament can be received unfruitfully without its being also invalid.

If a person received a sacrament unfruitfully without being aware of his unworthiness, and subsequently committed no mortal sin, the requisite disposition for the revival of the sacrament is attrition. If a person received the sacrament unworthily with full consent, or if after receiving the sacrament he committed mortal sin, the condition for revival is perfect contrition or the reception of the sacrament of Penance.

The doctrine of the revival of the sacraments illustrates very clearly the mercy and the goodness of God. Even in the case of those who make use of His sacraments without the due dispositions, He is willing to give the graces of the sacraments subsequently, as long as the recipient is in need of these graces and the sacrament cannot be repeated.

9. The Sacramental Character

Three of the sacraments — Baptism, Confirmation, and Holy Orders — imprint on the soul of the recipient a spiritual mark called a character. This is an article of faith from the Council of Trent.[9] By these sacraments there is given to the soul a spiritual entity which survives after the rite has passed away and even after the grace of the sacrament has been lost. This entity is what began to be commonly called the character in the thirteenth century.

The character is a spiritual, supernatural quality, probably of that species which is called *power*. It is indelible, at least in the present life, and very probably in the future life. Hence, once a sacrament conferring a character has been validly received, it can never be received again.[10] The character gives the recipient a right to special graces corresponding to the state to which it raised the recipient; it distinguishes him from all those who have not received this particular sacrament; it deputes him to the exercise of divine cult; and it makes him a participant in the priesthood of Christ. The character of Baptism gives the power to receive the other sacraments and to join in the offering of the Mass; the character of Confirmation deputes one to defend the faith publicly; the character of Holy Orders gives the power to offer Mass, to absolve from sins, etc.

FOOTNOTES

1. *DB*, 844.
2. *Summa*, III, q. 65, a. 1.
3. Mt. 28:19.
4. Lk. 22:19.
5. Jn. 20:23.
6. Jn. 3:5.
7. 2 Tim. 1:6.
8. James 5:15.
9. *DB*, n. 852.
10. Can. 732.

CHAPTER II . . . *BAPTISM*

1. *The Existence of the Sacrament of Baptism*

The New Testament frequently alludes to a rite of ablution established by Christ Himself, for the purpose of giving the soul a new life and remitting sin. Thus, our Lord said to Nicodemus: "Unless a man be born again of water and the Spirit, he cannot enter into the kingdom of God."[1] When He was about to leave this world, He commanded the Apostles to baptize, "in the name of the Father and of the Son and of the Holy Spirit,"[2] and declared: "He who believes and is baptized shall be saved."[3] Frequent mention of this ceremony is found in the Acts of the Apostles and in the Epistles.[4] Early tradition also makes frequent mention of Baptism — e.g., the Didache, the writings of St. Justin and Tertullian.

It seems that Christ had already instituted Baptism before the Last Supper, since the Apostles there received the Holy Eucharist, and this presupposes Baptism. However, the necessity of this sacrament for all was *promulgated* for the first time on Pentecost.[5]

2. *The Essence of Baptism*

The remote matter of Baptism is real, natural water. As far as validity is concerned it makes no difference whether this is taken from a spring, a lake, the ocean, rain, etc. Even if a small amount of extraneous matter is included, the validity of the sacrament is not impaired, as when there is salt in the water taken from the ocean. However, even though a substance is chemically composed, for the greater part, of water, but not recognized as or called water by ordinary people, nor regarded as suitable for washing, it is not valid matter since the common estimate of mankind must be taken into consideration when the matter of the sacraments is being determined. Thus milk, saliva, tears, wine, fruit juice, etc., are not valid matter for Baptism. Diluted milk and weak soup might perhaps be valid matter.

The proximate matter is the external washing of the recipient. This can be done either by complete immersion, by sprinkling, or by pouring. When one of these last two is used, the water must flow on the skin of the person's head. Moreover, the ablution must be performed by the person who pronounces the words. When immersion is used (as in the Baptism of a fetus), emersion (the drawing of the recipient out of the water) must also be performed by the minister to complete the significance of washing.

The form in the Latin Church is: "I baptize thee in the name of the Father and of the Son and of the Holy Ghost." In the Greek Church it is: "The servant of God is baptized in the name of the Father and of the Son and of the Holy Ghost." As is evident, the sense is substantially the same in both. The words must be pronounced *while* the ablution is being performed. Moreover, the words must be pronounced *audibly*.

3. *The Necessity of Baptism*

The necessity of this sacrament is proclaimed by Christ Himself: "Unless a man be born again of water and the Spirit, he cannot enter into the kingdom of God."[6] The tradition of the Church emphasizes the same doctrine, especially the writings of St. Augustine. That this necessity is a matter of *means,* and not merely of *precept,* is also clear from the tradition of the Church, and is indicated in the words of Christ, establishing Baptism as a spiritual *rebirth;* for birth is necessary by its very nature for the attainment of life.

The necessity of Baptism for the attainment of the life of grace was promulgated for the first time on Pentecost.[7] The obligation for individuals to receive this sacrament seems to have spread gradually throughout the world, as the Gospel was gradually announced. The more common teaching is that it became of universal obligation when *per se* all could have received the message — that is, by the end of the first century. However, there are some who hold that this obligation has accompanied the actual promulgation of the Gospel, so that Baptism became the necessary means of salvation in America only in the fifteenth and sixteenth centuries, and even today it has not become actually a necessary means of salvation in some lands where the Gospel has not yet been preached. In this supposition the pre-Christian religious rite whereby infants were justified after birth (circumcision or the *remedium naturae*) is still effective in those lands.

The necessity of Baptism is *extrinsic* and *relative,* because Christ's determination that it would be a necessary means admitted two exceptions, known as the Baptism of desire and the Baptism of blood. The former is an act of divine charity or perfect contrition; the latter is the acceptance of death for the faith of Christ or some Christian virtue. The person concerned is one who, through no fault of his own, has not received the Baptism of water. As is evident, these means are not independent of the sacrament; they presuppose in the recipient at least the implicit will to receive this sacrament. However, even an infant can gain the benefit of the Baptism of blood if he is put to death by a person actuated by hatred for the Christian faith — e.g., the unbaptized child of Catholic parents, killed by an atheist through hatred for the faith of the parents.

Children who die without Baptism do not attain the supernatural goal of the beatific vision; but it is commonly held that they enjoy a purely natural beatitude for all eternity in Limbo.

4. The Minister of Baptism

Anyone possessing the use of reason, who performs the rite of Baptism properly with the required intention, confers this sacrament validly. However, a lay person is allowed to baptize only when a consecrated minister is not available, and a child's parents should not baptize him if another person can be procured. The ordinary minister of *solemn* Baptism, conferred with all the ceremonies prescribed by the Church, is a priest. Under ordinary circumstances the pastor of the place where the recipient resides, or a priest deputed by him, is the proper minister of Baptism. In certain circumstances a deacon can be delegated by a bishop or a pastor to administer solemn Baptism as extraordinary minister.[8]

Every Catholic should be familiar with the method of baptizing, and should not hesitate to confer this sacrament when necessity urges — e.g., when an infant (unbaptized or probably unbaptized) is dying in an accident. The lay person who baptizes should understand full well that he should make no condition depending on a future circumstance, such as, "I intend to baptize only if the child is going to die," or "only if the priest does not get here in time," for such a condition would invalidate the sacrament.

5. The Recipient of Baptism

Since this sacrament imprints an indelible character and cannot be repeated, only an unbaptized person can receive it. One who has reached the use of reason must have an intention of being baptized in order to receive this sacrament validly.

Any infant can be lawfully baptized, even against the will of the

parents, when the child is in so great danger of death that it is prudently judged that he will die. Apart from this case, however, it is
forbidden to baptize the child of nonbaptized parents against the will
of these latter; and the Church commands that the same rule be
observed in regard to the children of baptized non-Catholics. The
Church will not baptize a child apart from the danger of death
unless there is some assurance that it will be brought up as a Catholic.[9]
The law of the Church prescribes that the children of Catholics be
baptized *as soon as possible* after birth,[10] and it seems that a month
is the longest period that can be understood by *as soon as possible* —
better, three weeks.

6. *The Effects of Baptism*

Baptism confers sanctifying grace on all recipients who have no
impediment. In the case of an adult this means that the recipient has
made an act of faith and (if he has committed any mortal sin) of
contrition (at least imperfect). The sacramental grace of Baptism includes the right to those actual graces that are needed in order that
the recipient may lead a truly Christian life. In addition, this sacrament takes away all the debt of eternal and temporal punishment
due to the recipient for previous actual sins. An adult, who because
of lack of the proper dispositions does not receive grace when the
sacrament is conferred, can later receive this grace through the
revival of the sacrament.

Baptism, when validly (even though unfruitfully) conferred, imprints on the soul an indelible character. This character gives the
recipient the power to receive the other sacraments validly and also
makes him a member of the Church, with the obligation to obey
its laws.

7. *Sponsors at Baptism*

It is the law of the Church that at solemn Baptism there be at least
one sponsor or godparent; there may be two of different sexes.[11] It is
the duty of a sponsor to regard the baptized person as a spiritual son
or daughter, and to provide this person with proper religious and
moral training if the parents are unable or unwilling to do so.

The Church has laid down certain laws determining who may
validly accept the office of baptismal sponsor and who may do so
lawfully. Excluded from valid sponsorship are the unbaptized, those
belonging to a non-Catholic religious denomination, the parents or

husband or wife of the person being baptized, and those on whom a condemnatory or declaratory sentence of excommunication has been inflicted. Excluded from lawful (though valid) sponsorship are persons under thirteen years of age, those who do not know even the rudiments of faith, priests and religious (unless they have received permission from their respective superior), and those who have been excommunicated for a notorious offense, without a declaratory or condemnatory sentence. However, for a good reason the minister of Baptism can allow a child under thirteen to be a godparent.[12]

The godparent must physically touch the recipient during the actual conferring of the sacrament, or (in the case of baptism by immersion) immediately afterward raise him from the font or receive him from the hands of the minister. A person can act as godparent through a proxy, or representative, who goes through the ceremony in the name of the real godparent. But it is necessary that the real godparent agree to this. Thus, the parents of the child could not delegate someone to act as a proxy for a relative who knows nothing about the matter.

When baptism is conferred privately (without the solemn ceremonies) a godparent should be had if it is easy to procure one,[13] but the obligation to procure a sponsor in this case is not grave.

A godparent contracts a spiritual relationship with the baptized person, which constitutes an impediment to their marriage. A similar relationship is formed between the minister and the recipient of the sacrament.[14] Thus, if a boy baptized a girl in danger of death, he would be forbidden afterward to marry her.

FOOTNOTES

1. Jn. 3:5.
2. Mt. 28:19.
3. Mk. 16:15.
4. Acts 2:38–41; 8:12, 38; 10:48; Eph. 5:26.
5. Acts 2:38.
6. Jn. 3:5.
7. Acts 2:38.
8. Can. 738–742.
9. Can. 750, 751.
10. Can. 770.
11. Can. 762, 764.
12. Can. 765, 766.
13. Can. 762.
14. Can. 768, 1079.

CHAPTER III . . . *CONFIRMATION*

1. *Existence of Confirmation*

The Gospel makes no mention of the sacrament of Confirmation, but the Acts of the Apostles[1] describes a rite, consisting of the imposition of hands and a prayer, whereby the Holy Spirit was given to those already baptized. This, supported by constant tradition, indicates an efficacious rite for the supernatural strengthening of those who have received Baptism. By this sacrament of the Holy Spirit the life given to the soul in Baptism is brought to maturity. It is not certain when our Lord established this sacrament, but it seems probable He did so when He promised that the Holy Spirit would be given to all who believed in Him,[2] or perhaps at the Last Supper.[3]

The Apostles did not receive Confirmation as a sacramental rite; but they (and our Blessed Lady and many of the disciples) received the effects of the sacrament when the Holy Spirit descended on them on Pentecost Sunday.[4]

2. *Essence of Confirmation*

At the present time in the Latin Church the essence of Confirmation consists in the imposition of the hand of the minister on the head of the recipient, with the anointing with chrism, and the words: "I sign thee with the sign of the cross and I confirm thee with the chrism of salvation, in the name of the Father and of the Son and of the Holy Ghost. Amen." The other ceremonies, such as the general extension of hands at the beginning and the blow on the cheek afterward, are not essential.

Chrism, the remote matter of this sacrament, is a mixture of olive oil and balm, blessed by the bishop at the Mass of Holy Thursday. It is a disputed point whether or not a priest could be deputed by the Holy See to bless chrism. As far as is known, such a deputation has never been given.

The proximate matter is the laying on of the hand, with the anointing. The anointing is made in the form of a cross, on the forehead, to indicate that the soldier of Christ must openly profess the faith.

193

The form consists of the words quoted above. In the Oriental churches the form is: "The seal of the gift of the Holy Ghost is given to thee." It is disputed whether the essence of this sacrament has remained the same down through the centuries. Many scholars believe that in the early Church only the imposition of hands was given. If that be true, it follows that Christ must have determined the matter of this sacrament generically only, leaving to the Church the right to make the specific determination, which could thus vary in the course of time.

3. The Minister of Confirmation

The ordinary minister of Confirmation is a bishop only. This is corroborated by tradition, and is most fitting, since it is congruous that the sacrament which gives fullness to the life of grace should be given (ordinarily, at least) only by one who possesses the fullness of the priestly power.

However, it is also evident from tradition and from the legislation of the Church that a priest can be deputed to administer Confirmation.[5] This faculty is given to cardinals who are priests and also to some missionaries. Since January 1, 1947, a pastor may confer Confirmation within the limits of his parish on a person in danger of death from sickness or accident if a bishop is not available.

4. The Subject of Confirmation

Confirmation can be received only by a baptized person; but, on the other hand, every baptized person is capable of receiving this sacrament validly. In other words, it is a normal procedure of the Christian life to be brought to spiritual maturity.

To receive Confirmation fruitfully it is obligatory to have the state of grace. Moreover, the recipient who has reached the age of reason should be instructed adequately in the dignity and the effects of this sacrament. It is the wish of the Church that children of the Latin rite be confirmed at about the age of seven. But in danger of death or for some other good reason the infant may be confirmed.[6] In some Oriental rites it is usual for children to be confirmed immediately after Baptism.

The reception of Confirmation is not necessary for salvation by necessity of means. It is a disputed point whether or not it is necessary by necessity of grave precept. The negative view is sufficiently probable to be followed in practice; hence, we may not assert that a person is guilty of mortal sin if he refuses to be confirmed. It is, however, the earnest desire of the Church that all receive this sacrament. It is especially called for before the reception of the clerical tonsure and the sacrament of Matrimony.[7]

5. *The Effects of Confirmation*

Confirmation impresses on the soul an indelible character, deputing the recipient to be a soldier of Christ — that is, to defend and to proclaim the faith. The grace of this sacrament is the grace of spiritual maturity and strength. It is analogous to the grace received by the Apostles at the descent of the Holy Ghost on Pentecost. The gifts of the Holy Ghost are given in a special way in Confirmation, though not exclusively, since they accompany every infusion of sanctifying grace.

Because of its special sacramental effects Confirmation is aptly designated as the sacrament of Catholic Action.

6. *Sponsors at Confirmation*

Just as in Baptism, so in Confirmation the Church commands that the recipient have a sponsor or godparent. The sponsor must be a Catholic who himself has been confirmed. The other requirements are the same as those described in the previous chapter as the conditions for the validity or the lawfulness of sponsorship in Baptism. It is the ruling of the Church that one person shall not be godparent to more than two recipients at the same Confirmation ceremony, but for good reasons the bishop can permit the same person to be sponsor for a large group.[8] Between the one confirmed and his sponsor there is a spiritual relationship, involving on the part of the latter obligations similar to those contracted by the sponsor in Baptism. However, this relationship does not constitute an impediment to marriage.[9]

FOOTNOTES

1. Acts 8:5–14; 19:1–6.
2. Jn. 7:39.
3. Jn. 14:16.
4. Acts 2:1–4.
5. Can. 782.
6. Can. 788.
7. Can. 787, 974, 1021.
8. Can. 794.
9. Can. 1079.

CHAPTER IV . . . *THE HOLY EUCHARIST*

The Holy Eucharist, the most excellent of the sacraments, will be considered in three sections: The Real Presence, The Holy Eucharist as a Sacrament, and The Holy Eucharist as a Sacrifice.

Section I. The Real Presence

1. *The Catholic Doctrine and Its Opponents*

The Catholic Church teaches that in the Holy Eucharist, under the appearances of bread and wine, are contained truly, really, and substantially the body and blood, together with the soul and divinity, of Jesus Christ — and hence the whole Christ.

Before the sixteenth century there were few calling themselves Christians who denied this doctrine. In the ninth century it may have been denied by Scotus Eriugena; in the eleventh century it was denied by Berengarius, who later retracted his denial.

A great number of views prevailed among the Protestants of the sixteenth century regarding the presence of Christ in the Blessed Sacrament. Luther admitted the real presence, though he held consubstantiation instead of transubstantiation. Most of the Reformers, however, denied the real presence and held that Christ is present only metaphorically or symbolically or (Calvin) through His spiritual power.

Nowadays the real presence is denied by most Protestants, who hold that the bread and wine represent Christ's body and blood, although High Church Anglicans and Episcopalians hold that our Lord is truly present in the Eucharist. The real presence is believed also by the dissident Oriental churches.

2. *Proof From Scripture*

The first proof from Scripture for the real presence is found in the sixth chapter of St. John's Gospel. Our Lord had just worked two miracles, the multiplication of the loaves and the walking on water, and was preaching in the Synagogue of Capharnaum. There, He began to speak about the "bread of God" (v. 33), and gradually became more definite, finally saying that He was the living bread (v. 51), and that all must eat His flesh and drink His blood in order to have life (v. 54). Evidently the people understood Him to speak of His own body and blood, for some of them protested that this was too hard a saying (v. 61) and left Him (v. 67). But Christ only insisted more emphatically on the acceptance of His teaching (v. 68), from which we know that He did speak of His living body and blood as the food and drink of men's souls.

The second proof is the account of the Last Supper, which is contained in the Gospels of SS. Matthew,[1] Mark,[2] and Luke,[3] and in the First Epistle of St. Paul to the Corinthians.[4] In all accounts, the words of Christ, simple and direct, if taken literally must signify the real presence, and not a mere symbolic presence. He said: "This is my body. . . . This is my blood."

The third scriptural proof is found in St. Paul[5] who clearly asserts that he recognizes the chalice as the communication of the blood of Christ and "the bread that we break" as the participation of His body. Later,[6] he tells us that one who eats or drinks unworthily is guilty of the body and blood of the Lord.

3. Proof From Tradition

Many early writers clearly profess their faith in the real presence. Thus Tertullian, in the beginning of the third century, says: "Our flesh feeds on the body and blood of Christ." St. Justin, in the second century, says that Christians have been taught that they partake of the flesh and blood of the Incarnate Jesus. St. Cyril of Jerusalem, in the fourth century, says: "What seems to be bread is not bread, but the body of Christ, and what seems to be wine is not wine but the blood of Christ." Undoubtedly, there was a constant tradition in the Church accepting unhesitatingly the doctrine of the real presence, which was not interrupted until the eleventh century when Berengarius appeared. And there was no widespread denial until the sixteenth century. Anyone who admits Christ to be God must be forced to admit that, if the whole Church was wrong from the beginning for so many centuries, He was to blame for not explicitly teaching that the Holy Eucharist is only a symbol of His body. But it would be blasphemy to attribute such deception to the Son of God.

4. Transubstantiation

It is an article of faith from the Council of Trent that the real presence is effected by a change called *transubstantiation*. This means that the *entire* substance of the bread is changed into the body and the *entire* substance of the wine into the blood of Christ, while there remain only the appearances of bread and wine. To understand this we must realize that the greatest substantial change wrought in the realm of nature is a *transformation* — a change of one substance into another, in which only a new *form* is produced, while the *matter* remains the same. By the matter of material substance we mean that element which it has in common with all other material things; by the form we mean that element which distinguishes it from all other material things. But when consecration takes place, both matter and form of the new substance — the body and blood of Christ — are distinct from the matter and form of the bread and wine.

However, the species (or appearances) of bread and wine remain, as is evident to our senses. By species we mean the accidents — taste, color, etc. Since the accidents of a substance are really distinct from it, there is no intrinsic reason why they cannot be supported in existence after the substance itself has ceased to exist. These accidents are upheld by the power of God, without any substance in which to inhere. And, since they are thus supported in existence, they continue to act as if the connatural substances of bread and wine were still present.

The real presence endures as long as the substance of bread (or wine) would remain if this wondrous change had not taken place. Another way to express it is that the real presence endures as long as the accidents of bread and wine remain unchanged. If with the consecrated wine some other liquid is mingled in a relatively large quantity, the real presence also ceases — e.g., if a large amount of water were poured into the chalice after consecration.

The *whole* Christ is present under each species both of bread and of wine. Furthermore, the whole Christ is present under every part of each species, for He is present there after the manner of substance which is wholly in every part of a material thing.

5. *The Real Presence Relative to Reason and Speech*

The doctrine of the real presence is above reason, not against reason. It is true, there are many wonders contained in this doctrine, especially the presence of the whole body of Christ in the small host, and the presence of the same body in thousands of hosts. But, with the scholastic explanation of accidents, and especially quantity, in mind, we can see that no argument can be brought up that will disprove the real presence. We do not claim to be able to prove the possibility of the real presence positively, but we can show that any arguments against it have no weight.

In our speech we should avoid attributing to the body of Christ what is proper to the accidents in their own being. Thus, we could not say that the body of Christ is corrupted or the blood of Christ is soured, when such changes take place in the accidents. We can apply to the body and blood of our Lord what really is proper to the species insofar as these are the sign of Christ's presence. Thus, we can say that we eat and drink the body and blood of our Lord.

The Blessed Sacrament gives us the humanity of Christ, which is hypostatically united to the Person of the Word, and as such worthy of the highest type of honor. Under the species of the bread, His body is present by virtue of the words of consecration, while His blood, soul, and divinity are present by virtue of concomitance. Similarly, under the species of wine His blood is present by virtue of the words of consecration, while His body, soul, and divinity are present by virtue of concomitance.

Section II. The Holy Eucharist as a Sacrament

1. *The Nature of the Holy Eucharist as a Sacrament*

That which constitutes the Holy Eucharist as a sacrament is the body and blood of Christ together with the sacramental species. This is a permanent sacrament — that is, it begins to exist as a sacrament as soon as the consecration takes place, and not merely when it is received, as in the case of the other sacraments.

The remote matter of this sacrament is bread made from wheat, and wine made from grapes. Bread from any other cereal, such as rye or barley, would not be valid matter, since our Lord used wheaten bread at the Last Supper. It makes no difference, as far as validity is concerned, whether the bread is fermented (leavened) or not. In the Latin Church the use of unleavened bread is commanded; in the Oriental churches for the most part leavened bread is used. All priests are obliged to follow their own rite in this matter.[7] Only wine from grapes is valid; but again, as far as validity is concerned, it may be fermented or unfermented. The Church commands for lawfulness fermented wine.

The form of this sacrament is made up of the words spoken by

Christ: "This is *my* body. . . . This is the chalice of *my* blood. . . ."
Probably the words which immediately precede are necessary for
validity — that is: "On the night before he suffered, he took bread . . ."
because otherwise it would not be clear whose body and blood are
being made present. It is also probable that a priest cannot validly
consecrate one species without the intention of consecrating the other.
The argument for this opinion is that the *sacrament* of the Eucharist
is made present through the offering of the *Sacrifice* of the Mass, and
unless a priest intended to consecrate both species he would not have
the intention of offering Mass. A priest is never allowed to consecrate
one species without the other, or even both species outside of Mass.[8]
Only an ordained priest can validly consecrate the Holy Eucharist.
However, once the Blessed Sacrament has been consecrated, a deacon
can be deputed to administer It in Holy Communion. In extraordinary
circumstances (especially to protect the Blessed Sacrament from pro-
fanation) even a lay person could administer Holy Communion to
himself or to others.

2. *The Necessity of the Holy Eucharist*

The Holy Eucharist is not necessary for salvation by necessity of
means. Certainly the Church would not allow baptized children to
die without receiving this sacrament if it were necessary in this way.
But the reception of this sacrament is necessary for all baptized persons
who have come to the use of reason by necessity of a *divine-ecclesiastical precept*. The divine precept is evident from the words of Christ:
"Amen, amen I say to you, unless you eat the flesh of the Son of
Man, and drink his blood, you shall not have life in you."[9] Our Lord
left it to the Church to determine how frequently the Holy Eucharist
must be received, and the Church has determined that this must take
place at least once a year, in the paschal season.[10] Moreover, when a
person is in danger of death from any cause whatsoever he is bound
to receive the Blessed Sacrament as Viaticum, probably by divine
precept. Even if a person has already received Holy Communion out
of devotion that same day, he can receive the Viaticum if danger of
death arises. A person in danger of death can continue to receive the
Viaticum daily.[11]

The divine-ecclesiastical precept binds all those who have attained
the use of reason. Hence, even a child of five or six, who has actually
attained the use of reason, is bound to receive Holy Communion at
least once a year. Moreover, when a child is in danger of death he

may be given the Viaticum, even though he has not attained the full use of reason, as long as he has enough knowledge to distinguish the Blessed Sacrament from ordinary bread and to give It due honor and reverence.[12]

The Catholic Church holds that it is sufficient to receive the Holy Eucharist under only one species, the basic reason being that Christ is whole and entire under each species. Moreover, the custom and the law of the Church support this practice.[13] The Council of Trent stated that those who receive one species are not deprived on this account of any grace necessary for salvation.[14]

3. *Dispositions for the Reception of the Holy Eucharist*

By ecclesiastical law a person is bound to be fasting from midnight in order to receive the Holy Eucharist lawfully.[15] The Apostolic Constitution *Christus Dominus,* promulgated on January 16, 1953, decrees that natural water does not break the eucharistic fast. Moreover, by virtue of this same Constitution, those who are sick and would find it gravely inconvenient to observe the eucharistic fast strictly may take medicine and nonalcoholic beverages before receiving Holy Communion, with the advice of a confessor. Furthermore, even those who are not sick, but must do onerous work before receiving Holy Communion, or wait for a late hour, or take a lengthy journey, may (with the advice of a confessor) take liquid nourishment (nonalcoholic) up to one hour before receiving Holy Communion. Priests in these same categories enjoy the same privileges with respect to the celebration of Mass. Where evening Masses are allowed, Catholics may receive Holy Communion at these Masses provided they abstain from solid food for at least three hours previously, and for one hour from beverages. In the observance of the eucharistic fast for the evening Mass a person is allowed light alcoholic beverages, such as beer and wine, at the meals he may take previously. But no "hard" liquors are allowed from midnight, and even the milder alcoholic beverages may not be taken outside of meals. Priests who celebrate evening Masses enjoy similar privileges with the time computed to the beginning of Mass.

The disposition of soul necessary for the worthy reception of the Holy Eucharist is the state of grace. Pius X, in his decree advocating frequent Communion, added, "a right intention," but this is only a general condition for any good work, since one who would receive Holy Communion from a bad motive, such as vanity, would certainly not be properly disposed. A person in mortal sin who receives Holy Communion with good faith (unconsciousness of his unworthiness) and attrition very probably thereby receives the state of grace. It is a law of the Church (and perhaps also a divine law) that a person who has committed a mortal sin may not receive Holy Communion until he has first been to confession, even though he may have regained the state of grace by an act of perfect contrition. But an act of contrition suffices when there is some urgent need for one to receive Holy Communion (e.g., to avoid scandal) and a confessor is not available.[16] But a person may not use this exception in order to receive Holy Communion without going to confession merely because others might be surprised or suspect him of sinning gravely if he does not approach the altar rail.

4. *Effects of the Holy Eucharist*

Like all the sacraments, the Holy Eucharist gives sanctifying grace; and this is given in a measure corresponding to the dispositions of the recipient. It also gives a sacramental grace, which actually is the sanctifying grace with a special adaptation toward the attainment of the purpose of this sacrament. It seems that the special sacramental grace of the Holy Eucharist is to be considered as, in general, the intimate union of the recipient with Christ — abiding in Him.[17] This general grace actually embraces several particular graces, especially the increase of actual divine charity, the union of the members of the Church with one another, the preservation from sin, remission of venial sins, an added title to eternal glory. The essential effects of this sacrament are given at the moment of the *eating* of the sacred species, since to this action our Lord promised the graces of this sacrament.

A person cannot receive Holy Communion for another in the sense that he can transfer to this other the essential graces of the sacramental reception, but he can do this in the sense that he can apply to this other person the satisfactory and the impetratory value of the prayers he says on the occasion of Holy Communion. Moreover, he can transfer to a soul in purgatory the indulgences that may be annexed to the reception of the Holy Eucharist.

SECTION III. THE HOLY EUCHARIST AS A SACRIFICE

1. *Proof of the Doctrine*

A sacrifice, generally speaking, is a sacred rite in which a victim is offered to God, and in some way destroyed or immolated. Sacrifices were common in the Old Law, at the express command of God; and the death of Christ on the cross was the great Sacrifice of all time, infinite in its value to adore and thank God, to atone for sin, and to obtain favors. That the Mass is a sacrifice is proved, first, from the prophecy of Malachias, in which the prophet contrasts the sacrifices of the Old Law with a great and clean oblation which in messianic times is to be offered everywhere: "From the rising of the sun even to the going down my name is great among the gentiles, and in every place there is sacrifice, and there is offered to my name a clean oblation."[18] It is to be noted that the prophet is speaking in the name of God. Second, when our Lord instituted the Holy Eucharist, He used words that indicated that He was then performing a sacrificial act: "My Body, *which is being given for you*,"[19] "My Blood . . . which is being *shed for many unto the forgiveness of sins*."[20] It is to be noted also that in the original Greek this is in the *present* tense; moreover, in St. Luke, the "shed" is applied to the *chalice* then before Him. All this indicates that the Last Supper was a sacrificial act. Now, the Mass is the renewal of the Last Supper, in obedience to our Lord's Command, "Do this in remembrance of me." Consequently the Mass is a sacrifice. This is corroborated by tradition from the earliest ages.

The Catholic Church does not claim that the Mass is an *independent* sacrifice — that is, entirely distinct from the Sacrifice of the cross. Indeed, it derives all its value of bestowing grace and pardon from the Sacrifice of Calvary; hence, it is called the renewal and the representation of the Sacrifice of the cross. But it is, nevertheless, a *true* sacrifice, and not merely a commemoration of the Sacrifice offered by Christ.

2. *The Nature of the Eucharistic Sacrifice*

The nature of the Holy Sacrifice of the Mass is the object of much discussion. A view which can be explained easily and has much in its favor is that which was proposed a few years ago by Father de la Taille, S.J. He held that the basic act of sacrifice is offering; immolation has come in only because of man's sin. The offering signifies that God is the supreme Lord of all; the immolation signifies that man has sinned and in consequence deserves destruction, but he is seeking pardon through the symbolism of destroying some creature, such as an animal.

Our Lord made the offering of His one great Sacrifice at the Last Supper; that offering continued through the crucifixion in which He was immolated. Now, although He has been glorified, He still remains an immolated victim for all eternity. The value of the immolation of Calvary remains forever. Every time a priest celebrates Mass, he renews the *offering* of the *immolated* victim. This takes place at the Consecration, in which there is a mystical (or representative) immolation of Christ, in that the separate consecrations vividly portray the separation of His body and blood on Calvary. Thus, the Mass is an offering of a victim *who has been immolated*.

3. *Those Who Offer the Mass*

We can distinguish the offerers of the Mass under four headings — Christ, the Church, the priest, and the faithful co-operating.

a) Our Lord in His human nature is the Chief Priest in every Mass. At least remotely our Saviour fulfills this function, insofar as He gave the commission and the power to His priests to renew His offering. Many theologians hold that He also is the immediate offerer of every individual Mass.

b) The Church, as the society authorized to give God divine worship, also offers each Mass through the ordained priest, an official of the Church.

c) The priest receives his commission from the words of Christ, "Do this in remembrance of me."[21] The Holy Sacrifice can be offered by one priest or by several concelebrants. Concelebration is quite common in the Oriental rites, but in the Latin rite it is practiced nowadays only at the ordination of a priest or at the consecration of a bishop.[22]

d) The faithful can be said to offer the Mass in the sense that they are members of the Church, which offers through the priest. Moreover, they can offer in a particular way by serving the Mass, singing in the choir, providing the bread and wine or the stipend, etc. However, it must be emphasized that the laity do not offer the Mass in the same sense that the priest offers it, and hence it is not advisable to invite them to "*offer* Mass with the newly ordained priest."

4. *The Effects of the Mass*

Every Mass produces four effects — adoration, thanksgiving, satisfaction, and impetration. The first two are given to God, the other two are for the benefit of men. These last two are called the *fruits* of the Mass. That the Mass produces these four effects is an article of faith from the Council of Trent.[23]

These effects are produced primarily by the Mass as the offering of Christ. The effects from this source are said to be *ex opere operato* inasmuch as they cannot be frustrated by the unworthiness of the other offerers. In addition, the Mass receives some value from the good dispositions of the other offerers — the Church, the priest, and the faithful co-operating.

The effects of the Mass from the standpoint of satisfaction and impetration (fruits) are merely the application of the benefits gained by the Sacrifice of Calvary. These fruits are fourfold, by reason of the recipients — the most special fruit (given to the priest), the special fruit (given to those of the faithful who actively co-operate in the Mass, such as the server and the choir), the intentional fruit (given to the one for whom the Mass is offered by reason of a stipend or other such title), and the general fruit (given to all the members of the Church, the souls in purgatory, and even in some measure to those who are not members of the Church).

Adoration and thanksgiving are always given to God by every Mass. The impetratory fruit of the Mass may be applied to either spiritual or temporal favors, and it is infallible in the sense that something — at least some actual grace — is always given to the person or persons for whom the Mass is applied. The satisfactory fruit of the Mass, as regards the remission of the debt of temporal punishment, is also infallible for a living person, if the one to whom it is applied has a debt of temporal punishment and is properly disposed to receive its remission. We do not know how much of the debt is remitted. A Mass said for a particular soul in purgatory may be accepted for this soul, or God may choose to direct the satisfactory fruit to some other soul. As far as the satisfactory value of the Mass for the guilt of sin is concerned, we can only say that the Mass obtains for sinners *some* graces that will aid them toward forgiveness, if they will use them.

5. *Mass Stipends*

For many centuries the Catholic Church has sanctioned the custom of the acceptance by a priest of a sum of money, known as a stipend, for which he binds himself in justice to offer a Mass or Masses according to the intention of the person giving the stipend. The stipend is not a price paid for the Mass, since the Holy Sacrifice is a spiritual object of immeasurable value; but the stipend is a person's contribution toward the support of the priest, in return for which he agrees to exercise his priestly function by applying the intentional fruits of the Mass to the purpose desired by the donor. When stipends are given in the form of the regular interest from a legacy the capital is called a Mass foundation.

The amount of the stipend is determined by the bishop for the particular diocese.[24] A priest may not celebrate more than one Mass for a stipend on the same day — e.g., on a Sunday when he offers two Masses — except on Christmas day, when he may take stipends for three Masses. Moreover (with the same exception) a pastor who is bound to celebrate Mass for the intentions of his people on Sundays and certain other days may not on such a day celebrate another Mass for a stipend.[25]

FOOTNOTES

1. Mt. 26:26–29.
2. Mt. 14:22–25.
3. Lk. 22:19–20.
4. 1 Cor. 11:23.
5. 1 Cor. 10:16.
6. 1 Cor. 11:27.
7. Can. 816.
8. Can. 817.
9. Jn. 6:54.
10. Can. 859.
11. Can. 864.
12. Can. 854, #2.
13. Can. 852.
14. *DB*, n. 932.
15. Can. 808, 858.
16. Can. 856.
17. Jn. 6:57.
18. Mal. 1:11.
19. Lk. 22:19.
20. Mt. 26:27; Lk. 22:20.
21. Lk. 22:19.
22. Can. 803.
23. *DB*, n. 950.
24. Can. 831.
25. Can. 824.

CHAPTER V . . . PENANCE

1. *The Meaning of Penance*

The word *penance* in its primary significance means that virtue whereby a person detests his own personal sins. We cannot therefore have penance in the strict sense for the sins of others or for our own original sin. Penance can be understood in a general sense as sorrow arising from any motive — e.g., love of God, gratitude, fear of punishment; or in a special sense, as that which is motivated by the desire to make up for sin as an injustice against God. This latter is a potential part of the virtue of justice.

The chief act of penance is designated as *contrition*. If the motive of such an act is one that is applicable to all sins, it is *universal* contrition. Such is the contrition (with reference to mortal sin) that arises from love of God or from fear of hell. If it is a motive that is applicable to only a certain type of sin, it is called *particular* contrition. Such is that which arises from the consideration of the loathsomeness of sins against temperance, as degrading to human nature.

God will not forgive any actual sin unless the sinner makes an act of contrition. This is true of all types of sin, venial as well as mortal.

2. *Existence of the Sacrament of Penance*

Our Lord promised the Apostles the general power of binding and loosing with the assurance that what they bound or loosed on earth would be bound or loosed in heaven,[1] and He promised the same power to Peter in a special way also.[2] From these words we can argue with some probability that He intended to give them the power to forgive sins, or to loose men from guilt. He clearly and explicitly granted such a power to the Apostles on Easter Sunday, when He told them: "Whose sins you shall forgive, they are forgiven them; and whose sins you shall retain, they are retained."[3] It is to be noted that in this text the Greek word for *forgive* is the same that is used in other parts of Scripture to designate the forgiveness of sins by Christ Himself.[4] Certainly, in this latter case, there is question of true forgiveness; consequently, we logically conclude that the power granted by Christ to His Apostles was a real power of *forgiving,* and not merely the power to *declare sins forgiven* through faith, as is the contention of many Protestants.

Since the powers granted to the Apostles were intended to be transmitted to their successors in the ministry, it is evident that the power to forgive sins has been handed down to the bishops and priests of the Church. Tradition fully substantiates this, for the authority of bishops and priests to forgive sins committed after Baptism has been claimed by the Church and admitted by Christians from the beginning.

The specific characteristic of the power to forgive sins granted by Christ is that it is intended to be exercised *judicially.* In a judgment there is an investigation of the case and an authoritative sentence by the judge. Now, since Christ gave the power both to forgive and to retain, there must be an investigation of the penitent's sins to find out if they should or should not be forgiven. Moreover, since what the minister decides is ratified by God — "whose sins you shall forgive, they are forgiven" (by God) — there is an authoritative sentence. However, there are many differences between a criminal trial in a civil court and the judicial act of Penance. The purpose of the former is to punish the guilty; the purpose of the latter is to reconcile him to God. The civil trial is concerned only with external acts; the sacramental judgment is concerned also with internal acts. In a civil trial witnesses bring accusations against the defendant; in the sacrament he accuses himself.

3. *The Essence of the Sacrament of Penance*

The remote matter of the sacrament of Penance is every sin committed after Baptism. Mortal sins committed after Baptism and not yet properly confessed and absolved constitute *necessary* matter — that is, they must be confessed according to their nature, number, and circumstances changing the nature of the sins, even if they have already been forgiven by perfect contrition. Mortal sins which have previously been properly confessed and forgiven in the sacrament of Penance, and also all venial sins, constitute *free* matter — that is, they need not be confessed, but nevertheless they suffice for the reception of this sacrament. The reason why a person can again receive sacramental forgiveness for a sin previously forgiven is that he can be truly sorry for it, and thus receive from the sacrament the grace which would forgive this sin if it were still on his soul. Thus, he can receive an addition to his measure of sanctifying grace by repeating and repenting of previously forgiven sins.

The form of the sacrament of Penance is composed of the words spoken by the priest to the repentant sinner after confession, "I absolve thee from thy sins, in the name of the Father and of the Son and of the Holy Ghost. Amen." The essential element of the sacramental form is the words: "I absolve thee from thy sins."

The proximate matter of the sacrament of Penance, according to the most common theological opinion, is the three acts of the penitent — contrition, confession, and satisfaction. Of these, the first two constitute *essential* matter, the third *integral* matter — that is, contrition and confession are necessary that the sacrament may be validly administered, satisfaction is required for the full perfection and efficacy of the sacrament.

CONTRITION: Contrition embraces detestation and sorrow for the past and the purpose of amendment in the future. To be beneficial for the remission of sins, contrition must be based on a supernatural motive, must be in the will and not merely on the lips, must be sovereign in appreciation (that is, accompanied by the conviction that sin is the greatest evil and the will to endure every evil rather than commit mortal sin), and universal (that is, it must extend to all the penitent's mortal sins at least). It seems that an implicit purpose of amendment (in regard to *all* mortal sins, at least) ordinarily suffices.

Contrition is perfect if it is based on the realization that sin is opposed to the goodness of God. Such contrition is actually an act of love for God. It justifies the sinner, even before he actually approaches the sacrament, but he must have the intention of confessing his mortal sins, in order to receive the judicial remission of them. In the meantime, he is in the state of grace, but he is forbidden to receive Holy Communion until he has been to confession.[5]

Imperfect contrition or attrition is that which is based on a motive inferior to love of God — e.g., fear of punishment, the recognition of the heinousness of sin, its ingratitude, etc. Such contrition does not justify a person outside the sacrament, but it suffices for sacramental absolution.

CONFESSION: Our Lord indicated the necessity of confession of sins when He gave the Apostles and their successors the power to *forgive* and to *retain* sins. It is only through the confession of the penitent that the priest can know whose sins are to be forgiven, whose to be retained.

Our Lord laid down no explicit command as to how frequently the faithful must confess their sins, though it is evident that this must be done at least when one is in danger of death. For one is certainly obliged to obtain the judicial pardon of his sins before he leaves this world. By the law of the Church the faithful are obliged to confess their sins at least once a year.[6] Only those are bound by this precept who have necessary matter to confess. The year is generally computed by the Easter season, rather than by the calendar year.

The confession must be *integral;* that is, it must contain all mortal sins (at least) which the penitent is bound to confess, their number, their specific nature, and any circumstances that change the specific *nature* of the sin, by adding a specifically different malice. If a person is not sure of the number, he satisfies his obligation by telling approximately the number.

There are times when a person can receive the sacrament of Penance without telling all his mortal sins in detail; namely, when there is a good reason for not mentioning some or even all of them individually. Such would be the case when a large number of soldiers are on the way to battle and have no time to confess individually. Then it suffices that the soldiers state by word or sign merely that they have sinned and that they are sorry and desire absolution. Another occasion would arise if there were danger that a person's confession would be overheard, as in a crowded hospital ward. It must be noted, however, that the obligation to confess integrally still binds, and when one next goes to confession he must tell according to number, specific nature, and requisite circumstances the sins thus confessed in only a general way.

The *intrinsic* difficulty of confession does not excuse one from omitting any sin. That is, the embarrassment of telling one's sins to a priest is no excusing cause, for our Lord foresaw this when He imposed the obligation of confession; though it would seem that some very extraordinary circumstance might excuse, such as the fact that the only confessor available is a person's brother or son. Similarly, a person is not justified in going to Communion after a mortal sin, with only an act of contrition, merely because of the embarrassment of being noticed as not approaching the communion rail.

SATISFACTION: The main purpose of satisfaction, or the sacramental penance, is the remission of the temporal punishment that may remain after sin has been forgiven. Another purpose is to help the penitent get rid of bad habits. The priest is bound to give a penance, and ordinarily he must give a grave penance for mortal sins.

The penance can be prayer, almsgiving, or works of self-denial such as fasting. A work which is already of obligation can be imposed, such as attendance at Sunday Mass, but the priest is counseled to give at least some other penance. A light penance binds under pain of venial sin, a grave penance under pain of mortal sin. However, if the penitent had the intention, when he went to confession, of accepting and fulfilling the penance, his sins remain forgiven even though later he neglects to say the penance. The penance should be performed without too great delay, though there is no obligation of fulfilling it before receiving Holy Communion, or even before the next confession. If the penitent forgets the penance and cannot return to the priest except with great trouble he is free from the obligation of performing any penance. Moreover, if a penitent has a reason for obtaining a commutation of the penance, he can obtain this either from the same confessor or from another. In the latter case, he must give the priest at least a general knowledge of the nature and gravity of the sins he confessed.

4. The Minister of Penance

The minister of Penance is a priest or bishop. Besides the power of orders, he must possess the power of jurisdiction over the penitent, for the sacrament of Penance is exercised as a judgment, and a judgment is valid only if the judge has jurisdiction over the accused. The jurisdiction of the priest may be either ordinary or delegated. Ordinary jurisdiction is that which is connected with an office. Such jurisdiction for the sacrament of Penance is possessed by the Pope (and Cardinals) over the universal Church, by the bishop and vicar-general over a diocese, by the pastor over the parish. This ordinary jurisdiction is personal as well as local, so that a pastor could hear the confession of his parishioners and a bishop of his diocesans in any part of the world.

Delegated jurisdiction is that which is deputed to a priest by one having ordinary jurisdiction. Such, for example, is the jurisdiction of the curate. Not everyone having ordinary jurisdiction can delegate; e.g., the pastor has not this power. One who has jurisdiction for confessions, whether ordinary or delegated, in a certain territory can also hear the confessions of those who come into this territory as transients.

A priest who has faculties for confessions in his own diocese or in the port from which he sets sail or in any port on the way on a sea voyage can hear confessions on shipboard during the entire voyage (and even in a port where the vessel stops). Recently this same concession was extended to those priests who take a journey by air.

The Church supplies jurisdiction to all priests for the benefit of a person in danger of death. Moreover, the Church also supplies in the case when a priest is in a positive doubt whether or not he has jurisdiction and also in what is called *common error;* that is, when there is a general impression that he has jurisdiction, or even when some public act has been placed which would give such an impression. Thus, if a priest outside his diocese went into the confessional and began to hear confessions, his absolutions would be valid.

Sometimes a bishop reserves certain sins, so that ordinarily a confessor must receive a special delegation to absolve a person who has committed such a sin. Moreover, a person who has committed a sin to which an excommunication is attached, such as the sin of abortion or attempted marriage before a non-Catholic clergyman, must receive the forgiveness of the excommunication (from the bishop or priest to whom this power has been delegated) before he can obtain the pardon of the sin.

5. *The Recipient and the Effects of Penance*

Any baptized person who has committed sin after Baptism can receive the sacrament of Penance, and if he committed mortal sin, must do so. One who is a recidivist, that is, who has fallen back into the habit of grave sin after a previous confession without any effort at amendment, and thus shown that his mere assertion of contrition is unreliable, cannot ordinarily be absolved until he manifests special or extraordinary signs of contrition, for ordinarily the priest may not absolve unless he is morally certain of the penitent's dispositions.

One who is in the proximate occasion of grave sin, which occasion he can without great inconvenience avoid, cannot be absolved unless he promises to avoid it in future. At times a person is in a necessary occasion of sin, and in that event he must promise to use all reasonable means to make the proximate occasion remote.

The primary effect of penance is the remission of sin, and no sin is beyond the power of this sacrament. In the early Church a more rigorous practice prevailed than nowadays in regard to the pardon of very grievous sins and the infliction of satisfaction for them. Sometimes a person had to do penance a very long time before he could receive absolution; and it seems probable that in some instances absolution was refused even at the hour of death to those who had relapsed into grave sin after having once been absolved from grave transgressions. But this in no way indicated that the Church doubted its power to impart pardon of even the most grievous transgressions. The Church was simply taking this course (if this procedure actually took place) to impress the faithful with the heinousness of sin. The sinner could be justified by perfect contrition.

With the remission of sin the penitent receives sanctifying grace (or an increase of it, if he is already in grace), the infused virtues, the gifts of the Holy Spirit, and a special sacramental grace enabling him to remain in God's friendship. A measure of his temporal punishment is also taken away, especially by virtue of sacramental satisfaction. Moreover, the merits which he had acquired before losing the state of grace by mortal sin are restored.

6. *The Sacramental Seal*

It is most strictly forbidden to anyone who hears a person's confession to reveal that this person has confessed this sin. This obligation binds the priest primarily, but it also binds any other who chances to overhear the confession. It admits of no exception. This is what is meant by a direct revelation, and even if the sin revealed were very small, the revelation would be a grave sin. By an indirect revelation is meant a statement that is likely to lead to the knowledge of the sin confessed. This too is forbidden, and the sin is grave or light, according to the probability of the sin being manifested as committed by a certain individual. A priest who would directly reveal what he heard in confession would receive *ipso facto* an excommunication most specially reserved to the Holy See.[7]

It is also forbidden to use the knowledge one acquired in the sacrament to the detriment of the penitent. Thus if a sexton confessed sins of theft around the church, the priest would be forbidden to put locks on the drawers, etc., as a result of this confession. But to make use of this knowledge without detriment to the penitent, e.g., to pray for him, is not forbidden.

FOOTNOTES

1. Mt. 18:18.
2. Mt. 16:19.
3. Jn. 20:23.
4. Mt. 9:2.
5. Can. 856.
6. Can. 906.
7. Can. 889, 2369.

CHAPTER VI . . . *EXTREME UNCTION*

1. *Existence of Extreme Unction*

PROOF FROM SCRIPTURE: St. James, in his Epistle, says: "Is any one among you sick? Let him bring in the presbyters of the Church, and let them pray over him, anointing him with oil in the name of the Lord. And the prayer of faith will save the sick man, and the Lord will raise him up, and if he be in sins, they shall be forgiven him."[1]

The ceremony described by St. James has the elements of a sacrament. It is an external rite consisting of matter (anointing with oil) and form (prayer), which confers grace (it will *save* the sick man, and *forgive his sins*). The institution by Christ is not clear from this text, though the phrase, "in the name of the Lord," may be understood to imply this. But the general principle that all the effective signs of grace in the New Law were established by Christ can be adduced.

TRADITION: At least from the fourth and fifth century we have explicit evidence that the rite described by St. James was in use in the Church: e.g., in the Euchology of Serapion, and in the writings of St. Innocent I.

2. *Essence of Extreme Unction*

The remote matter of this sacrament is olive oil, blessed by the bishop (or priest with delegation) for use in the conferring of Extreme Unction. It is doubtful if the sacrament can be validly conferred if one of the other blessed oils — chrism or oil of catechumens — is used. At any rate, it is certain that the sacrament is invalid if the oil is not blessed, and it is also certain that a priest, without special delegation (which is never given to priests of the Latin rite), cannot bless oil for this sacrament. For the lawful, though not valid, administration of this sacrament, the oil should be that which was blessed the Holy Thursday immediately preceding, and it would seem to be of obligation (though not grave) to use oil blessed by the bishop of the diocese, if this is available.

The proximate matter is the anointing of the sick person. According to present-day legislation, six anointings are given — eyes, ears, nose, mouth, hands, and feet. For any reasonable cause the anointing of the feet can be omitted. Moreover, in urgent necessity one anointing suffices, given on any sense, though preferably on the forehead. If this latter method is used, the individual anointings should be supplied later, when the urgency of the situation has passed.

THE FORM: The words spoken by the priest at the individual anointing are: "Through this holy anointing and His most pious mercy, may the Lord forgive thee whatever faults thou hast committed through sight (or hearing, etc.). Amen." When only one anointing is given the words are: "Through this holy anointing may the Lord forgive thee whatever faults thou hast committed." It seems that as far as validity is concerned any prayer for the spiritual welfare of the sick person will suffice. The Church's ritual contains other prayers to be said both before and after the anointing; and these are of obligation, but are not necessary for the validity of the sacrament.

3. *The Minister and the Recipient*

The minister of this sacrament is a priest or a bishop. Any priest can validly confer it, but for lawfulness it is reserved to the pastor of the place where the sick person is staying, but he can give permission to another priest to confer it, and at times this permission can be reasonably presumed.[2] The pastor is obliged in justice to give this sacrament or to see that it is given by another priest to those who reasonably seek it within the limits of his parish.[3] Other priests are bound out of charity to give Extreme Unction to one who seeks it, if a priest having the duty to confer it is not available.

To receive Extreme Unction validly one must be a baptized person who has attained the age of reason and is in danger of death from some affliction actually present in the body.[4] Therefore, a child below the age of reason cannot be validly anointed, because he is incapable of the primary effect, the comforting of soul. One who is in danger of death from some imminent cause which has not yet afflicted his body, such as a criminal about to be executed, a soldier on his way to battle, cannot be anointed.

To receive Extreme Unction fruitfully one must *per se* be in the state of grace; but *per accidens* it will give sanctifying grace to a sinner in good faith who has attrition. It is uncertain whether or not there is a grave obligation to receive Extreme Unction.

4. *Effects of Extreme Unction*

It is not quite certain what constitutes the primary effect of Extreme Unction, but the best view seems to be that it is the comforting of the soul of the sick person, beset with the weaknesses arising from the grave affliction of body. To this primary effect are annexed other effects, such as the remission of venial sin, the eradication of the remains of sin (such as inclinations toward sinful conduct), and the remission of the temporal punishment due to sin. Indeed, it is quite probable that this sacrament is intended to dispose the soul for immediate entrance into heaven; that is, to remit all its temporal punishment so that it will not need to pass through purgatory. This last effect can be produced only if the recipient has contrition for all, even venial, sins.

Extreme Unction can also bring about the restoration of the sick person's bodily health. However, as regards this effect it must be noted: first, this effect is conditional on whether or not restoration to health will be beneficial to the sick person's spiritual welfare. As the Council of Trent expressed it, Extreme Unction sometimes gives health of body when it will be expedient for the health of the soul.[5] This effect is given, not necessarily, in a miraculous manner, but through the benefit conferred on the soul. For, when the soul is encouraged and comforted, there naturally flows some benefit to the body. Hence, the bodily effect of Extreme Unction is a combination of the supernatural and the natural.

The practical conclusion, then, is that Catholics should receive Extreme Unction as soon as they are in probable danger of death from sickness or other bodily ailment (including old age).

Extreme Unction may not be repeated in the same illness, unless the person has recovered somewhat and again fallen into danger of death.[6] If a person lives for several months after being anointed, even if there has been no notable improvement, he may be anointed again if death is near, on the presumption that there must have been some amelioration of his condition and a relapse.

FOOTNOTES

1. James 5:14–15.
2. Can. 938.
3. Can. 939.
4. Can. 940.
5. *DB*, n. 909.
6. Can. 940.

CHAPTER VII . . . *HOLY ORDERS*

Holy Orders and Matrimony are *social* sacraments; that is, they are intended primarily for the common good rather than the benefit of the recipient, as is the case with the other five sacraments.

1. *Existence of Holy Orders*

PROOF FROM SCRIPTURE: It is evident from the Gospel that Christ chose certain men to confer sacred rites in His Church, and wished that this office would be continued until the end of time. At the Last Supper our Lord gave the Apostles the power over the Holy Eucharist; on Easter Sunday He extended their power to the remission of sins. But the Gospel does not tell us that Christ wished this ministerial power to be transmitted by a *sacrament*. This, however, appears from other parts of the New Testament. For example, when the Apostles chose the first deacons, they gave them their official assignment by the ceremony of the laying on of hands.[1] St. Paul used this same ceremony in making Timothy a minister (bishop) of the Church.[2] From this we logically conclude that this ceremony must have been instituted or authorized by Christ, and that it gives the minister of the Church the right to perform sacred rights and the grace he needs for his ministry.

TRADITION: We have indications from the early centuries that the ceremony by which a man was made a minister of the Church gives grace. St. Augustine compares the effects of this rite with Baptism, which is surely one of the sacraments.

THE NUMBER OF ORDERS: In the Latin Church there are four minor orders — porter, lector, exorcist, and acolyte. The major orders are: the subdiaconate, the diaconate, the priesthood, and the episcopate. It is a disputed point whether the minor orders and the subdiaconate are sacramental orders, or only ceremonies of ecclesiastical origin. Undoubtedly the diaconate and priesthood are sacramental orders; but it is a disputed point whether the episcopate is a distinct order from the priesthood or only an extension of it.

2. Essence of Holy Orders

MINOR ORDERS: The remote matter of these orders is an instrument suited to the office — a key, a book, cruets and candle, etc. The proximate matter is the handing over of the instrument by the bishop to the candidate. The form is the words spoken by the bishop on this occasion.

MAJOR ORDERS: The remote matter of the subdiaconate is the chalice and paten (empty), and perhaps also the book of Epistles which is given to the candidates by the bishop; the proximate matter is the conferring of the remote matter; the form, the words then spoken by the bishop.

The matter of the diaconate is the imposition of hands; the form is the prayer after the nature of a preface, of which the essential words are: "Send into him we ask Thee, O Lord, the Holy Spirit, by which he shall be strengthened by the gift of Thy sevenfold grace for the faithful performance of the work of the ministry."

The matter of the priesthood is the first imposition of the bishop's hands; the form is the "preface," essentially the words: "Give, we ask Thee, omnipotent Father, to this Thy servant the dignity of the priesthood. . . ."

The matter of the episcopal consecration is the imposition of hands; the form is the "preface," essentially the words: "Fill out in Thy priest the fullness of the ministry. . . ." Pius XII, in an official decree, has authoritatively determined the essential factors of the ordination to the diaconate, the priesthood, and the episcopate. This was previously a subject of discussion among theologians.

3. The Minister and the Recipient

MINISTER OF HOLY ORDERS: The ordinary minister of Holy Orders is a bishop only. However, the Church can delegate a priest to confer the minor orders, as is evident from the legislation of the Code, which gives such delegation to certain priests, such as cardinals who are only priests, not bishops.[3] It is also certain from past practice that a priest can be delegated to confer the subdiaconate. A priest cannot be delegated to confer the priesthood or the episcopate, or (very probably) the diaconate.

The bishop normally authorized to ordain is the Ordinary of the diocese. However, he can grant permission to another bishop to ordain his subjects. A very severe penalty is decreed by the Church on a bishop who would confer Holy Orders without the proper testimonials and dimissorial letters.[4]

THE SUBJECT OF HOLY ORDERS: Only one of the male sex can be validly ordained. This is implied by the admonition of St. Paul, that women should be silent in the Church,[5] and is confirmed by the constant tradition of the Church. Only a baptized person can be validly ordained. A male infant can be validly ordained, but a bishop would never be allowed to ordain a child.

For the lawful reception of this sacrament the Church has laid down many laws concerning the preparation, the qualifications, etc., of the aspirant to the priesthood. There are certain impediments to the lawful reception of this sacrament and to the exercise of the functions of the ministry, known as irregularities. These are of two classes — ex defectu and ex delicto — insofar as respectively they imply no fault or arise from sin. Examples of the former are illegitimate birth, blindness, the fact that a person has been married twice. Examples of the latter are the crimes of murder, abortion, and attempted marriage by one already in sacred orders.

For ordination to the subdiaconate one must be at least twenty-one years of age, to the diaconate twenty-two, to the priesthood twenty-four, to the episcopate thirty. Moreover, no man will be admitted to Holy Orders unless he has acquired the proper knowledge, especially of theology. Only one who feels that he has received a divine call to this exalted state may seek the priesthood. He must first prove that he has the requisite virtue.

4. Effects of Holy Orders

EFFECTS BY DIVINE LAW: The sacrament of Holy Orders confers a character on the soul, empowering the recipient to perform certain sacred functions. A character is surely given by the diaconate and the priesthood, at least — and probably also by the other orders.

This sacrament also gives sanctifying and sacramental grace, the latter bringing with it a title to the actual graces the recipient needs in the course of his ministry to perform its functions in a proper manner and with suitable holiness.

EFFECTS BY ECCLESIASTICAL LAW: In the Latin Church with the subdiaconate come two obligations — perpetual celibacy and the duty of daily recitation of the Canonical Hours. In some of the Oriental rites married men may be ordained to the priesthood, but those who have received sacred orders may not marry afterward.

NOTE:

Anglican Orders. The Catholic Church, through the decree, Apostolicae Curae, of Leo XIII (September 13, 1896), has officially declared the ordination rites of the Anglican Church in succession to those of the sixteenth-seventeenth centuries to be invalid. The reason is that in the period from 1559 to 1662 there was lacking a proper form in the rite of ordination to the priesthood and episcopal consecration; consequently, even if afterward this defect were remedied, the hierarchy was extinct. Furthermore, it is evident that the intention of the early Anglican bishops was not to give the priesthood in the Christian sense of an order destined primarily to the offering of sacrifice.

FOOTNOTES

1. Acts 6:6.
2. 1 Tim. 4:14; 2 Tim. 1:6.
3. Can. 239.
4. Can. 2373.
5. 1 Cor. 14:34–35.

Besides being a sacrament, Matrimony, or marriage, is also a natural institution. That is, the very nature of human beings as they are created by God adapts them to married life and inclines them to this state. Hence, it is true to say that God instituted marriage by the very fact that He created men and women with the bodily and spiritual faculties and desires that are inherent in their nature. In addition, as we know from revelation, when the Almighty had created the first man and woman, He declared them to be husband and wife and gave a special blessing to their marital union.[1]

Hence, before considering marriage as a sacrament, we shall devote some attention to marriage as a natural institution.

1. *Marriage as a Natural Institution*

Marriage on the natural plane can be considered under a twofold aspect — first, as a contract; second, as a state. Under the first aspect marriage can be defined as a contract whereby a man and a woman mutually give and accept the right to sexual intercourse and the other rights connected with it, such as the right to cohabitation, fidelity, etc. Under the second aspect marriage is the permanent condition resulting from this contract, whereby the two parties remain united by a lasting bond, subject to the rights and duties which were transferred mutually when they made the marriage contract.

The primary purpose of marriage is the procreation and the proper rearing of children. In other words, God's first plan in establishing marriage is that married couples contribute toward the benefit of society by bringing children into the world and by providing for their bodily and spiritual needs until they are able to take care of themselves. Thus, marriage is primarily a social institution. The secondary ends of marriage are the providing of human beings with the helps and comforts that domestic life, properly conducted, brings to husband and wife, and also the allaying of the sexual urge by the lawful use of the procreative faculty.

To contract a valid marriage, as far as the laws of nature prescribe, a person must have sufficient knowledge of the rights and duties of the marital state to give an intelligent and free consent to the contract, and also the physical ability to perform his or her part in conjugal intercourse. As far as this latter condition is concerned, the natural law demands no more than that a person reasonably foresees that he will possess sexual potency at the normal stage of his maturity; and so, from the standpoint of the natural law, even a child of seven or eight could contract marriage. However, both civil and ecclesiastical laws require a more advanced age.

In making the marriage contract the parties can express consent by any mode of external expression — words, writing, signs, etc. A person can also give consent through a proxy or representative.

There are two essential qualities or properties of marriage — unity and indissolubility. The former signifies that marriage is intended by the law of nature to exist between one man and one woman, to the exclusion of polygamous unions. The basic reason is that the wholehearted love which should unite husband and wife is possible only when one man and one woman enter into the marriage. Indissolubility signifies that when a couple enter into the married state they are bound to remain husband and wife until the death of one of the parties. This property is opposed to divorce, the severing of the marriage bond with the understanding that each may contract another valid marriage. The fundamental reason for indissolubility is the well-authenticated fact that divorce renders the rearing of the offspring very difficult. Moreover, even the possibility of a divorce weakens the love and mutual trust that should exist between husband and wife.

2. Marriage as a Sacrament

Most Protestants deny that Christian marriage is a sacrament, though they admit that it is a sacred contract. The Catholic Church holds that matrimony is one of the seven sacraments instituted by Jesus Christ.[2] The churches of Eastern rite separated from Catholic unity also accept matrimony as a sacrament.[3]

The first argument for the doctrine that Christian marriage is a sacrament is found in the Epistle of St. Paul to the Ephesians,[4] where the Apostle compares the union of Christian husband and wife to the union between Christ and His Church. From this we argue that, just as the union between Christ and His Church is a sacred union, productive of supernatural grace, so the union between a Christian husband and wife is a sacred union that produces grace for the couple. In other words, it is an efficacious sign of grace, or a sacrament. And since Christ established all the sacraments, it follows necessarily that He instituted marriage as a sacrament. The Gospel does not, indeed, contain any explicit assertion to this effect, though it surely indicates that our Lord honored and extolled the married state.[5] However, not all that Christ taught is found in the Gospel;[6] and in the course of the forty days between His resurrection and ascension into heaven, He gave the Apostles many instructions regarding the Christian religion.[7] Doubtless it was at this time that He informed them that marriage among Christians was to be a sacrament.

The argument from St. Paul's words is corroborated by Christian tradition, which from the beginning regarded marriage as a very holy state, under the jurisdiction of the Church and comparable in some respects to the sublime dignity of Holy Orders,[8] all of which indicates that it is a sacrament. Naturally it can be received as a sacrament only by a baptized person, since the reception of Baptism is a necessary prerequisite for the valid reception of any of the other sacraments.

On the other hand, according to Catholic belief, the valid marriage of two baptized persons, whatever their particular belief, is *always* a sacrament, whether they are aware of it or not. For Christ elevated the very contract of marriage between baptized persons to the dignity of a sacrament, in such wise that there can be no valid marital contract between baptized persons which is not by its very nature a sacrament.[9] In other words, the contract itself between Christians is the sacrament. From this it follows that those who make the contract by that very fact confer on each other the sacrament of Matrimony. The Catholic Church requires for the validity of marriage, when at least one party is a Catholic, that a priest, as well as two witnesses, be present.[10] But the priest assists, not as the minister of the sacrament, but as the Church's representative, to bless the union and to attest that it took place with all the requirements for validity.

The remote matter of the sacrament of Matrimony is the conjugal right, which the parties mutually give and receive. The proximate matter is the giving of this right to the other; the form is the receiving of this right from the other. The contract can be expressed through any form of external sign, and can be made even through a proxy or representative.[11] The effects of this sacrament are sanctifying and sacramental grace, the latter including the right to the actual graces the couple need in the married life. Since Matrimony is a sacrament of the living, a person must be in the state of sanctifying grace to receive it worthily.

The marriage of two unbaptized persons, though a sacred contract, cannot be a sacrament, since only a baptized person can receive any of the other sacraments. However, if both parties of such a marriage afterward receive Baptism, their marriage most probably by that very fact becomes a sacrament. The marriage of a baptized person with one who is unbaptized cannot be a sacrament for the latter; and it is now practically certain that it is not a sacrament for the baptized person either, since it seems incongruous that the marriage bond of one of the parties should possess a higher dignity than that of the other. However, as in the previous case, their marriage becomes a sacrament as soon as the unbaptized party receives Baptism.

3. The Authority of the Catholic Church Over Marriage

Since marriage is a social institution, intended primarily for the benefit of society, it is necessarily subject to some public authority, in such wise that this authority can determine the conditions for the validity as well as the lawfulness of the contract. In the case of the marriage of two unbaptized persons this authority is exercised by the state. In the case of the marriage of two baptized persons the Catholic Church possesses this authority, since their marriage is a sacrament, and the jurisdiction over the sacraments was committed by Jesus Christ to His Church.

When one party of a marriage is baptized, the other unbaptized, the Church certainly has jurisdiction over the contract as far as the baptized person is concerned. Some theologians have held that the competent civil authority possesses jurisdiction over the marriage inasfar as it affects the unbaptized person; but the more common view is that the marriage in its entirety is subject to the jurisdiction of the Church. For it would be incongruous for two distinct authorities to be empowered to regulate the same marriage; hence, the Church, as the higher authority, should have full jurisdiction.

By virtue of its jurisdiction, the Church has established certain impediments to marriage by legislating that, if certain circumstances are present in a particular marriage, a marriage contract between the two would be unlawful or even null and void. An impediment is *prohibitive* if it renders the contract merely unlawful, but not invalid, such as the fact that one of the parties has a private vow of chastity. An impediment is *diriment* if it renders the contract also invalid. For a sufficient reason the Church can give a dispensation from the impediments established by ecclesiastical law; but the Church cannot dispense from an impediment of divine law, such as permanent sexual impotence or the relationship between parent and child. In other words, the Church could never sanction the marriage of a person who is permanently incapable of the act of sexual intercourse or the marriage of a person with his or her own child.

4. *Marriage Impediments in Particular*

The following are the marriage impediments laid down for persons of the Latin rite in the Code of Canon Law, which became effective on May 19, 1918. The impediments for persons of the Oriental rites are substantially the same, though different in some accidental respects.

a) Lack of Proper Age (Nonage). A baptized boy cannot contract a valid marriage until he has completed his sixteenth year, and a baptized girl until she has completed her fourteenth year. The Church, moreover, recommends that the accepted customs of the country be followed in the matter of the age at which young folks should marry.[12]

b) Blood Relationship. In the direct line of descent — child, grandchild, etc. — every degree of relationship invalidates marriage. In the collateral line — brother or sister, cousins — this diriment impediment extends to the third degree (second cousins).[13]

c) Affinity. There is a diriment impediment between a person who has previously been married and a brother or sister, aunt or uncle, first cousin, and direct ancestors or descendants in any degree of the previous spouse.[14]

d) Public Decency. If a man and a woman have lived together as husband and wife but actually are not married, each contracts a diriment impediment to marriage with the relatives of the other to the second degree in the direct line of blood relationship.[15]

e) Spiritual Relationship. Through Baptism a person contracts a diriment impediment of spiritual relationship with the one who baptized him and with the godparents.[16]

f) Vows. A private vow of virginity, celibacy, perfect chastity, or of receiving Holy Orders constitutes a *prohibitive* impediment. The same is true of the *simple* vows of religion taken in many religious congregations. However, the *solemn* vows of religion, such as are taken by the members of the older religious orders, are a *diriment* impediment to marriage. The same is true of the major orders in the clerical state — the subdiaconate, the diaconate, and the priesthood.[17]

g) *Adoption.* In a country where the civil law forbids the marriage of an adopted person with the one who adopted this person (or with near relatives) the Church also forbids it, making it a prohibitive or a diriment impediment according as the civil law makes it prohibitive or diriment.[18]

h) *Mixed Marriage.* The Catholic Church has established an impediment to the marriage of a Catholic with a non-Catholic. In the event that the non-Catholic is baptized the impediment is prohibitive; if he is unbaptized it is diriment. This law of the Church is based mainly on the fact that such marriages frequently result in the loss of faith to the Catholic party or to the children. Sometimes the Church grants a dispensation to a Catholic to contract a mixed marriage — namely, when there are good reasons for the marriage, the non-Catholic guarantees not to hinder the religious practices of the Catholic, both agree that all the children will be baptized and brought up in the Catholic religion, and there is moral certainty that these guarantees will be fulfilled.[19] The Church also urges her members not to marry persons who have rejected the Catholic faith, even though they have not embraced any other religion, and also Catholics affiliated with a forbidden society, such as the Masons, as well as public sinners or excommunicated persons.[20]

i) *Abduction and Fear.* There is a diriment impediment between a woman who has been abducted or been kept a prisoner by a man for the purpose of inducing her to marry him and this man, as long as she is in his power. Similarly, grave fear or violence unjustly inflicted on a person so that this person is forced to enter marriage in order to be free from the fear renders the marriage null and void.[21]

j) *Crime.* If a married person commits adultery and there is a mutual promise between the two that they will marry (or if they have even attempted a civil marriage) — or what is worse, if to the adultery one has joined the crime of murdering his legitimate spouse — there is a diriment impediment between these two sinners, even though they eventually become free to marry through the death of the lawful spouse or spouses. A similar impediment exists if, even without adultery, they collaborate in killing the spouse of one of them.[22]

5. *The Form of Marriage*

By the form of marriage is here meant the ceremony required by the law of the Church for the valid celebration of Matrimony. The ordinary law is that for validity the marriage of any Catholic (one who was baptized as a Catholic or was converted to the Catholic Church from a non-Catholic denomination), whether he marries another Catholic or a non-Catholic, must take place before an authorized priest and two witnesses. By an authorized priest is meant either the bishop or vicar-general (in the diocese) or a parish priest (in his parish) or another priest delegated by either of these within his respective territory. Usually the assistant priests in a parish have such delegation.[23]

However, there are two exceptions to this law, both supposing that an authorized priest cannot be had without grave inconvenience. Presupposing this circumstance, the couple can contract a valid marriage before two witnesses, without a priest, if one (at least) of them is in danger of death, or if they can prudently foresee that they will not be able to secure the services of an authorized priest within a month.[24]

The Church desires that the marriage of two Catholics be celebrated with a nuptial Mass, at which the bride receives a special blessing, ordinarily not given outside the Mass. A mixed marriage must usually be celebrated outside the church, though the bishop of the diocese can give permission for such a marriage in the church, for good reasons, but never with the celebration of Mass.[25]

6. *The Properties of Matrimony*

As was previously stated, the essential properties of marriage are two — unity and indissolubility.

a) Unity. The unity of marriage, excluding polygamy, is demanded by the law of nature, because the wholehearted mutual love of husband and wife, which is so necessary for a happy marriage, cannot exist in a polygamous union. God Himself added a positive command to this dictate of nature at the beginning of the human race, by revealing that marriage should consist of *two* becoming *one* flesh.[26] However, God Himself dispensed from this law for a period of time before the coming of Christ (at least from the time of Abraham), allowing men to have several wives. But our Lord restored the ideal of unity to marriage, and no exception for polygamy has been granted under the Christian Dispensation.

b) Indissolubility. This property, forbidding divorce with the right to remarry, is also demanded by the natural law, inasmuch as the proper rearing of children, one element of the primary purpose of marriage, cannot be satisfactorily fulfilled if the couple are separated. It might be objected that this argument would not apply to a childless union; but the answer is that the laws of marriage are based on what is the normal occurrence, not what is accidental or exceptional.

In the Old Law God gave a dispensation from indissolubility through the law of Moses which allowed a man to put away his wife "for some uncleanness" and to marry again.[27] In the New Law, Christ terminated this exception,[28] but nevertheless permitted, through the supervision and authority of His Church, certain exceptions. These are:

1) *The Pauline Privilege.* This means that if two unbaptized persons are married, and later one is converted to the Christian faith, and the other will not be converted also, or will refuse to live peacefully with the convert, or will be an occasion of sin to him, the Christian party may contract another marriage. With the contracting of this new union, the former bond is broken.[29]

2) *Nonconsummated Christian Marriage.* The Church can dissolve a marriage between two baptized persons or between a baptized and an unbaptized person, if it has never been consummated. This can be done either directly by the Holy See or by the solemn religious profession of one of the parties. That the Church possesses this power is evident from practice dating from the twelfth century.[30]

3) *Marriage of a Baptized Person With One Not Baptized.* From the practice of the Church it is also evident that the marriage of a baptized person with one who is unbaptized can be dissolved. This power of the Church is employed, not for the personal benefit of the parties involved, but for some reason connected with the faith. The power of the Church over such a marriage is based on the fact that it is not a sacramental marriage.

A marriage between two baptized persons, which has been consummated, cannot be dissolved by any power on earth, but terminates only with the death of one of the parties.[31] The marriage of two baptized non-Catholics has the same permanence and strength as the marriage of two Catholics.

Sometimes the Church is said to grant the annulment of a marriage. What is meant is a *declaration of nullity,* an official statement that there was no valid marriage from the beginning. It is very evident that this is entirely different from a divorce with the right to remarry.

For a very good reason the Church will allow a married couple to separate with the understanding that they are not to remarry. In the event that a married person has been guilty of adultery, the innocent party may separate permanently; but when a separation is granted for some other reason (e.g., habitual drunkenness or cruelty), conjugal life should be resumed when the cause for the separation ceases.[32]

7. *The Duties of Marriage*

A married person has the duty to render conjugal rights to the other, when seriously asked to do so. To refuse this, apart from a grave reason, would be a mortal sin. A sufficient reason for such a refusal would be the well-founded fear that another pregnancy would be very dangerous, or the fact that the husband is not fulfilling properly his duty to work for the support of the family. A proved case of adultery would justify the innocent partner in refusing the conjugal right permanently. Usually, however, it is better to forgive the erring one, if he is repentant. The obligation of cohabiting, of rendering each other love, fidelity, and mutual assistance is also the duty of a married couple.

Contraception is a very grave sin, which no situation can justify. There are occasions, however, in which only one party is guilty, and the other is guiltless, provided this latter protests sincerely against this abuse of marriage. The basic reason for the sinfulness of contraception is that it is a frustration of the primary purpose of the married state by the unnatural use of the generative faculty. The use of periodic continence, or the "Rhythm," is allowed to a married couple if they have serious reasons for avoiding children, either for the time being or permanently.

A married couple have the obligation of providing for the physical, intellectual, moral, and religious training of their children. In the case of Catholic parents this includes provision for the Baptism of the newborn child as soon as possible after birth, training of the child in Catholic doctrine, care that he receives the sacraments and a truly

Catholic education. This last includes sending the child to a Catholic school when this is possible.

8. *Preparation for Marriage*

A young person preparing for marriage should bear in mind that the choice of a life partner should be made, not on the basis of physical attractiveness, but rather on qualities of soul. A Catholic should always seek a good Catholic as his marriage partner. During the period of courtship they should receive the sacraments frequently and avoid all liberties that would arouse their passions. Even those who are engaged have no more rights in this respect than any other unmarried persons.

A Catholic should visit the priest at least a month before the planned date of the marriage in order to provide him with the necessary data and documents and to receive instructions about the great sacrament he is preparing to receive. Ordinarily the marriage takes place in the parish church of the bride.[33]

Catholics should enter marriage with the realization that it is a holy state, which brings great blessings to those who fulfill the obligations it entails according to the teaching of the Church. They should have the intention of making their home a place of holiness, so that it will resemble the most sacred household that the earth ever sheltered, the home of the Holy Family in Nazareth.

FOOTNOTES

1. Gen. 1:28.
2. *DB*, n. 971.
3. Connell, *Matrimony* (Brooklyn: Catholic Truth Society, 1938), p. 9.
4. Eph. 2:25-32.
5. Cf. Mt. 19:6.
6. Jn. 21:25.
7. Acts 1:3.
8. Cf. St. Augustine, *De Bono conjugali*, cap. 24, n. 32.
9. Can. 1012.
10. Can. 1094, 1099.
11. Can. 1089.
12. Can. 1067.
13. Can. 1076.
14. Can. 1077.
15. Can. 1078.
16. Can. 1079, 768.
17. Can. 1058, 1072, 1073.
18. Can. 1059, 1080.
19. Can. 1060, 1061, 1071.

20. Can. 1065, 1066.
21. Can. 1074, 1087. (Unjust fear is considered as an obstacle to consent rather than as a diriment impediment in Church law, but its effect is similar.)
22. Can. 1075.
23. Can. 1094, 1096, 1099.
24. Can. 1098.
25. Can. 1101, 1102, 1109.
26. Gen. 2:25.
27. Deut. 24:1.
28. Mk. 10:11-12.
29. 1 Cor. 7:12-15; Can. 1120-1124.
30. Can. 1119.
31. Can. 1118.
32. Can. 1128-1131.
33. Can. 1097.

INDEX

Compensation, occult, 129
Concelebration, 204
Concupiscence
  love of, definition, 81, 85
  See also Passion
Confession, 209–210
  frequency of, 210
  integral, 210
  intrinsic difficulty, does not excuse, 210
  necessity of, 209–210
"Confessions" extorted by violence, 15
Confirmation, 193–195
  character of, 186–187
  of children, 194
  effects of, 195
  essence of, 193–194
  existence of, 193
  form of, 194
  minister of, 194
  necessity of, 194–195
  proximate matter of, 193–194
  remote matter of, 193
  sponsors in, 195
  subject of, 194–195
Congregatio S. Officii, decrees of, 67
Connection of virtues, 61
Conscience, 38–48
  act of prudence, 101
  antecedent, 38
  certain, 40
  consequent, 38
  definition, 38
  division, 38–40
  doubtful, 40
  erroneous, 38–40
  kinds, 47–48
  lax, 47
  nature, 38
  perplexed, 47–48
  preceptive norm of morality, 20
  psychological, 38
  scrupulous, 47
  true, 38–39
  types, 38
  use of, 40–42
Consciousness, or psychological con-
    science, 38
Conscription, universal military, 140
Consent, in contracts, 132
Consequent conscience. *See* Conscience,
    consequent
Constancy, 161
Contraception, 47, 172, 231

Contraceptives, sale of, 95
Contracts, 132–141
  aleatory, 139–140
  bilateral, 132
  binding force, 133
  consent, 132
  definition, 132
  and error, 132–133
  failure to fulfill, 134
  and minors, 134
  nature, 132–134
  sinful, 134
  unilateral, 132
  violation, 134
  when binding, 132
  when rescindable, 133
Contrition, 209
  act of penance, 207
  imperfect, 209
  particular, 207
  perfect, 209
  perfect and imperfect, 86
  requirements for, 209
  universal, 207
Contumely, 130–131
Co-operation, 92–95
  formal, 92
  material, 93
  with respect to violations of fast and
      abstinence, 168
Co-operator(s)
  negative, in injustice, 122
  and restitution, 121–122
Correction, fraternal, 91–92
  conditions, 92
Council, ecumenical, 69
Councils and synods, 69
Council of Trent. *See* Trent, Council of
Counsel
  gift of the Holy Ghost, 60
  works of, as object of moral theology, 3
Credibility, motives of, 69–70
Crime, impediment to marriage, 228–229
Culpable ignorance. *See* Ignorance, kinds
Cult, 142
Cyril, St., Bp. of Jerusalem, on the real
    presence, 197

Damnification, and restitution, 117–119
Davis, Henry, S.J., quoted on state law,
    28
Decision, unjust, by judge, 140–141
Declaration of nullity, of marriage, 231

remote matter of, 208
sacramental
obligation, 211
purpose, 211
as satisfaction, 211
when to be fulfilled, 211
Perception, intuitive, of God, man's final
end, 10
Peregrini, 34
Perplexed conscience. *See* Conscience, perplexed
Perseverance, 161
Persons, acceptance of, 36
sin against distributive justice, 140
"Petting," 173
Piety, 155–156
gift of the Holy Ghost, 60
Pius X, Pope, decree on frequent Communion mentioned, 201
Pius XII, Pope
Humani Generis, 67
quoted on the gratuity of the supernatural order, 10
Place, sacred
and local sacrilege, 152
violation, 152
Pleasure, acting for, 22
Polygamy, 224, 229, 230
in the Old Law, 30
Popes
empowered to make ecclesiastical laws,
32
speaking *ex cathedra,* 69
Porter (Holy Order). *See* Minor Orders
Positivism, 17–18
Possession(s)
adverse, 113–114
temporal, classification, 91
Poverty, vow of, in respect to ownership,
110
Prayer, 142–143
attention, 143
definition, 142–143
ends, 143
necessary intention and attention, 143
necessity, 143
of petition, 143
and souls in purgatory, 143
Precept
nature of, 27
necessity of, 70, 72
Prescription, 113–115
acquisitive, 114–115

Church's recognition of, 113
liberative, 114
Presumption
beyond hope, 87
Lutheran, 84
opposed to hope, 83–84
Pelagian, 84
Price
ceiling, 136
common, 135–136
conventional, 136
fair, 136
legal 135
species, 135
Priesthood, 219
form of, 220
matter of, 220
Principles, reflex, 41–42
exceptions to use, 42–43
Prize fighting, 125–126
Probabiliorism, 44
Probabilism, as moral system, 44
Probabilists, 44
Professional secret, 157
Prohibited books, 78–80
to whom permitted, 80
Promised secret, 157
Promulgation of law. *See* Law,
promulgation
Property
private, limitations to, 108
right to, 108
right to possess, 109
Proxy in marriage, 226
Prudence
act of, 101
definition, 99
function of, 99, 100
governing, 100
in intellect, 57
natural, 99
nature of, 99–100
parts of, 100–101
personal, 100
supernatural, 60, 99–100
Prudence of the flesh. *See* Flesh, prudence
of

Quietists, 82
Quinquennial faculties. *See* Faculties,
quinquennial

Rape, 171